LOVE IN VIENNA

LOVE IN VIENNA

THE SIGMUND FREUD–MINNA BERNAYS AFFAIR

Barry G. Gale

An Imprint of ABC-CLIO, LLC

Santa Barbara, California • Denver, Colorado

Library of Congress Cataloging-in-Publication Data

Gale, Barry G. (Barry George), 1941– author.
  Love in Vienna : the Sigmund Freud-Minna Bernays affair / Barry G. Gale.
      pages cm
  Includes bibliographical references and index.
   ISBN 978-1-4408-4220-7 (print : alk. paper) — ISBN 978-1-4408-4221-4 (e-book)   1. Freud, Sigmund, 1856–1939.   2. Freud, Sigmund, 1856–1939—Relations with women.   3. Bernays, Minna.   I. Title.
  BF109.F74G346 2016
  150.19'52092—dc23   2015028277

ISBN: 978-1-4408-4220-7
EISBN: 978-1-4408-4221-4

20 19 18 17 16   1 2 3 4 5

This book is also available on the World Wide Web as an eBook.
Visit www.abc-clio.com for details.

Praeger
An Imprint of ABC-CLIO, LLC

ABC-CLIO, LLC
130 Cremona Drive, P.O. Box 1911
Santa Barbara, California 93116-1911

This book is printed on acid-free paper ∞
Manufactured in the United States of America

For Heather, Megan and Ian,
and
the magic that was Bruno Bettelheim

CONTENTS

Preface   ix

Acknowledgments   xiii

Part I: The Controversy   1

1   The Antagonists: Freud and Jung   3

2   The Rumor and Its Origins   9

3   The Freudian Response   37

Part II: The Affair and the Reality   53

4   Sorting Out the Arguments   55

Part III: Freud's Women   103

5   Freud and Minna   105

6   Freud and Martha   153

Concluding Thoughts   179

Notes   203

Bibliography   235

Index   241

PREFACE

For many decades, controversy has surrounded the exact nature of Sigmund Freud's relationship with his sister-in-law Minna Bernays. The idea that they had an intimate relationship was first mentioned by Carl Gustav Jung, an early supporter of Freud's and later a critic. He said that in 1907, when he and his wife first visited Freud in Vienna, Minna had revealed the affair in private conversations with him. She had sought his counsel.[1]

Freudians denied the allegations, but recently a German scholar, who is also a trained Freudian psychoanalyst, found evidence to support the contention. In a Swiss hotel registration book from the late nineteenth century he found the notation *Dr. Sigm. Freud u[nd] Frau/Wien* (Dr. Sigmund Freud and Wife/Vienna), written in Freud's handwriting. This was a holiday that Freud and Minna took alone.[2]

Freud and Minna traveled alone together on many occasions.[3] Even staunch Freudians, such as Peter Gay, now believe an affair may have taken place, though the matter is far from settled. A detailed article on the Freud/Minna relationship, including the new revelations, was published on December 24, 2006, in *The New York Times*.[4]

Love in Vienna: The Sigmund Freud–Minna Bernays Affair provides a critical look at the relationship and offers conclusions as to its nature and its implications for Freud's life and work. It examines the numerous arguments pro and con with regard to whether there was an affair—the first study to systematically do so—and concludes that Jung's recollections cannot be easily discounted, especially given how close Freud and Minna became. In a departure from previous scholarship, it also suggests that if anyone lied about the affair it was not Jung, as many have maintained, but might well have been Minna. Given her emotional needs, perhaps she was expressing her hope that such a romance had occurred, rather than asserting that it actually had.

What, if any, substantive contributions Minna made to the corpus of Freud's ideas is less clear. Yet it seems reasonably certain she provided Freud with something equally important and valuable: emotional support at a time when his self-esteem was at its nadir as he struggled to gain recognition for his ideas.

Love in Vienna argues that Minna Bernays, starting in the mid-1890s and continuing for some years beyond the turn of the century, became, in essence, Sigmund Freud's second wife, and in some ways the better, more desirable one—a cultured woman who was vivacious, interesting, supportive, and funny. It explores the transition in Freud's affections from his wife Martha (and family) to Minna (and work) throughout this period.[5]

We see Minna performing the same domestic duties as Martha, including caring for Freud's six children, helping with household management, and protecting Freud against unwanted distractions and intrusions. We also see her acting in ways Martha could not or did not want to: providing solace, showing empathy, taking Freud's ideas seriously, offering criticism, sharing his elitist, often sardonic outlook on life as well as his secularism, becoming his favorite travelling companion, playing cards with him, reading his manuscripts, checking his translations ... in essence, becoming his irreplaceable confidante and muse.[6]

It is not without significance that in a May 21, 1894, letter to his Berlin friend and colleague Wilhelm Fliess, Freud refers to Minna as "my closest confidante."[7]

In this study, after providing background information on Freud and Jung, our chief antagonists in this story (Chapter 1), I present the views of those who believe there was an affair (Chapter 2), as well as those who think there was not (Chapter 3). I then look critically at both sides of the argument and attempt to sort out the various pros and cons while I weigh the available evidence (Chapter 4).

I then explore in detail the Minna/Freud relationship (Chapter 5), followed by Freud's relationship with his wife, Martha (Chapter 6). I will show how different these two relationships were and will argue that in those differences lies the key to understanding an affair between Minna and Freud.

I will conclude by summarizing my findings and touching upon several additional, related topics: the impact Jung's own sexual infidelities might have had on his view of the Freud/Minna relationship and how, in some striking ways, Jung emulated Freud's "two wives" situation in his own life.

I will also examine what I call the powerful Fortress Freud mentality that dominated life at Berggasse (and still pervades the work of Freud scholarship now), and how this mentality may have covered up an affair between Freud and Minna as a way of protecting Freud and psychoanalysis.

Finally, I will assess the implications for psychoanalysis of Freud's affair with Minna Bernays. While I don't believe that Freud's sexual dalliance in any way impacted the validity of his life's work—the value of psychoanalysis has to be assessed by objective criteria that have nothing to do with his particular sexual desires—I do believe that looking carefully at the reasons for his affair, and especially as these pertain to his relations with both Minna and Martha, can tell us much about Freud the man and how his personality contributed in a positive way to the development of psychoanalysis at the beginning, as well as how in the long run it negatively impacted his efforts to find long-term adherents to his ideas.

ACKNOWLEDGMENTS

I owe thanks to many people who helped me put this work together, unfortunately too many to mention all of their names here. Of particular importance was the editorial staff of Praeger, especially Catherine Lafuente and Nicole Azze, and Peter Feely at Amnet. Their constant support and encouragement was invaluable as was their ability to answer my numerous questions in a thoughtful and helpful way. I also want to thank Dr. Robert Schulmann, my roommate at the University of Chicago, who went on to a distinguished career as an historian of Einstein. He read an early draft of *Love in Vienna* and made many helpful suggestions. His daughter, Vera Schulmann, who lives in Europe with her family, did yeoman service in translating the many German texts that for the first time now appear in English in this work. She helped supplement in a major way my own rather meager college German. Finally, I want to thank the many librarians without whose help I could not have produced this volume. Michele Missner, formerly of the University of Wisconsin, was especially helpful as were the staffs of the Arlington County Library, Arlington, Virginia, and the Library of Congress in Washington, DC.

PART I

THE CONTROVERSY

THE ANTAGONISTS: FREUD AND JUNG

Before I turn to the issue at hand—the alleged affair—it would be useful to remind the reader of something about Sigmund Freud and Carl Gustav Jung. While the focus of this study is on Freud's alleged affair with his sister-in-law, the two main antagonists in our story, as you will see, are actually Freud and Jung.

THE POSITIVIST SCHOOL

Sigmund Freud was born in the Moravian town of Freiberg in the Austrian Empire on May 6, 1856. He was the son of Galician Jewish parents, his father Jakob an impecunious wool merchant.[1] Looking for brighter business prospects, Jakob moved his growing family first to Leipzig, Germany, in 1859 and then to Vienna, Austria, in 1860.[2] There the family settled, and in 1865 Freud entered the *Sperl Gymnasium*, where he excelled, graduating *summa cum laude* in 1873.[3]

Later that same year he entered the University of Vienna as a medical student. At the university, he came under the influence of the positivist school of thought. Practitioners of this philosophy included Berlin professors Emil Du Bois-Reymond and Hermann Helmholtz and his own University of Vienna professor Ernst von Brücke. Positivism sought to apply the findings and methods of the natural sciences to the investigation of all human thought and behavior. It rejected the influence of mysticism, vitalism, and supernatural powers. Everything, it was thought, could be explained by common physical-chemical forces, without the need to appeal to divine powers.[4]

This vision of a "physics" of nature, with its secular perspective on the world, became ingrained in Freud. This is important to remember, in order to better understand Freud's reaction later, when confronted with the occult and spiritualist tendencies of Jung. The two men always saw the world from two very different philosophical points of view. How they ever came together for as long as they did is a greater mystery to me than why they eventually went their separate ways.

ENTERING PRIVATE PRACTICE

Freud graduated with an MD in psychiatry and neurology in 1882 and began work at the Vienna General Hospital, where he remained for three years. He was not interested in practicing medicine[5]—he felt much more comfortable doing research—but in June 1882 he had become engaged to Martha Bernays, Minna Bernays's sister, and was not in a financial position to support a family on a university teacher's salary, among other reasons why a university career seemed out of reach.[6] While at the hospital Freud became interested in clinical work, especially in Theodor Meynert's psychiatric clinic. In 1885, based on promising research completed to date, Freud was awarded the coveted position of *Privatdozent,* or lecturer, at the university, in the field of neuropathology.[7]

In 1886 Freud resigned his hospital post and entered private practice specializing in "nervous disorders." The year before, Freud had been awarded a travelling fellowship to study with Jean-Martin Charcot, who was experimenting with the use of hypnosis at his Paris clinic, *La Salpêtrière.* Freud saw the impact that hypnosis could have on patients exhibiting hysterical symptoms. Also, Charcot was taking hysteria seriously, diagnosing it as a genuine ailment rather than what some had called a "malingerer's refuge."[8]

THE BEGINNING OF PSYCHOANALYSIS

Returning home, Freud began to apply hypnosis to hysterical patients under his care. He used a method developed by Dr. Josef Breuer, a close personal friend and eventual collaborator. In 1895 the two published *Studies on Hysteria,* a collection of case studies.[9] Breuer's method differed from Charcot's in that it did not use suggestion. Breuer put patients under hypnosis and asked them to talk about memories and traumatic incidents associated with the onset of their symptoms (one of Breuer's patients called it the "talking cure"), and the very act of remembering seemed to reduce the severity of the symptoms. Eventually, Freud abandoned hypnosis altogether (his results with it had been mixed) and adopted a variation of Breuer's method, which Freud called "free association," in which he asked his patients to say anything that might come into their minds. He also found that patients' dreams could be usefully analyzed. They often revealed important unconscious mechanisms of repression that may have been the original source of their symptoms. He also saw the importance of sexual factors in the etiology of the neuroses.[10]

By 1896, Freud had labeled his new system of treatment "psychoanalysis," describing both his clinical methods of treatment as well as a theory of the mind that formed the basis for those methods. During this same time, Freud was experiencing periods of severe depression, which he realized were linked to the recent death of his father. This led him to embark upon an exhaustive "self-analysis," focusing on an examination of childhood memories as well as of his own dreams. What he learned from this effort helped him refine his theories of infantile sexuality. This, in turn, led eventually to his promulgation of his concept of the Oedipus complex and other basic tenets of psychoanalysis.

JUNG AND *THE INTERPRETATION OF DREAMS*

Over the next several years, Freud produced seminal works expanding and further elucidating his theories of the psychogenic origin of hysterical symptoms with an emphasis on repression and infantile sexuality. These included *The Interpretation of Dreams* (1900), *The Psychopathology of Every Life* (1901), *Jokes and Their Relation to the Unconscious* (1905), and *Three Essays on the Theory of Sexuality* (1905).[11] Beginning in 1902, a small group of followers began to form around Freud, and a regular Wednesday evening discussion group (eventually called the Wednesday Psychological Society) was established. This group included Alfred Adler, who, like Jung, was later to break with Freud and start his own "school."[12]

Eventually, Freud's theories began to attract the attention of a wider medical audience, including Jung, who at the time was a brilliant young psychiatrist serving as assistant to Eugen Bleuler at the prestigious Burghölzli Mental Hospital in Zürich. Jung had been familiar with Freud's work since 1900, when Bleuler had asked him to read Freud's *The Interpretation of Dreams*. In 1906 the two began a correspondence culminating in Jung's visit to Freud in 1907, Jung's meeting with Minna, and her revelations about her affair with Freud. An intense collaboration between Freud and Jung continued for the next six years.[13]

A MOST UNUSUAL CHILDHOOD

Carl Gustav Jung was born on July 26, 1875, in Kesswil on Lake Constance in the Swiss canton of Thurgau. He was the fourth but first surviving child of Paul Achilles Jung, a well-educated but poor country pastor of the Protestant Swiss Reformed Church, and Emilie Preiswerk, his unhappy and often unstable wife. In 1879, Paul Jung was transferred to a new parish located in a small suburb of Basel.[14]

Jung's parents' marriage was not happy; turbulent marriages seem to have been a tradition in the Jung family.[15] Jung's mother was an eccentric woman who talked to spirits she claimed visited her at night. She also grew careless about her personal appearance and became obese, remaining so for the remainder of her life. While often tender with young Carl, she could also frighten him with her strange behavior.[16] Jung's father had shown great promise in his youth as a brilliant student of Oriental languages at Göttingen University in Germany, but he had a depressive personality, and was often quarrelsome and bad-tempered when with his family.[17] In 1875 Jung's parents separated for a period, his mother spending some time in a mental hospital.[18]

Jung was a solitary and introverted child, often feeling lonely, inferior, and depressed.[19] At about the age of four he developed a morbid fascination with death.[20] He soon became convinced he had two personalities: one living in the present, the other an historical figure living in the past.[21]

In 1886, Jung entered the *Humanistisches Gymnasium* in Basel, the school to which the best families in Basel sent their sons.[22] Poor compared to his peers, the young boy often displayed raucous behavior, including pranks and fights with classmates. Jung recalled that most of his teachers thought him stupid and crafty.[23] After an accident, he also became susceptible to fainting spells, which he attributed to his dislike of school, where he found the work boring and one subject, mathematics, particularly taxing. He would rather have spent time "drawing battles and playing with fire," he afterward remembered.[24] In his later school years, he began to settle down and take his studies more seriously, particularly after overhearing his father lament to a friend that he did not know what to do with his difficult son and he wondered whether young Carl might someday ever be able to earn a living.[25] Between the ages of sixteen and nineteen, Jung felt his depressive moods begin to lighten and eventually disappear, and he soon made friends and became more engaged in his studies.[26]

At the end of his school days he had no clear notion as to what he wanted to become—his interests alternated between science and the humanities, and his father, based on personal experience, had strongly urged him to stay away from theology and the clergy. Carl finally settled on science and, in the spring of 1895, began the study of medicine at the University of Basel.[27] Too poor to pay the tuition, his father applied for and received a stipend to help defray the costs of his son's university education. The fact that he needed financial support greatly embarrassed Jung.[28]

Soon after Carl entered the university, Jung's father died, but family members helped support his education. He also took steps to support himself, working as a junior assistant in anatomy at the university and helping his aged aunt dispose of her modest collection of antiques, receiving a small percentage of the sales.[29] In 1898, Jung, though interested in surgery and internal medicine, chose psychiatry as his area of specialization.

THE BURGHÖLZLI

Following graduation, on December 10, 1900, Jung took a position as an assistant at the Burghölzli, which Eugen Bleuler then headed. Here Jung began an intensive study of psychiatric techniques, and his interests in psychotherapy and Freud first emerged.[30] He was impressed by Freud's *The Interpretation of Dreams*. Jung felt that Freud's work was a landmark (he would later call it "a masterpiece"),[31] the first to introduce psychology into psychiatry, even though Freud himself was trained as a neurologist. At the time Jung had already begun diagnostic association studies, with the aim of trying to understand what takes place within the minds of the mentally ill, and Freud's work seemed to confirm much of what Jung was discovering about the unconscious mind and repression.[32]

In 1903 Jung published his dissertation, "On the Psychology and Pathology of So-Called Occult Phenomena," and in the same year he married Emma Rauschenbach, who came from a wealthy Swiss family.[33] In 1905 he became a lecturer in psychiatry at the University of Zürich and was promoted to senior physician at the Burghölzli.

SUPPORTING FREUD

By this time, Jung, although skeptical of the importance Freud placed on the role of the libido (sexuality) in mental functioning, had become an open supporter of Freud's, despite the risk to his own career. Jung later recalled that Freud's ideas at the time were *persona non grata* in academic circles because of their strong emphasis on the sexual etiology of symptoms. "At congresses," Jung would remember, "he [Freud] was discussed only in the corridors, never on the floor."[34] But Jung believed that psychoanalysis, and especially its techniques of dream analysis and interpretation, could shed valuable light on schizophrenic forms of expression, a topic in which he was at the time engrossed.[35] In 1906 Jung's *Studies in Word Association* appeared, a copy of which he sent to Freud, and the correspondence between the two men began.

A SHORT BUT INTENSE RELATIONSHIP

The Freud-Jung collaboration, one of the most turbulent in the history of psychiatry, did not last long. Hoping that Jung's support for psychoanalysis would help bring his theories recognition beyond his small group of supporters in Vienna, Freud planned to name Jung his heir and successor. But Jung never felt comfortable with Freud's emphasis on sexuality, and Freud had trouble accepting any deviation from his disciples when it came to what he considered the core principles of psychoanalysis. By 1913 the two men had chosen to go their separate ways.

CHAPTER 2

THE RUMOR AND ITS ORIGINS

The rumor of an affair between Freud and his sister-in-law did not become the subject of serious research until a published account of it appeared in 1969. Analyses followed which sought to corroborate that an affair had taken place.

AN UNLIKELY BEGINNING

It is odd that the first public mention that there might have been some alienation of affection in Freud's marriage began not with someone claiming that it was true, but with a staunch Freud supporter protesting that it was not: Freud's colleague and loyal biographer Ernest Jones.[1]

The most prominent English-speaking proponent of psychoanalysis and its leading spokesperson in the United Kingdom during the first half of the twentieth century, in 1953 Jones published Volume I of his three-volume authorized biography of Freud. By 1957 all three volumes had appeared. The work was enormous in scope, but, unfortunately, often hagiographic in tone.[2]

In Volume I, Jones tell us something about Freud the man and his sexual and moral rectitude. Freud was undoubtedly, Jones asserts, "monogamic in a very unusual degree, but for a time seemed to be well on his way to becoming uxorious," or excessively devoted to his wife.[3] Jones then adds,

"He always gave the impression of being an unusually chaste person—the word 'puritanical' would not be out of place."[4]

As far as Minna Bernays and Freud went, according to Jones they were close but not dangerously so: "*Tante* Minna was witty, interesting, and amusing, but she had a pungent tongue that contributed to a store of family epigrams. She and Freud got on excellently together. There was no sexual attraction on either side, but he found her a stimulating and amusing companion and would occasionally make short holiday excursions with her when his wife was not free to travel."[5]

All of this, Jones continues, gave rise to "the malicious and entirely untrue legend that she displaced his wife in his affections. Freud always enjoyed the society of intellectual and rather masculine women, of whom there was a series in his acquaintanceship."[6] Minna appears to have been the first of this group.

In Volume II, published in 1955, Jones returns to the subject and uses the occasion to criticize Helen Walker Puner's biography of Freud, which had appeared almost a decade before: "It is desirable to say something about Freud's married life, since various strange legends seem to be in vogue about it. In particular, Helen Puner's picture of it is very remote from that familiar to anyone with personal knowledge. His wife was assuredly the only woman in Freud's love life, and she always came first before all other mortals."[7]

On the next page Jones turns to Minna Bernays, so it seems we can assume that at least in Jones's mind there is some connection between "the only woman in Freud's life" (meaning Martha) and Martha's sister Minna. Jones writes, "One of [Freud's] sons remarked to me that 'Tante Minna' deserved a book to herself, so interesting and decided was her personality. She certainly knew more about Freud's work than did her sister, and he remarked once that in the lonely nineties Fliess and she were the only people in the world who sympathized with it."[8] Freud, Jones continues, "no doubt appreciated her conversation, but to say that she in any way replaced her sister in his affections is sheer nonsense."[9]

What we have learned from Jones thus far is that Freud was chaste, almost puritanical, loved only Martha, liked Minna but not that much— not in a romantic sense, anyway—and what Helen Puner says in her biography about Freud, Martha, and Minna just isn't so. And what does Jones claim Puner says? Remember, right after commenting that "Helen Puner's picture of [Freud's married life] is very remote from that familiar to anyone with personal knowledge," Jones adds, "His wife was assuredly the only woman in Freud's love life." This certainly appears to imply that

Helen Puner said something different—that Martha Freud wasn't the only woman in her husband's life.

In reading through Helen Walker Puner's biography it is impossible to find any direct reference to an affair between Minna and Freud or hints that such an affair took place, or even that Minna might have somehow superseded Martha in Freud's affections. The information in Puner's work is a bit muddled. Admittedly, Puner presents a tough, critical look at Freud's relationship with Martha. She finds it pretty much devoid of love— as well as respect. She writes: "Outwardly, the marriage was ... correct. ... Inwardly ... it lacked luster and joy. It was as if Freud's capacity for love, naturally great, were encased in a block of ice."[10] Pretty strong stuff, but no hint of an affair. Puner continues: "In [Martha's] domain of catering to [Freud's] physical comfort and shielding him from the routine stresses of everyday living, she remained superlative. But she could not be as immediately sensitive to the other needs of his nature."[11]

And what exactly are these "other" needs? Puner does not say. They could be sexual, they could be intellectual, they could be both, or neither; we just don't know. But this sounds a bit suggestive. Martha could satisfy certain of her husband's needs, but not others. Is the implication that perhaps another woman, Minna, could? It is not clear.

Puner portrays Freud's relationship with Minna in a favorable light, especially when compared to how she describes the rather passionless nature of his life with Martha. Freud's marriage to Martha, Puner notes, was not "a marriage built ... on the mutual respect of two equals, but on the limitless subservience of the woman to the man." Minna, on the other hand, "because of her independence and intellectual stature was always more companionable to Freud than his wife."[12]

But elsewhere Puner disabuses readers of any notion that she might be thinking that Freud could find greater happiness with Minna. In fact, it seems she believes the opposite, and this is where things get confusing. Puner writes: "Frau Freud [Martha] oiled the incomparably efficient household machinery with the measured, temperate kindliness that was natural to her. Tante Minna ... might be more forthright and more aggressive. She might lend to her few, pungent words a decidedly epigrammatic turn. She might understand more clearly the importance of the work Sigmund Freud was doing. ... Certainly she had more time for, and was fonder of reading and could evaluate what she read with discrimination and wit. But her slimmer, smaller sister, who had neither the time nor the zest for intellectual pursuits, had a kind of deep, albeit restrained and delimited humanity to offer in place of Minna's more clearly defined individuality."[13]

Unless I am misunderstanding what Puner is saying, I don't see any suggestion of a Freud/Minna affair in Puner's description of the two sisters' roles vis-à-vis Freud. More significantly, at one point in her book Puner flatly denies that possibility. She notes: "Sigmund Freud would never once swerve from the path of marital rectitude that grew from the seed of his general rigid morality. ... Freud never deviated from the straight path of his righteousness, any more than he could deviate from the fixed character traits which gave rise to that righteousness."[14]

Why is Jones apparently associating Puner's book with these so-called strange legends about an affair between Freud and Minna or at least some sort of alienation of affection? There doesn't seem to be any reason to do so. Don't forget, Jones identifies Puner "in particular."

Daniel Burston, in his 2008 article, "A Very Freudian Affair: Erich Fromm, Peter Swales and the Future of Psychoanalytic Historiography,"[15] asks the same question about these so-called malicious "legends." However, Burston mistakenly attributes the origins of the legends to Kurt Eissler's 1953 interview with Jung in which, Burston says, "Jung revealed that, during his visit to the Freud household in 1907, Jung and Minna shared a few private moments together, and that she confided in him." I have read that interview, which is in German. It was released to the public by the Freud Archives at the Library of Congress in 2013, and Jung does not say that. More on the interview later in this chapter.

I suspect Jones hated Puner's book for its stark depiction of an autocratic Freud and his loveless marriage to Martha, for Jones took every opportunity in his biography of Freud to zing Puner. In essence, Puner's was the biography of Freud which Jones wrote his *against*. I count at least eight instances where he singles her out for criticism.[16] No other source is treated in a similar way. In Paul Roazen's introduction to the 1992 Transaction Edition of Puner's study, he points out Puner's book was one of the reasons Anna Freud authorized an official biography of her father, against his stated wishes: in order to set the record straight, given Puner's characterization of Freud and his family.[17]

But what record is Jones trying to set straight? If we can't find the rumor of a Freud/Minna affair in Puner's book, what are these so-called strange legends about Freud's marriage that Jones seems to be upset about? Remember, he refers to "legends" twice: first the "'malicious and entirely untrue legend that [Minna] displaced his wife in his affections,"[18] and then the "various strange legends [which] seem to be in vogue about it [Freud's marriage]."[19]

I don't know where Jones got his information, but I have certain suspicions. I believe he must be referring to various rumors current at the time

he was writing his biography (the early 1950s) or rumors about Freud and ?
Minna he had heard in the past. Or probably both.

RAISING EYEBROWS

Some things we do know. The several holiday trips that Minna and her
brother-in-law took alone apparently raised eyebrows within the Freud
family. Franz Maciejewski points out, "Years later, Freud's niece, Judith
Bernays Heller, would recollect that there had been lots of gossip within the Lot3?
family; wicked tongues had spoken of Sigmund's 'second wife.'" Albrecht
Hirschmüller has described the gossip about the trips as "vicious" with references to the "other woman."[20] The Freuds might have been secretive, but
they were not stupid. And they were not blind. Just imagine how such gal-
livanting alone through the mountain resorts of Austria, Switzerland, and
Italy by a man and his sister-in-law would appear today in a much more
sexually emancipated world. And Minna was unmarried.

But of course Freud and Minna had a special relationship, an especially   yes...
close one. She was an integral part of the family, so perhaps some of their
behavior could be justified in those terms. It still looks unusual, and apparently some members of the Freud family thought so as well. We can expect
that, if there was talk in the family, Jones would probably have heard about
it, as close as he was to Freud at the time.[21]

Freud himself knew there was a rumor circulating about him and Minna,
as Kurt Eissler reveals in his 1993 book *Three Instances of Injustice*. Eissler
was the founder and first director of the Freud Archives at the Library of
Congress and a staunch Freudian. According to him, a woman named Eva
Rosenfeld, who was being treated by Freud and who "moved in his circle"
told Eissler in an interview that "Freud expressed surprise that she [Rosen-   ?
feld] never brought up … the rumor she must have heard about him and his
sister-in-law."[22] The same story also involving Eva Rosenfeld is told by Paul
Roazen in his book *Freud and His Followers*. Roazen writes: "On at least
one occasion Freud raised the issue of his relationship with Minna in an
analysis; Freud chided the patient, 'So you believe in my famous love affair
with Minna.' But when the patient disavowed the idea, Freud seemed a bit
miffed, as much offended for Minna's sake as for his own." Roazen gives the
reference as an "Interview with Eva Rosenfeld, November 3, 1966."[23]

Yet Eva Rosenfeld was no ordinary patient and not only someone who
"moved in his [Freud's] circle." She was Anna Freud's first intimate friend,
before Anna became involved with Dorothy Burlingham, the daughter of
Louis Comfort Tiffany, whose children Freud was treating and who rented
the apartment directly above the Freuds at Berggasse 19.[24]

If Freud knew about the rumor, we can assume that others did as well, perhaps even before Freud did. In matters like this, the subjects of gossip are often the last to find out. Thus, many decades before Jones's biography appeared in the early fifties, it seems probable that a rumor about Freud and Minna must have been making the rounds, and Jones, I suspect, was aware of this.

There is a curious sentence in Peter Gay's 1988 biography of Freud, where he addresses the Freud/Minna rumor. He asks: "Did Freud have an affair with his sister-in-law Minna Bernays? The first to have made the charge was apparently Carl G. Jung, in private (it is reported) and then in 1957 in an interview with his friend, John M. Billinsky, who published it in 1969."[25] We will be getting to Jung and Billinsky momentarily. Right now I want to focus on the "in private (it is reported)" part of Gay's statement. Who reported it? Gay does not say, but it could have been many people.

One person who did hear the story directly from Jung was Dr. C. A. Meier, an acquaintance of Billinsky, a confidante of Jung, and a friend of Kurt Eissler. We know this because Eissler reported as much, again in the aforementioned 1993 *Three Instances of Injustice.*[26] Eissler says Meier had heard the exact same story Jung had told Billinsky in 1957. Meier, with whom Eissler had worked on a collection of Freud/Jung letters and whose reliability, according to Eissler, "is above doubt," did not indicate when he first heard the story or when he told Eissler about it. We will learn later from Peter Gay that Meier apparently heard the story "years before."[27] In any case, I suspect Meier is one of the people Jung told "in private," and since Eissler knew about it his close friend Jones must have known as well.

It is interesting that Gay also finds Jones's defense of Freud a little awkward—as in, the loyal biographer doth protest too much. Gay observes: "Ernest Jones's pertinent comments [about Freud and Minna] hint, not so much perhaps that Jung's story is necessarily true, but that it had been circulating and seemed persuasive enough (at least to some) to deserve explicit refutation. Certainly, Jones is emphatic enough on the matter to cause the suspicious to wonder whether he is not being a little defensive."[28]

THE EISSLER INTERVIEW

Another possible source of the rumor for Jones—a source which has come to my attention only recently—is the aforementioned 1953 Kurt Eissler interview of Jung, which, like Billinsky's, took place at Jung's home in Küsnacht in Switzerland.[29] It is an interview that Eissler never talked about publically, as far as I am aware. The transcript of it was embargoed

for sixty years on orders from Eissler and was released for public review
only in 2013, as indicated earlier.

The Eissler interview is very interesting in at least one regard, for purposes of our discussion here. It is clear from Eissler's aggressive questions
on certain delicate topics that he already knew what Jung had said about
an affair between Minna and Freud and he was attempting to tease out of
Jung whatever details the latter might be willing to share on the topic. Jung
is very coy, however. After all, he is meeting with the "enemy," the ultimate
Freudian, and he seems to know exactly what Eissler is attempting to do.
We will be discussing this interview at considerable length, with excerpts,
later in this study, so I will not now go into detail. But the point here is that
I suspect someone had already informed Eissler about the "Minna matter"
(perhaps C. A. Meier or a member of the Freud family), so Eissler knew
about Minna's confession at least four years before Jung related the same
story to Billinksy. Thus if Eissler knew in 1953, one can assume his close
friend and colleague Jones knew as well and therefore Eissler is another
possible source of the rumor or "strange legend" that Jones is trying so
hard to combat. Unfortunately for Puner, Jones conflates these so-called
legends with her critical look at Freud and family, and actually reads more
into her book than is really there.

BILLINSKY'S REVELATIONS

The first and only public report that Freud and Minna had an affair came
with the publication in 1969 of John M. Billinsky's 1957 interview of Jung.

Billinsky was born in 1917 in Philadelphia and educated at the Hartford
Theological Seminary, Harvard University, and the C. G. Jung Institute in
Zürich. I think it would be correct to plant him firmly in the Jungian camp.
At the time the interview was published, Billinsky was a professor of psy-
chology and clinical studies at Andover Newton Theological School and on
the staff of the Boston City Hospital.[30]

On September 5, 1969, Billinsky tells us, an article appeared in *Time*
magazine,[31] where it was reported that thirteen letters between Freud and
psychologist and Clark University President G. Stanley Hall were found
in Clark University's library basement.[32] Most of the letters "abound with
expressions of gratitude and courtesy," Billinsky says.[33] But one of the letters, Billinsky emphasizes, is of a sharper tone and "replied to Hall's suggestion that Prize Disciple Carl Jung's bitter split with Freud was a classic case
of adolescent rebellion."[34]

In his return letter to Hall dated August 28, 1923, Freud points out "if
the real facts were more familiar to you, you would very likely not have

thought that there was again a case where a father did not let his sons develop, but you would have seen that the sons wished to eliminate their father, as in ancient times."[35]

It is obvious that Freud's letter of August 28, 1923, with its apparent sharp criticism of Jung—you will understand why I use the word "apparent" in a moment—angered Billinsky and forced him into publishing his 1957 interview with Jung. He did so in order to reveal the *real* reason for Jung's break with Freud: namely, Freud's affair with Minna and his unwillingness to share with Jung personal details associated with dreams that might be related to that affair; in other words, Freud's autocratic exercise of "authority." These dreams are the so-called (by Jung) "triangle" dreams, involving Freud, Martha, and Minna.

Presented with the *Time* article containing the quotation from the August 28, 1923, Freud letter to Hall, Billinsky appears to have felt the need to set the record straight and give Jung's side of the argument, even though by doing so he is forced to reveal intimate details of Freud's private life. The information Billinsky had was potentially explosive. That is probably why he held it back for so long and why, when he finally did decide to go public with it, he tried to soften what Jung had told him, presumably to reduce embarrassment to Freud's family.

An additional factor which might have driven Billinsky into publication is that the article appeared in *Time* magazine, which had the largest circulation of any news magazine in the world at the time, and still retains that title. *Time*'s circulation in June 2013 was 3,301,056.[36] I suspect that in 1969 its circulation was even larger. And the article about Freud's criticism of Jung did not appear in some out-of-the-way section of the magazine, but in its popular "People" page. Above the article in the upper right-hand corner of the page is a picture of a smiling, handsome Sigmund Freud, cigar in hand, captioned with his name—and below that, "Eliminating father."[37] Talk about pouring salt into an open wound! Billinsky must have been furious. My bet is that if a similar article had appeared in some out-of-the-way scholarly journal, Billinsky would not have hurried to publish the information he had about Minna and Freud—at least, not as quickly as he did.

GETTING IT WRONG

But there is one odd twist to this story, and it is an important one. It is one of those that makes history stranger than fiction, and fun for those interested in pursuing the profession. I think it ironic that the primary reason Billinsky published his interview with Jung (with the story of Freud's infidelity) appears to have been to get back at Freud for bashing Jung in his

August 28, 1923, letter to Hall. I say this because, in that letter, *Freud does not bash Jung at all!* In the letter *Time* (and later Billinsky) quotes, Freud is bashing Alfred Adler, not Jung. Like Jung, as mentioned before, Adler was originally a disciple of Freud and later broke with him. Freud feared that Hall was moving away from psychoanalysis and into Adler's camp, and apparently wanted to disparage Adler in Hall's eyes. If only Billinsky had looked closely at the *Time* article and researched more carefully, he would have realized that in the August 28, 1923, letter to Hall Freud does not even mention Jung.

So this whole controversy about Jung, Freud, and Minna came to light because of an aggressive *Time* reporter who got it wrong, followed by an anxious and angry Jungian psychologist who also got it wrong. Of course the argument can be made that the complaints Freud had about Alfred Adler trying to "murder" the father (Freud) could be applied equally to Jung, and that is true, but the fact is that in the letter cited Freud was not attacking Jung.[38] Ten years earlier, in a letter to G. Stanley Hall dated November 21, 1913, Freud mentions Jung, but it is less in the form of a criticism than an announcement—that a divorce had taken place. Freud writes: "The only inauspicious changes in the psychoanalytic movement concern personal relationships. Jung, with whom I shared my visit with you, is no longer my friend, and our collaboration is approaching complete dissolution." Freud then adds laconically, "Such changes are regrettable but inevitable." No mention of Jung trying to depose him.[39]

THE BILLINSKY INTERVIEW

Billinsky interviewed Jung on May 10, 1957. The interview began at approximately 4:30 P.M., and Billinsky recorded (wrote out) Jung's remarks later the same day.[40] Jung was eighty-two years of age at the time. He tells Billinsky that he, along with his wife Emma and a young protégé at the Burghölzli, Ludwig Binswanger, visited Freud's apartment in Vienna during the week beginning March 3, 1907. It was Jung and Freud's first meeting, although, as you'll recall from Chapter 1, Jung and Freud had begun corresponding in 1906.

Jung remembers:

> Soon I met Freud's wife's younger sister. She was very good-looking and she not only knew enough about psychoanalysis but also about everything that Freud was doing. When, a few days later, I was visiting Freud's laboratory, Freud's sister-in-law asked if she could talk with me. She was very much bothered by her relationship with Freud

and felt guilty about it. From her I learned that Freud was in love
with her and that their relationship was indeed very intimate. It was
a shocking discovery to me, and even now I can recall the agony I felt
at the time.

Two years later Freud and I were invited to Clark University in
Worcester [Massachusetts], and we were together every day for some
seven weeks. From the very beginning of our trip we started to analyze each other's dreams. Freud had some dreams that bothered him
very much. The dreams were about the triangle—Freud, his wife, and
wife's younger sister. Freud had no idea that I knew about the triangle
and his intimate relationship with his sister-in-law. And so, when
Freud told me about the dream in which his wife and her sister played
important parts, I asked Freud to tell me some of his personal associations with the dream. He looked at me with bitterness and said,
'I could tell you more but I cannot risk my authority.' That, of course,
finished my attempt to deal with his dreams. During the trip Freud
developed severe neuroses, and I had to do limited analysis with him.
He had psychosomatic troubles and had difficulties in controlling
his bladder [incontinence]. I suggested to Freud that he should have
complete analysis. ... If Freud would have tried to understand consciously the triangle, he would have been much, much better off. ... It
was my knowledge of Freud's triangle that became a very important
factor in my break with Freud. And then I could not accept Freud's
placing authority above the truth. This, too, led to further problems
in our relationship. In retrospect it looks like it was destined that our
relationship should end that way. It was full of questions and doubts
from the very beginning.[41]

Years later Jung would describe, a bit salaciously, the topic of Freud's "triangle" dreams as "hot material" to his friend Karl Schmid.[42]

Earlier in the Billinsky interview, just before Jung talks about Minna's
confession, he also comments on Martha Freud. He does so in rather
unflattering terms, in sharp contrast to the effusive praise he bestows upon
Minna. Jung, again from the Billinsky interview:

When I arrived in Vienna with my young and happy wife, Freud came
to see us at the hotel and brought some flowers for my wife. He was
trying to be very considerate and at one point he said to me, "I am
sorry that I can give you no real hospitality; I have nothing at home
but an elderly wife." When my wife heard him say that, she looked
perturbed and embarrassed. At home that evening,[43] during dinner,

I tried to talk to Freud and his wife about psychoanalysis and Freud's activities, but I soon discovered that Mrs. Freud knew absolutely nothing about what Freud was doing. It was very obvious that there was a very superficial relationship between Freud and his wife.[44]

It's almost as if Martha is an embarrassment to Freud; that there really isn't much substance to their marriage, at least from Jung's point of view.

It is important to note that Jung connects Minna's confession directly to the Freud "triangle" dream episode which occurred when the two were together in America. It is only because of what Minna had confessed to Jung about her affair with Freud in 1907 that Jung knows Freud is withholding vital information when they begin to interpret Freud's "triangle" dream. These two incidents, the confession and the "triangle" dream episode, are inextricably linked in Jung's mind—linked historically as well as conceptually.

I suspect that if Jung had not heard Minna's confession two years previously he would not have been as upset as he was when Freud refused to give further details about the "triangle" dream. I think he might have simply dismissed Freud's reluctance as a desire not to deal with matters of a personal nature. But since Jung did know, Freud's appeal to "authority" was seen as an act of concealment and a lack of trust and candor on Freud's part, which obviously offended Jung. I suspect there would have been other reasons for their eventual breakup, given the ideological differences between the two men and how really different each man's psychological makeup was, but that is another story.

As mentioned, after the interview with Jung, Billinsky transcribed his notes that same day—May 10, 1957. University of Florida professor Peter Rudnytsky indicates that the notes are much more graphic than Billinsky's published version of the interview. Rudnytsky is one of only a few people who have had access to Billinsky's original notes. The difference between the published version and the notes is significant. In the published version, Billinsky writes that Minna told Jung her relationship with Freud "was indeed very intimate." This could mean they were having sex or any number of other possible things. Yet in the original notes, Rudnytsky points out, Billinsky records Jung telling him that Minna said she and Freud had "sexual relations." There can be no doubt about what that means.[45]

CONFIRMATION

I have received confirmation of Rudnytsky's assessment from Billinsky's son, John M. Billinsky Jr., who is a psychiatrist in North Carolina and who remembers reading the notes before they appeared in published form.[46] I had tried through Rudnytsky's good offices to obtain a copy of the notes, but my efforts were blocked by the person who had shared the notes with Rudnytsky. This is ironic because that same person had been someone who has complained vehemently against the practice, rather common in the world of Freud scholarship, of denying some researchers access to documentary materials, while allowing others a free hand. More on this in our final chapter.

Billinsky's son tells me he looked for his father's notes of the Jung interview following his death, but could not find them. However, he suspects his sister might have them. I think perhaps that's how they ended up in the hands of at least one researcher. Billinsky Junior also informs me that the publication of his father's article created a bit of a hullabaloo. He recalls that a nephew of Freud's went on *The Tonight Show*, with Johnny Carson, to denounce the article and that his father received a letter from Dino DeLaurentis, the movie producer, offering to buy the copyright to the article. DeLaurentis was apparently thinking of making some sort of spicy film biography of Freud based on Billinsky's interview with Jung.

THE 1907 VISIT

The 1907 visit of Jung to Freud was important for both men. Freud was looking for converts to psychoanalysis, especially beyond the narrow group of Jewish adherents he already had in Vienna. He wanted international recognition for his ideas. He was convinced psychoanalysis was unique and revolutionary. At fifty-one years of age, he was also seeking a young and capable heir to carry on the work of psychoanalysis, spread the gospel, so to speak, convert even more people to its special insights. And Jung, as we have seen, had been Freud's chief advocate at the Burghölzli—at some risk to his own career—so Freud had evidence of the younger man's courage and missionary zeal. Also, Jung and Bleuler had made the Burghölzli the first institution where psychoanalytic techniques were formally taught to doctors and applied systematically to patients.[47]

Jung, on the other hand, only thirty-two at the time of his visit to Berggasse, was attempting to understand and investigate the psychology of the individual patient[48] and had been deeply impressed with Freud's theories, especially Freud's work on dreams and his concepts of repression and the unconscious, both of which neatly dovetailed with Jung's own work on word associations. Ambitious as Freud, Jung was thrilled to be able to meet a man he thought of as great. He remembers in his autobiography that Freud was "the first man of real importance I had encountered." Until that time, "no one else could compare with him." Jung found the older man "extremely intelligent, shrewd, and altogether remarkable."[49] Jung had apparently discovered in Freud the strong, intellectually daring father he had always felt he sorely lacked. Years later, Jung's son Franz would recall, "Father was very disappointed in his own father."[50]

Jung, his wife Emma, and Binswanger arrived at the Freud home on Sunday, March 3, 1907. They stayed for five or six days.[51] They arrived for lunch, and then Jung and Freud went into Freud's study on the upper ground floor, where they talked alone for the next thirteen hours, ending their marathon session at two o'clock the next morning. At the beginning Jung talked for three hours without pause, but then Freud intervened, suggesting that they organize their conversation for more productive results.[52] Years later, in his 1953 interview with Kurt Eissler, Jung remembers that discussion as if it had occurred just the day before, so strong was its impression on him.

Jung also attended Freud's regular Wednesday Psychological Society meeting that was held on the evening of March 6.[53] These meetings, begun in 1902, were by then a tradition and were held in Freud's waiting room off his study. Among those who attended was Alfred Adler, the subject of the famous August 28, 1923, Freud letter to G. Stanley Hall. Jung did not say much. He wasn't sure he completely understood all of Freud's ideas. He also did not think much of those in attendance. He later described them to Ernest Jones as "a medley of artists, decadents and mediocrities" and "deplored Freud's lot in being surrounded by them."[54] The Wednesday evening meeting was followed by private discussions between Freud and Jung.

Minna and one of Freud's daughters took Emma Jung shopping several days, and on one of those days Jung joined in.[55] He had lunch with the Freuds once or twice and also attended some dinners; it is not clear how many. The rest of the time during the week he had free, as Freud was busy with his regular schedule of patients.

Freud had hoped that Jung would have visited him at Easter, when Freud would have had more time—in Austria, as well as in other parts of Europe, Easter is celebrated on both Sunday and Monday—but Jung's schedule would not allow for that. Freud writes him on February 21, 1907: "I am somewhat disappointed that you cannot come at Easter time, since otherwise I am taken up every day from eight to eight with the occupations known to you. But on Sundays I am free, so I must ask you to arrange your visit to Vienna in such a way as to have a Sunday available for me."[56]

Freud was quite impressed with Jung; he liked his "vitality, liveliness and, above all, his unrestrained imagination."[57] Freud's son Martin, who met Jung only once, was impressed with the power of Jung's personality. He

remembered Jung's "ability to project his personality and to control those
who listened to him." He had a "commanding presence. He was very tall
and broad-shouldered, holding himself more like a soldier than a man of
science and medicine. His head was purely Teutonic with a strong chin, a
small moustache, blue eyes and thin close-cropped hair."[58]

No wonder Minna might have felt comfortable confiding in the mag-
netic Jung.

TWO YEARS BETWEEN

Following this first meeting, which both men felt to be very successful, their collaboration intensified rapidly. When Jung returned to the
Burghölzli, he wrote Freud to say how impressed he had been with him
personally, as well as with his ideas, and vowed to work for psychoanalysis,
even though he still had some reservations about Freud's strong emphasis
on sexuality. "I am no longer plagued by doubts as to the rightness of your
theory," Jung writes confidently on March 31, 1907, from the Burghölzli.
"The last shreds were dispelled by my stay in Vienna, which for me was an
event of the first importance."[59]

The American psychoanalyst A. A. Brill, then studying at the Burghölzli,
remembers Jung at that time being an "ardent and pugnacious Freudian.
You could not express any doubt about Freud's views without arousing his
[Jung's] ire."[60]

At the beginning of August 1907, Jung travels to Amsterdam, for the
First International Congress for Psychiatry, Psychology, and the Assistance
to the Insane.[61] Unsure of the reception his presentation on psychoanalysis might receive in such an august meeting, Jung expresses concern to
Freud. But the latter is reassuring. What Freud says is quite revealing not
only about how he views himself, but what he sees as Jung's advantages in
terms of charm. Freud writes Jung on September 2, 1907, "I have always
felt that there is something about my personality, my ideas and manner of
speaking, that people find strange and repellent, whereas all hearts open
to you."[62] At the Congress, Jung outlines Freud's psychoanalytic ideas and
indicates how his own clinical work confirms them. Freud's reassurances to
the contrary notwithstanding, Jung gets a cold reception.[63]

In the months following the Congress, contacts between Jung and Freud
become sporadic, and Freud expresses concern about their diminishing
nature. With remarkable candor, Jung confesses he believes he is keeping his distance because the veneration he has for Freud has turned into a
"religious" crush with "undeniable erotic undertone." He explains that as
a child he was sexually abused by a man he had once venerated, and as his

relationship with Freud became more intimate, at least from an emotional point of view, he felt the need to pull back.[64] Freud seeks to reassure him on this matter as well.[65]

In the spring of 1908, beginning April 27, a congress in Salzburg is held devoted solely to Freud's ideas, the first of its kind. Ernest Jones attends the congress, as does Karl Abraham, who had studied under Bleuler and Jung at the Burghölzli and now had a private psychoanalytic practice in Berlin. The thirty-five-year-old Sándor Ferenczi from Hungary, who had met Freud a few months before and had become acquainted with his ideas through a colleague of Jung's at the Burghölzli, is also there, as are Eugen Bleuler and A. A. Brill.[66] Jung is made editor of a new psychoanalytic journal, *Jahrbuch für psychoanalytische und psychopathologische Forschungen*. At the congress, Freud's Viennese followers are envious of the new people, but Freud holds firm in his belief that if psychoanalysis is to survive, it must find recognition beyond Vienna.[67]

Beginning September 18 of 1908, Freud visits Jung at the Burghölzli. This is his first visit. He tries to convince Jung to apply psychoanalytic ideas to psychotic states, as he had done to the neuroses, since Jung and Bleuler were not attributing sexual causes to schizophrenia but rather talking about toxins in the brain as the cause of the disease. During Freud's stay, the two men go hiking and mountain climbing together and have a wonderful time. Jung loves Freud's stories, which make him "laugh down to his shoes."[68]

Six months later, on March 25, 1909, Jung visits Berggasse for a second time. He is greeted warmly by Freud. He tells Freud he has decided to leave the Burghölzli for private practice and to build a house at Küsnacht on Lake Zürich. Earlier, on March 7, 1909, Jung had written Freud revealing that he had developed a strong transference to a brilliant young Russian woman, Sabina Spielrein, who he was then treating. But Jung claims he is innocent of any wrongdoing. "She [Spielrein] has kicked up a vile scandal solely because I denied myself the pleasure of giving her a child. I have always acted the gentleman toward her, but before the bar of my rather too sensitive conscience I nevertheless don't feel clean, and that is what hurts the most because my intentions were always honourable."[69] Significantly, Freud replies two days later (March 9, 1909) with a strong defense of Jung. Freud writes, "To be slandered and scorched by the love with which we operate—such are the perils of our trade."[70] Freud is obviously referring to the process of transference that occurs between patient and doctor (and sometimes between doctor and patient, so-called counter-transference) within the therapeutic setting. Freud had already witnessed a similar dangerous transference in the case of his friend and colleague Josef Breuer.[71]

Freud already knew what was happening between Jung and his patient. Sabina Spielrein's mother had written Jung warning him not to take his relationship with Sabina beyond the bounds of friendship. Jung had written back assuring Frau Spielrein that he had no intention of going beyond those bounds. But he also warns her: "You do understand, of course, that a man and a girl cannot possibly continue indefinitely to have friendly dealings with one another without the likelihood that something more may enter the relationship. For what would restrain the two from drawing the consequences of their love?" This excerpt from Jung's letter to Frau Spielrein is quoted by Sabina Spielrein in a letter she sends to Freud dated June 10–11, 1909.[72] She had asked Freud to help sort things out between Jung and her.

Jung's message to Sabina Spielrein's mother is significant in light of what he had already learned from Minna about her affair with Freud. The lesson: men and women just can't be friends—at least not for very long. After being close for a while, "something more" might enter the relationship. Witness what happened to Minna and Freud, Jung seems to be saying.

THE CLARK UNIVERSITY CELEBRATIONS

In late 1908 and early 1909 Freud and Jung are invited to Worcester, Massachusetts, by G. Stanley Hall, president of Clark University, for the celebration of the university's twentieth anniversary. They were asked to deliver lectures and were scheduled to receive honorary degrees. Freud invites Ferenczi to join them.[73] The event was to include twenty-seven distinguished psychiatrists, neurologists, and psychologists. It represented a watershed in the acceptance of psychoanalysis in North America and would give both Freud and Jung international recognition, something which both men had eagerly sought—not only for the prestige but for the new patients that would invariably come with international standing.[74]

Freud arrives in Bremen on the morning of August 20, 1909. Jung and Ferenczi are already there. The three men stop for lunch at the famous old Essinghaus Restaurant. According to Jung, during lunch he happens to mention a report he read about corpses found in bogs near Bremen, and Freud faints. Freud sees in Jung's repeated emphasis on the story a death wish toward him, which Jung denies. Freud remembers the incident differently. He thought he fainted because he had had very little sleep the evening before, on the long train ride from Vienna to Bremen, or he might have consumed his wine too quickly. Saul Rosenzweig, who has examined the incident in detail, does not find Freud's version compelling, and I agree.[75]

In any case, the next day the three men board the *George Washington* of the North German Lloyd line. They had planned to go to America a little early in order to do some sightseeing before the ceremonies at Clark, which were scheduled to commence on September 10. Freud, Jung, and Ferenczi all booked first-class accommodations.[76]

The ship departs Europe on Tuesday, August 24. It arrives at Hoboken, New Jersey, on August 29. A. A. Brill had arranged for someone to meet the Freud party at the dock, and for the next six days, prior to their departure for Worcester, they go sightseeing, though not always together. For his part, Freud tries to visit his brother-in-law Eli Bernays and sister Anna, but finds they are still on vacation. Freud does get to see Eli and his family on his return trip to New York, prior to departing for Europe.[77]

The important date for us during this visit is Thursday, September 2. This is when—at the invitation of Brill—Freud, Jung, and Ferenzci visit the Psychiatric Clinic at Columbia University. Brill works there as a clinical assistant in order to supplement his income from his private practice.[78] Details of this visit come from a July 6, 1951, interview between Rosenzweig and Jung that took place at Küsnacht. Rosenzweig tells us the interview lasted seventy minutes, and afterward he walked to a small restaurant and wrote out the contents of the interview in detail. He then boarded a train for Zürich and his hotel.[79] This is an important interview, and I think it unfortunate that Rosenzweig has not published it in full. At least I have not been able to find it. Rosenzweig provides only excerpts from it in his book.

According to what Jung told Rosenzweig, following the Columbia University visit and while viewing the New Jersey Palisades from Riverside Drive across the Hudson on the Manhattan side of the river, Freud experiences a personal mishap: he accidentally urinates in his trousers. Jung whisks him back to their hotel, where Freud changes clothes. Freud is concerned that a similar accident might occur at some time during their visit to Clark University, and Jung suggests that an analytic intervention might quickly clear up the problem, which he diagnoses as a neurosis. Jung tells Rosenzweig that Freud agrees.

During Jung's analysis of Freud, one of the so-called "triangle" dreams comes up. Jung feels that if he is to be able to interpret the dream in a way that might be helpful, he will need additional information from Freud, including any personal associations he might have. But Freud's response is the same as Jung describes to Billinsky; Jung tells Rosenzweig that Freud pauses, thinks carefully, then declines, declaring he cannot "risk his authority." Jung tells Rosenzweig that at that point Freud lost it, from Jung's point of view, and that "this incident started the break between us."[80] Remember,

Freud is not aware of what Jung already knows about the "Minna" issue, so it is reasonable to assume he would want to keep secret any associations which might reveal that an illicit relationship might exist between him and his sister-in-law.

Why was Jung so open with Rosenzweig about these events in America? I am not certain, but perhaps it was because Rosenzweig, like Billinsky, was a Jungian—or more of a Jungian than a Freudian. Rosenzweig had studied under Jung's disciple H. A. Murray at the Harvard Psychological Clinic, so that may provide something of a clue.[81] In any case, Jung tells Rosenzweig essentially the same story about Freud's incontinence, the triangle dream, and Freud's reluctance to share personal details—his shutting off the discussion by invoking his "authority"—that he would tell Billinsky six years later.

It is approximately thirty months between Jung's first visit to Freud, where he hears Minna's confession, to the incontinence incident and "triangle" dream episode in New York (March 1907 to September 1909), so it is obvious that what Jung learned from Minna had made a deep impression on him—in fact, so deep that he was still telling the same story more than forty years later, in his interviews with Rosenzweig and Billinsky. As we shall see in the next chapter, he will share similar information with the arch-Freudian Kurt Eissler.

CORROBORATIVE STUDIES

Following the publication of Billinsky's interview and its revelations about an affair between Freud and Minna, a number of articles began to appear in support of Jung's story, a few going so far as to suggest that Minna became pregnant and had an abortion. Some of these studies were based on analytic interpretations of Freud's writings and letters, with numerous inferences and assumptions, while others relied more heavily on a re-examination of existing materials from varying and sometimes new perspectives. Before I get to these analyses, I want to briefly mention two studies which add plausibility—one might even say, provide corroborating evidence—to the story of an affair and, as such, ought to be considered in conjunction with Billinsky's revelations.

One of these studies is by the German sociologist Franz Maciejewski. Searching through various mountain resorts that Freud and Minna visited on their 1898 holiday together—the second trip they are known to have taken alone—Maciejewski found in a guestbook, or *Fremdenbuch*, at the Schweizerhaus Inn in Maloja, Switzerland, the log entry, *Dr. Sigm. Freud u Frau/Wien*, in Freud's handwriting. The Schweizerhaus *Fremdenbuch* contained registration records dating back to 1883. Maciejewski found the Freud notation under the date August 13, 1898. Freud and Minna occupied Room 11, Maciejewski tells us, a standard double room.[82]

It was August 1898, and Freud and Minna "exited Austria's North Tyrol at the Italian border near Trafoi, then wended their way into Switzerland." The last place they stayed was in Maloja, at the westernmost reach of the Upper Engadine. There they registered at the Schweizerhaus.[83]

Maciejewski sees his discovery solving the "Minna Question," and in essence vindicating "Jung's testimony very powerfully." He argues that by "any reasonable standard of proof, Sigmund Freud and his wife's sister Minna Bernays had a liaison. They not only shared a bed; they were even up to misrepresenting their relationship to strangers as that of husband and wife—a subterfuge they surely then maintained whenever feasible during subsequent holidays together in faraway places."[84]

Maciejewski points out that Freud, in a postcard to Martha dated August 13, 1898, or the first day Freud and Minna spent at the inn, describes the Schweizerhaus as a "modest Swiss house."[85] Yet it was anything but modest. It is described in a contemporary *Baedecker* guide book as an old inn, *Osteria vecchia,* a rather venerable and grand place.[86]

I wonder why Freud would send such a message to Martha. Did he feel guilty about staying at too nice a place, spending too much money, not economizing with Minna while he always economized with Martha? We will later learn that Martha and the rest of the household often travelled third class while Freud travelled first. Or was it important for him to send a message that he and Minna were not having too good a time together, as a cover for the fact that maybe they were having a great time? Whatever the motive, I suspect Freud was very carefully managing the information he provided Martha when he and Minna were on holiday together.

Maciejewski's argues that Freud was an impatient traveler, and would hardly stay more than one night at any given place. As evidence, he quotes an August 6, 1898, letter which Minna and Freud send to Martha, in which Minna indicates that Freud loves "to sleep every night in a different bed."[87] Maciejewski points out that Freud's desire not to stay long at any one place is confirmed in a December 26, 1912, letter from Sándor Ferenczi to Freud. Ferenczi writes, "You once took a trip to *Italy* [emphasis Ferenczi's] with your sister-in-law (*voyage de lit-à-lit*)"[88] [traveling from bed to bed or, in other words, quite rapidly]. But when the couple reach the Schweizerhaus, things are different. Maciejewski says they alter their original plan of going on to Chiavenna, Italy, and remain at the Schweizerhaus for three days and three nights before heading home to Austria.[89] And they seem to have had a wonderful time. In a letter a few days later, dated August 20, 1898, Freud writes to Wilhelm Fliess about the "pleasures" of "our trip." "It really was glorious," Freud exults; "the air made me feel giddy."[90]

Maciejewski hopes that his discovery at the Schweizerhaus will lead authorities at the Freud Archives at the Library of Congress in Washington, D.C., to immediately declassify the interview that the founder of those archives, Kurt Eissler, had with Jung in 1953. Originally, Eissler had embargoed use of it for fifty years. Even after that time authorities had added a further restriction which forbade researchers from making copies of the contents of the interview until 2013.[91] As mentioned, this 1953 interview will be discussed later in our study. We will see what light, if any, it throws on the importance of Maciejewski's discovery.

In a follow-up article that appeared two years later,[92] Maciejewski paints a broad overview of the Freud/Minna relationship, emphasizing how Freud felt attracted to Minna from their first meeting (when he also met Martha—both sisters were apparently visiting Freud's sisters at the Freud apartment at the time); how tender and intimate his letters to Minna were; and how several of Freud's dreams reveal that his affection for Minna continued unabated thereafter.[93]

Somewhat further afield, Maciejewski argues that two dreams from the summer of 1898 confirm "that the emotional attitude of an incestuous connection to Minna dominates the period prior to" Freud and Minna's holiday trip, and that the "Minna affair" does not run counter to Freud's psychosexual development, but actually fits the patterns he had learned in childhood.[94]

The other evidence of special important can be found in Peter L. Rudnytsky's article, "Rescuing Psychoanalysis from Freud: The Common Project of Stekel, Jung, and Ferenczi."[95] Rudnytsky's findings appear to corroborate at least part of what Billinsky said Jung told him. Rudnytsky discusses Sándor Ferenczi's *Clinical Diary* entry of August 4, 1932,[96] and his October 19, 1911, letter to Freud.[97]

In the *Clinical Diary* entry, Ferenczi recalls "the incontinence incident on Riverside Drive." As mentioned, he was with Freud and Jung at the time. In Ferenczi's October 19, 1911, letter to Freud, which accompanies a letter that Emma Jung had sent to Ferenczi (which has since been lost), Ferenczi seems to be referring to Freud's assertion of authority about the "triangle" dream issue—an assertion that so soured Jung on Freud. Ferenczi writes: "Frau Jung ... could be partly right in her assertions (where she talks about your antipathy toward giving completely of yourself as a friend). It is certainly false that it is your 'authority' that you want to protect."[98]

Rudnytsky speculates, and I agree, that Jung must have told his wife about the incident involving Freud's "authority," and she must have quoted that back to Ferenczi in her letter to him.[99] Rudnytsky also points out that Jung, in a December 3, 1912, letter to Freud, reminds the latter of what he had said in New York about risking his "authority." Jung writes: "Our analysis, you may remember, came to a stop with your remark that you 'could not submit to analysis *without losing your authority.*' [Emphasis Jung's.] These words are engraved on my memory as a symbol of everything to come."[100]

The evidence Rudnytsky points to does not bear directly on what Jung told Billinsky about Minna's confession, but at the very least it independently verifies Jung's story about the incontinence incident on Riverside drive and Freud's invocation of "authority" when pressed by Jung for details regarding the "triangle" dream. I think it would be difficult to interpret it any other way.

If one part of Jung's story is verifiable, does that mean that the other parts may be true as well? Especially the story of Minna's confession, the most important element of all? No, but it makes it *more likely* that everything Jung said might be true. Don't forget, these two pieces of the story are inextricably linked by Jung.

Also, it is important to remember that we should not expect to be able to independently verify the other part of Jung's story, the part dealing with Minna's confession, because that involved only Jung and Minna. No third party was present; no one apparently witnessed it or overheard it, as far as we are aware. And we do not know if Minna told anyone else about the affair.

AFTER-THE-FACT, INTERPRETIVE ACCOUNTS

There are also after-the-fact accounts which, through interpretation and inference, see in certain of Freud's works ("Screen Memories," *The Psychopathology of Everyday Life*, and *The Interpretation of Dreams*, for example), as well as some of Freud's letters, evidence that Freud and Minna had an affair. I want to focus on two of these—one by Peter J. Swales, the other by Michael T. O'Brien. Swales even suggests that Minna became pregnant and had an abortion, though neither author pretends to have discovered a "smoking gun," as Maciejewski does with regard Freud's handwritten notation in the Schweizerhaus logbook.

In Swales's 1982 paper, "Freud, Minna Bernays, and the Conquest of Rome,"[101] he juxtaposes two sets of data: one historical, the other interpretive. The historical data deal with the fact that in August 1900 Freud began a six-week-long holiday. Swales uses Ernest Jones's biography of Freud as a source for his information about that trip,[102] and Jones in turn had used an unpublished letter from Freud to Wilhelm Fliess (dated September 14,

1900) as his source. In 1985 this letter was published in J. M. Masson's *The Complete Edition of the Letters of Sigmund Freud to Wilhelm Fliess*.[103]

The holiday in question starts with Freud and Martha traveling to Trafoi in the Italian South Tyrol (which was still part of Austria at the time), then to Sulden, and then via Merano on to Mendola, where they meet Dr. Lustgarten, an old medical friend who had emigrated to New York, and other Viennese acquaintances. Martha then goes home and, at her suggestion, Freud continues on with Lustgarten to Venice, where Freud meets his sister Rosa and his brother-in-law Heinrich. Together the whole group travels to Berghof on Lake Ossiach, where Freud runs into his sister Anna Bernays and her "American" children. This is the sister who had married Eli Bernays, Martha's brother, and whose family was now living in America. A day later Freud's brother Alexander arrives.

On August 26 Minna also arrives, to Freud's relief, as he points out in his letter to Fliess. Freud and Minna then take off alone—first through the Puster Valley to Trient, or Trentino, as Freud calls it, where they visit the "dreamlike" Castello Toblino, then on to Lavarone and Lake Garda, where they stay for five days at Riva. They then sail from Pallanza to Stresa, where they spend the night, and the next day Freud drops Minna off in Merano, where she is to remain for some time in hopes of recovering from tuberculosis. Freud then returns to Vienna via Milan and Genoa.[104]

Swales says that Minna was with Freud from the beginning of the trip, and that the phrase "with his wife and Minna," included in the earlier, English version of Jones's biography was amended in the later, American version, the "and Minna" phrase being dropped.[105] Yet in the letter from Freud to Fliess of September 14, 1900, upon which Jones bases his description of the holiday, Minna only seems to arrive on August 26. What Freud writes is this: "Finally—we have now reached August 26—came relief. I mean Minna, with whom I drove through the Puster Valley to Trentino [Trient], making several short stops along the way."[106] We will examine more of this letter in a moment.

This sounds as if Minna first joins Freud on August 26, 1900, and not before—though alternatively it could mean that she was already part of the group and then on August 26 she and Freud took off alone together. Freud begins the September 14, 1900, letter to Fliess by saying "we drove to Trafoi," which Masson interprets as meaning that Martha and Freud drove to Trafoi. I interpret it the same way, for I think Freud would have mentioned that Minna was with them. He often mentions her name in other letters to Fliess.[107] Perhaps Jones had mistakenly included the phrase "and Minna" in the earlier English edition and then corrected his mistake in the later, American one?

I am not certain Swales had access to the letter of September 14, 1900, since Masson's edition of the Freud/Fliess letters only appears in 1985, or four years after Swales wrote his article.

Freud's letter is interesting because of the tone of joy it exhibits after Minna arrives to join him. After outlining for Fliess the various places visited on the holiday, Freud continues:

> Only when I was completely in the South did I begin to feel really comfortable; under ice and snow something was missing, though at the time I could not have defined it. The sun was very amiable in Trentino, in no way as intolerable as in Vienna. From Trentino we made an excursion to the extraordinarily beautiful Castel Toblino. ... There I saw my beloved olive tree again. Minna wanted a taste of a high-altitude sojourn; therefore we went over a spectacular mountain road to Lavarone ... a high plateau on the side of the Valsugano, where we found the most magnificent forest of conifers and undreamed of solitude. The nights began to be cool, however, so I headed directly for Lake Garda. ... We finally stopped for five days at Riva, divinely accommodated and fed, luxuriating without regrets, and untroubled. ... Two long boat trips took us one time to Salò and the other to Sirmione. ... On September 8 I took Minna to Merano, where she is supposed to stay for either a few weeks or a few months to cure her pulmonary apicitis [inflammation]. I believe I have told you that the recurrence of this affliction, for which she was sent to Sicily at the age of seventeen, casts a shadow on the immediate future. I arrived feeling outrageously merry and well in Vienna.[108]

Note the "undreamed of solitude" Freud and Minna experience together, the "luxuriating without regrets, and untroubled."

Swales tells us he retraced the various places Freud and Minna visited on this trip and found in records deposited in a local museum in Merano, where Freud dropped Minna off, that she registered at the Hotel Erzherzog Johann sometime between September 5 and 12, then on September 26 moved to a rest home in nearby Obermais, where she stayed for no less than four and a half months, or until mid-February 1901.[109]

That is the factual part of the story. Now for the interpretive part. Swales theorizes that at Merano Minna may have had an abortion, having been impregnated by Freud. He bases this conjecture on a textual re-examination of some of Freud's works. His line of argumentation is complicated and is rooted in a belief that much of Freud's work is more autobiographical than he was willing to admit. I cannot give due justice to all the subtle nuances and connections Swales touches upon and the various assumptions he makes. I admit that at times I have had trouble following his argument. Suffice it to say that a key part is based on Freud's analysis in Chapter 2 of *The Psychopathology of Everyday Life* ("Forgetting of Foreign Words").[110] In this chapter Freud describes a travelling companion's inability to remember the Latin word *aliquis* ("someone") from a line in Virgil's *Aeneid* and Freud's conclusion, based on this young man's associations to that word, that his failure to remember it is due to a fear that his Italian girlfriend has become pregnant, having missed her period, and might require an abortion. Swales sees this not as a fear expressed by Freud's so-called traveling companion, but really, because that man is a thinly disguised Freud, Freud's fear that Minna has become pregnant and might, as a result, require an abortion.

One important part of Swales's argument is connected to the reason Minna might have stayed at Merano. In Jones's account, it is to "pass some time in the hope of recovering from her tuberculosis."[111] Swales is skeptical. If Minna had stayed at Merano for legitimate medical reasons, as Jones suggests—as opposed to needing to recover from an abortion, as Swales maintains—it takes some of the bite out of Swales's argument that Minna went to Merano to have an abortion. Of course, theoretically Minna could have had both: a cure and an abortion. To bolster his argument that Minna's stay was primarily for the latter reason, Swales offers several arguments which question the "curative" reasons for her being at Merano. One of these is the "fact" that the only reference to Minna having tuberculosis in the whole Freud literature, as Swales puts it, is the one provided by Jones; hence Swales wonders whether she really had tuberculosis. In addition, in photographs of Minna dating from circa 1898 and circa 1912, she certainly does not look consumptive. Further, she seemed fit enough to accompany Freud on his rather exhaustive holiday tour prior to being dropped off at Merano. Finally, Swales argues, Merano was not really the place to go for patients afflicted with tuberculosis.[112]

I suspect many of these arguments can be challenged, and I know that several already have been. With regard to Swales's suggestion that Minna may not have been tubercular, there is of course Freud's September 14, 1900, letter to Fliess, to which Swales in 1982 apparently did not have access, where Freud indicates that Minna's pulmonary condition was an old and perhaps persistent one, which had necessitated her having been sent at age seventeen to Sicily for a cure.

I have only touched upon a few of Swales's major lines of argument here in order to provide an introduction to some of his thinking on the matter. To cover all his arguments in detail would require much more time and space than I have available. However, in the next chapter I will return to

Swales's ideas when we consider several critiques of his work offered by those who doubt that Freud had an affair with Minna.

In 1991 Michael T. O'Brien published an article titled "Freud's Affair with Minna Bernays: His Letter of June 4, 1896,"[113] in which the author argues that while the manifest content of a June 4, 1896, Freud letter to Wilhelm Fliess does not appear to concern an affair between Freud and Minna, the context of the letter does. The letter in question was written at a time when Freud and Minna were at home alone for a period of several days and, as O'Brien puts it, "Freud had thoughts of an affair, coitus, and sexual intercourse on his mind."[114]

O'Brien suggests that one way to test the strength of his hypothesis is to look at various sections of Freud's *The Interpretation of Dreams*. O'Brien argues when that is done the theme of personal trauma emerges, in which Freud is connected with the birth and death of an illegitimate child by a second woman who shares characteristics with both Martha and the "Irma" of Freud's specimen dream in that work, "The Dream of Irma's Injection." This woman, O'Brien contends, can be construed to be Minna, with the implication that she and Freud did have an affair.

O'Brien offers additional "interpretive" ideas—references to other Freud works and letters—in an attempt to bolster his argument.[115] We will have an opportunity to look again at O'Brien's ideas in Chapter 4.

A MOST DANGEROUS METHOD

John Kerr's 1993 book, *A Most Dangerous Method: The Story of Jung, Freud, and Sabina Spielrein*, adds useful information about the Freud/Minna affair,[116] although his focus is primarily on Jung, Freud, and Jung's alleged affair with Sabina Spielrein. Although a supporter of Swales, Kerr suggests that Swales's interpretation of Freud's writings might indicate the fantasy of an affair rather than a real one. Kerr suggests the names of others to whom Jung might have shared his story of Freud and Minna. Like Rudnytsky, Kerr has the original notes upon which Billinsky bases his published interview, and he has the same reaction as Rudnytsky does: the notes indicate that Billinsky softened Jung's remarks about Freud and Minna in the published version.[117]

Kerr points out that while the affair had been kept secret for many years, after Billinsky published his article, it became an open secret that hardly anybody would discuss. C. A. Meier, who, as we have seen, was a close confidante of Jung's and a friend of Billinsky's, was apparently perturbed when Billinsky published the interview and pressured him to drop the whole matter. Kerr speculates that Meier did not want to open old wounds with the Freudians, and I think Kerr is correct in that judgment. Meier is also surprised that Jung had been so open with Billinsky, who was not a close friend or acquaintance. Kerr quotes Meier saying: "I was convinced up to that moment that this story was only known to Toni Wolff and me— nobody else. ... I would never think of publicizing a thing like this. What is the use? But apparently not so Billinsky."[118]

Toni Wolff was from an old and distinguished Swiss family and was originally Jung's patient, undergoing treatment beginning in 1910. By 1913 she had become Jung's mistress. An unorthodox but open *ménage à trois* consisting of Jung, Wolff, and Emma Jung continued for the rest of Jung's life, with Emma tolerating though certainly not comfortable with her husband's extramarital interest.[119]

So Meier and Wolff also had heard the same story Jung told Billinsky. We will see in the next chapter, when we discuss the views of Peter Gay and Kurt Eissler, who both argue against there having been an affair, that Meier had also confirmed Jung's story to them. Kerr mentions several other people who were also apparently told by Jung, including the Harvard psychologist Henry Murray, who was interviewed on November 11, 1968, by Dr. Gene Nameche for the *Jung Oral History Archive* (59); John Phillips, an analyst in training, who told Kerr on September 27, 1984, what he had heard about the affair from Jung; and the Italian journalist Hugo Charteris's short description, "in passing," as Kerr describes it, quoted in Vincent Brome's biography of Jung.[120] Charteris remembers Jung stumbling over the subject as they discussed a variety of topics: "'He said to me—"I thought it—so it must be true"—imagine. ... But his wife's younger sister. She appreciated the old man.' Jung laughed mischievously and then said more soberly: 'I don't know what happened. Once I think ... I think he slept with her once ... he told me.' His voice trailed off."[121]

Brome's reference, according to a note in Brome's book, is "from a partly unpublished manuscript" of Charteris.[122] No year is given, but I suspect it is 1957 or later. I find Charteris's memory of what Jung said strange. It is different from all others I know of, in which Jung has always attributed the story of the affair to Minna, not Freud. There is no evidence that I have found which indicates that Jung ever talked to Freud about the matter.

Kerr also indicates there were contemporaneous rumors about such an affair. We have already seen what Eva Rosenfeld had reported to Eissler.[123] Kerr also points out that Dr. Oskar Rie, a family friend and physician to the Freud children, had commented on what seemed to have been readily observable to all who were close to the household. "For children, Freud went with Martha; for pleasure, he took Minna," Rie is reported to have said.[124] Of course, Freud could have found pleasure with Minna as a traveling companion without having had an affair with her.

THE "MINNA WARS"

Other studies have also appeared since Billinsky published his famous interview supporting the notion of a Freud/Minna affair. In a 2007 article titled "What Happens in Maloja Stays in Maloja: Inference and Evidence in the 'Minna Wars,'"[125] Barry Silverstein argues that Freud might have felt that sex with Minna was permissible, given his growing lack of sexual satisfaction with Martha. Silverstein writes: "it is not unreasonable to conclude that the forty-two-year-old Freud's state of mind during his 1898 trip with Minna [their second alone together][126] was full of sexual frustration, resentment toward Martha, and a vulnerability to give in to impulses to taste the forbidden fruit to which he by then may have decided he was entitled."[127]

Silverman sees in several of Freud's works and letters an effort to establish the idea of the superior human being: someone not bound by standard moral constraints, and hence a person who can do sexually whatever he wishes, whether it involves "incest" or not. In this sense Freud might have felt justified in having an affair with Minna.[128] To bolster the idea that an affair might have taken place, Silverstein cites the recollections of Esti Freud about Minna. Esti was Martin Freud's estranged wife. In conversations with Paul Roazen, Silverman points out, Esti repudiates the idea of a liaison, yet at the same time refuses to rule out the possibility the Minna "had had more than a platonic relationship with Freud." Esti, who always hated Minna, feels Minna had "made a play" for Freud; "there was no doubt of that," she insists.[129]

Silverstein suggests that Minna might have been much more aggressive toward Freud away from the Freud home.[130] Or, I would add, more aggressive toward Freud than any of us might have imagined, given the shadowy, spinster-like woman many scholars have sought to portray.

But, Silverstein asks, why would Freud do something so risky as to have an affair with his own sister-in-law, possibly exposing her to an unwanted pregnancy? The question is a formidable one, Silverstein admits, if we assume that Freud was a strictly rational human being. But what about a deeply frustrated man in love and unable or unwilling to constrain a pent-up sexual drive? In this case, Silverstein argues, wouldn't passion trump reason?[131] Silverstein's idea is intriguing.

In 2008, in a paper titled, "A Very Freudian Affair: Erich Fromm, Peter Swales, and the Future of Psychoanalytic Historiography,"[132] which we have already briefly referenced, Daniel Burston argues that despite denials by several Freudians of a possible Freud/Minna affair, Maciejewski's discovery of Freud's handwritten notation in the Schweizerhaus registration book (*Dr. Sigm. Freud u Frau/Wien*) makes "outright denial" that Freud and Minna did have an affair "no longer an option."[133]

Burston sees the publication in 1975 of the Freud/Jung correspondence[134] providing evidence that "Martha and Sigmund Freud were ... deeply estranged from one another."[135] He also references a paper by Richard Schoenwald, who, Burston says, in light of the Freud/Jung letters, sees Billinsky's account of his conversation with Jung as quite plausible and thinks Freud's affair with Minna a strong possibility. Having read Schoenwald's paper, I think Burston accurately characterizes his position. Schoenwald had a chance to talk to Billinsky directly, and that, among other things, left him convinced of the veracity of Jung's story.[136] As Schoenwald writes: "A few writers more critical of Freud than Jones have suggested that something beyond just good talk must have been going on between Freud and Minna. My own careful consideration of Billinsky's evidence, and a conversation which I had with him about the strongly confirmatory response to his release of the interview, leave me quite sure that we can accept and use Jung's testimony."[137]

Burston also strongly defends Swales's theories about Freud and Minna, though he believes that in later work Swales goes too far—such as the latter's suggestion that Freud made a pact with the Devil and that he had devised a plan to murder his sometime friend Wilhelm Fliess, a plan that was never carried out.[138] Burston sees a Freud/Minna affair as validating Erich Fromm's views of Freud as someone estranged from his wife (and other women) as well as autocratic and manipulative in the way he often treated his friends and followers, as opposed to the idealized view of the man promoted by Freudian orthodoxy.[139]

CHAPTER 3

THE FREUDIAN RESPONSE

While there are many scholars who suggest there was an affair between Freud and Minna, there are an even larger number who maintain there was not.

"NOT A TATTER OF EVIDENCE"

We have already seen Ernest Jones maintain that there was no sexual attraction between Freud and Minna and that strange "legends" about an affair are "sheer nonsense."[1] In Ronald W. Clark's 1980 biography of Freud,[2] the idea of an affair between Freud and Minna is likewise dismissed out of hand. Freud's interest in sex was merely professional, Clark maintains. There is not "a tatter of evidence" that "an unsublimated randy young man … grew into an unsublimated randy old man … the known context of his life makes it distinctly improbable," Clark contends.[3]

Curiously, Clark says the Jung rumor about Freud and Minna has Jung "approached by both Martha and Minna, who separately spoke of Freud's passion for his sister-in-law."[4] I wonder where Clark got this information. I checked Clark's footnotes and found no source for his assertion, and I notice that Clark does not include Billinsky's paper in his bibliography. The paper had appeared a decade previously, in 1969, so Clark had ample opportunity to consult it.

"SUPPOSITIONS OF GUILT"

In a 1982 article appearing in *Psychology Today*,[5] Alan C. Elms finds Jung's account of Minna's confession highly suspect. Elms argues that Jung's phrasing, as reported by Billinsky, leaves unclear what Minna actually told him as opposed to what he might have inferred. Also, Jung was a complete stranger a decade younger than Minna, and spent very little time with her during his visit to Berggasse. In addition, isn't it odd that Jung's first letter to Freud following the 1907 visit is filled with enthusiasm for Freud, given what he had just been told by Minna?[6] Elms is referring to Jung's letter to Freud of March 31, 1907, where Jung says, "I hope my work for your cause will show you the depths of my gratitude and veneration. I hope and even dream that we may welcome you in Zürich next summer or autumn. A visit from you would be seventh heaven for me personally." Immediately before those sentences in the same letter, Jung talks of "the tremendous impression you [Freud] made on me."[7]

Perhaps more importantly, Elms asserts, Jung himself was becoming deeply involved in a love affair of his own with one of his patients (Sabina Spielrein, though Elms does not mention her by name), and he apparently never mentioned a word of the Freud/Minna affair to her. That seems strange to Elms as well.[8]

While Elms argues that Jung's credibility can be dismissed with relative ease, given his "obvious bias against Freud, plus his own history of repeated affairs with female patients," he finds Swales's views of the affair a tougher nut to crack, though not much tougher.[9] He attacks Swales on several fronts. While not having any obvious reason for bias, Elms argues, Swales has put together what amounts to an argument that relies on "elaborate suppositions, confidently asserted," wherein "suppositions of guilt are ... no more probable than the equivalent suppositions of innocence."[10] Elms hones in on Swales's examination of Freud's *aliquis* anecdote in Chapter 2 of *The Psychopathology of Everyday Life*. Don't forget, one key element in Swales's argument is that the young man in the tale is actually Sigmund Freud, and the young man's concern about his Italian girlfriend becoming pregnant (missing her period) is really Freud's own concern about Minna's pregnancy. Yet, Elms maintains, the parallel breaks down at least in one important respect: the young man expresses a desire to inflict vengeance on his oppressors (those preventing Jewish people like himself from achieving their full potential), and Freud interpreted this as a wish by the young man for descendants. Yet Freud already had six potential avengers (three boys and three girls), so how does the parallel hold?[11]

Elms sees no need to assume that Freud made up the character of the young man. He didn't need to, for the person in question, Elms hypothesizes, is probably Alexander Freud, Freud's younger brother, who fits the character of the young man in many respects, including the facts that he was known to be an avid womanizer and there is evidence that Freud had always worried about that aspect of his brother's behavior.[12]

"I FIND IT VIRTUALLY IMPOSSIBLE ..."

In his 1988 biography of Freud, Peter Gay is skeptical that an affair between Freud and Minna ever happened. Gay discusses Minna and acknowledges the important role she played in Freud's life and work. He calls her "one indispensable ingredient in Freud's domestic arrangements."[13] Gay tells us that Freud, during his engagement to Martha, had written Minna "intimate and affectionate letters" and signed himself "Your Brother Sigmund" and called her "My Treasure."[14] After the death of Minna's fiancé, Ignaz Schönberg, in 1886, Minna apparently resigned herself to spinsterhood and began to let her appearance go: she "grew heavier, more jowly," Gay writes, "becoming exceedingly plain; she looked older than her sister Martha, though she was in fact four years younger."[15]

Always a welcome visitor to Berggasse, Minna became a permanent fixture in the mid-1890s. Gay calls her "the intellectual sister," witty, able to follow Freud's thinking—"at least some of the way." In the early years, Freud thought of her as his "closest confidante," along with Wilhelm Fliess.[16] Minna remained close to Freud, Gay tells us: "in summer, the two occasionally visited Swiss resorts or Italian cities alone."[17] Having said all that, Gay believes "the rumor, launched by Carl G. Jung, that Freud had an affair with Minna Bernays lacks convincing evidence." He discusses the issue in a bibliographical essay toward the end of his book.[18]

"What is one to make of this [story of an affair]?" Gay asks, after quoting liberally from Billinsky's 1957 interview with Jung. Not very much, he implies.[19] He sees several problems with the validity of Jung's story. One is that Jung was not a reliable reporter, as his "contradictory autobiographical comments suggest," although Gay does not tell us what those contradictory comments are. Also, he believes that Freud's refusal to "interpret one of his own dreams aboard ship may be true enough," since Jung repeated it several times, once even to Freud, and "Freud never denied it." But in all other respects, Gay has his doubts.[20]

Another problem for Gay is that Freud did not have a "laboratory," where Jung tells Billinsky Minna first approached him with information about an affair. Gay admits that Freud did have a consulting room next to his study, and maybe that is what Jung meant, but still the expression, Gay feels, "remains a strange one."

In addition, photographs do not show Minna to have been "very good-looking," as Jung describes her. Freud may have thought so, but, Gay argues, "it seems highly implausible that Jung, who had an eye for feminine beauty and was himself sexually quite active during these years, beyond the bounds of marriage, would really have found her so." Gay reveals that Dr. Max Schur, who became Freud's private physician in March 1929, and who Gay admits knew Minna Bernays "only in relatively advanced age, found her quite unattractive," according to what Helen Schur, Dr. Schur's wife, told Gay in a June 3, 1986, interview.[21]

Also, Gay continues, it seems "quite improbable" that Minna would have confided such an intimate matter to Jung, who at the time was a total stranger, "alien to her in religion and culture and professional interests." This is similar to Elms's point, though Gay does admit that perhaps that is just the sort of person—one who was soon to depart—she might have wanted to confide in. Still, Gay maintains, "I find it virtually impossible to visualize the scene" in which Jung and Minna might have met privately.[22]

Gay finds Peter Swales's 1982 paper, in which he says Swales offers "confident conjectures as demonstrated fact," sadly lacking in terms of evidence of an affair. Gay says Swales employs what he calls the Siegfried Bernfeld method, which reads certain of Freud's texts "as disguised autobiographical revelations." This method can be useful, Gay admits, but it can also be risky. Gay sharply rebukes Swales's methodology: "When a statement that Freud makes concerning someone else may well apply to himself, Swales accepts it as evidence; when a statement fails to fit, he accused Freud of disguising the material, or of brazen deception."[23]

Gay concludes that if "dependable, independent evidence" should emerge—as distinct from what he refers to as "conjecture and clever chains of inferences," and I assume he means Swales here—he would be willing to revise his "text accordingly," but for now, he says, "I must accept the established, less scandalous view of Freud as correct." I assume from Gay's argument that he does not find Jung's account of Minna's confession "dependable, independent evidence."[24]

A year later, in 1989, Gay published an article in *The New York Times* book section titled, "Sigmund and Minna? The Biographer as Voyeur."[25] The occasion for the piece was the opening of the Library of Congress' file of letters that Freud and Minna exchanged over the years. To clarify, I should add that Gay is talking about those letters that had not been labeled "restricted," for later in this chapter we will see Kurt Eissler make the distinction between those letters and a cache of "restricted" ones.

According to Gay, the letters show no passionate passages, though he admits, "I knew that the absence of erotic material in these letters could offer no conclusive demonstration one way or the other." He notes that while Minna may have been Freud's confidante in psychoanalytic matters, the correspondence "offers inklings of their confidentiality," but also "its limits." An example of the limits is when Freud complains to Minna, "in a rapid-fire series of notes," about how bored and lonely he felt studying hypnosis with Hippolyte Bernheim at Nancy in 1889, yet at the same time told her nothing "about the work for whose sake he had made the trip."[26]

Dreams, however, are a different matter. Gay points out that as early as 1893 (in a letter dated April 27, 1893) Freud shares with Minna his growing interest in the subject, even before he does the same with his other confidante of the period, Wilhelm Fliess.[27]

Gay also admits that Freud and Minna were close enough to exchange letters in secret, with an eye toward keeping her mother from reading them. "Dear Minning," Freud writes on April 28, 1887, using one of his pet names for Minna, "my effort to appear as an affectionate son-in-law, in addition to my lack of time, has led to the cessation of our private correspondence." Freud wanted to resume it, Gays tells us, especially because he sensed that Minna was in a bad mood, "for which I do not want to be even partly responsible."[28]

Gay indicates that one troubling aspect of the present set of Freud/ Minna letters is that many appear to be missing. Gay points to a large gap between Freud's letter of April 27, 1893, and one of July 25, 1910. In terms of the numbering system employed, he points out, letters 95 to 160 are missing. "The years 1893 to 1910," Gay admits, "were the very years when an affair between Freud and his sister-in-law would have taken place, if it did."

But Gay doubts that it did. Even if those letters did show up, and he assumes they probably no longer exist, he says he thinks it "exceedingly unlikely that they would substantiate the rumor that Jung was the first to float … Jung is too unreliable a witness, the conjectures of others are more ingenious than persuasive." Once again, Gay does not mention why he feels Jung is "too unreliable a witness."

Gay points out that Freud, in a letter to James J. Putnam of July 8, 1915, had indicated that while he stood for greater sexual freedom than bourgeois society thought proper, he admits that he himself had taken little advantage of it. Was Freud lying? Gay asks.

The problem that I see is that Gay leaves out a critical next sentence of Freud's. Gay had paraphrased what Freud wrote; let me quote Freud more fully. He writes: "I stand for a much freer sexual life. However, I have made little use of such freedom, *except in so far as I was convinced of what was permissible for me in this area.*" The emphasis is mine. This fuller reading of what Freud wrote seems to imply that it was "permissible" in Freud's mind to have an affair with Minna. This is a key question that needs to be addressed, and we will do so later in this study.[29]

Finally, Gay, in his 1989 *New York Times* piece, provides a brief history of the Freud/Minna letters. When Anna Freud turned over a "substantial cache" of documents to the Library of Congress in 1972, "she could not bear to part with certain letters," he tells us—namely, those between herself and her father and those between Freud and Minna. These remained at 20 Maresfield Gardens in London, now a Freud Museum. Dr. Harold Blum, Eissler's successor as director of the Freud Archives, took charge of them and transported them to the Library of Congress in two separate trips: one in 1986, then again in 1987. Although Gay does not say this, apparently somewhere in this overall process letters 95 to 160 disappeared.

In 1990, Gay reprises and expands his *New York Times* article as a chapter in his book *Reading Freud: Explorations and Entertainments.*[30] Two references he adds to the revised essay are of special interest. In one Gay indicates: "C. A. Meier, a longtime intimate of Jung and an eminent professor of psychiatry in Zürich, has confirmed the accuracy of Billinsky's recollection: Jung had told Meier precisely the same thing years before." Gay indicates that this information is based on a personal communication he had with Meier on February 15, 1989.[31] This confirmation by Meier is important if for no other reason than that it bolster's Billinsky's credibility, if not Jung's.

The second reference is of equal importance and solves a puzzle that had bothered me for some time. Gay refers to a diagram of the Freud apartment as it existed in 1938. It is reproduced in *Berggasse 19: Sigmund Feud's Home and Offices, Vienna 1938.*[32] I remember picking this book up at one of my visits to Freud's Berggasse apartment, now the Freud Museum in Vienna. The diagram shows the only entrance to Minna's bedroom as being through the master bedroom, the one shared by Martha and Freud. In one sense, this arrangement could be seen as potentially erotic, if indeed Freud, Martha, and Minna engaged in a *ménage à trois*, which I don't believe they did. On the other hand, Minna having access to her bedroom only though Freud's seemed a reason to believe that there was no affair, at least at Berggasse, because of Martha's probable nearby presence. Gay now solves this problem. He has learned that this was indeed Tante Minna's bedroom, but *only after 1920.* Before then, it was occupied by Anna Freud. Thus Minna had her bedroom elsewhere in the sprawling Freud apartment during the years prior to 1920, when it is most likely that an affair might have occurred.[33]

One might think the fact that Minna's bedroom was some distance from Freud's would argue against an affair between them, but I believe it's just the opposite. Since Freud never went to bed before two or three in the morning,[34] and Martha always expected that, he could quite easily have dropped in on Minna after finishing his day's work and before joining Martha in their bedroom. So if Freud did have an affair with Minna, their lovemaking might not have been restricted to the several journeys alone which they took during holidays in Switzerland and Italy, but actually could have continued regularly at Berggasse itself. At the very least, this new information provides Freud and Minna added *opportunities* for intimacy.

Where might Minna's bedroom have been prior to 1920? I have no idea, but if she and Anna simply switched bedrooms, which seems most likely, Minna's bedroom prior to 1920, based on the apartment diagram, would have been as far from the master bedroom as one could get within the Freud apartment. Perhaps the most vivid way to describe where it was located is that while the master bedroom (Martha and Freud's) looked out over the inner courtyard of the building, Minna's bedroom, if she did trade with Anna, looked out over the street at the opposite end of the apartment. And Freud would not have had to go through someone else's room to reach Minna's, for her room (Anna's old one) was directly off one of the foyers.

Following the publication of Franz Maciejewski's paper in 2006, with its revelations about the Schweizerhaus log book, Gay seems to have softened his position on the Minna issue a bit, becoming more open to the possibility that an affair between Freud and Minna did occur. Queried by Ralph Blumenthal, the author of the December 12, 2006, article in *The New York Times* about Maciejewski's discovery, Gay responded, "It makes it very possible that they slept together. It doesn't make him or psychoanalysis more or less correct." When I asked Blumenthal how he got this information, he said he recalled talking to Gay on the phone.[35]

"THIS MUCH IS UNQUESTIONABLE"

Kurt Eissler provides the most extensive critical response to Billinsky's revelations about Freud and Minna. In his 1993 book *Three Instances of Injustice*, in a chapter titled "C. G. Jung, A Witness or the Unreliability of Memories," he devotes seventy-seven printed pages to a rebuttal[36] Implicit in Eissler's critique is the assumption that if you can discredit the messenger (Billinsky), you can discredit the message; and if you can't do that, you must discredit the source of the message: Jung. Eissler tries, at least initially, to do both.

With regard to the messenger, Eissler tells us, there seems to be so much that is "contradictory, improbable and even bizarre" in what Jung is supposed to have said that he feels Billinsky's interview with Jung is an "invention."[37] Eissler cites an interview he had with E. A. Bennet, a close friend of Jung, in 1972. Bennet, he reports, is certain Jung never made the statements attributed to him by Billinsky, if only "because [Jung] would have made himself guilty of an unpardonable indiscretion by conveying extremely confidential matters to a person with whom he was only distantly acquainted."[38] Yet, almost in the same breath, Eissler admits that C. A. Meier, the Jung confidante Gay had also talked to, assured Eissler that Jung had given him the exact same account, and Eissler feels Meier's reliability "is above doubt."[39] As mentioned in the previous chapter, Eissler worked closely with Meier on the production of the joint Freud/Jung letters which appeared in 1974, and apparently in that process Eissler and Meier became good friends.[40] Anyway, so much for Billinsky's credibility; it remains intact.

What's left? Jung's credibility, of course. Here Eissler is relentless. I only select some of the highlights of his critique. Eissler believes that Freud's disparaging description of Martha, as reported to Billinsky by Jung, lacks authenticity. You'll recall, this occurs when the two men first meet in Jung's hotel. Billinsky reports Jung saying: "When I arrived in Vienna with my young and happy wife, Freud came to see us at the hotel and brought some flowers for my wife. He was trying to be very considerate and at one point he said to me, 'I am sorry that I can give you no real hospitality; I have nothing at home but an elderly wife.' When my wife heard him say that, she looked perturbed and embarrassed."[41] This, Eissler avers, was a tactless remark and completely out of character for Freud: "No one else ever heard Freud make such a disrespectful, indeed vulgar, remark about his wife."[42]

Also puzzling, Eissler says, is what Freud could have meant by saying he can provide Jung "no real hospitality." Eissler explains that earlier (February 21, 1907), Freud had written Jung about what to expect on his visit. We have seen that Freud regretted Jung could not come at Easter, when Freud would have had more time to spend with him.[43] "[Normally] I am taken up every day from eight to eight with the occupations known to you," Freud had written. He also asked Jung to dine with him and his family on the "few evenings" he might be spending in Vienna and then meet the rest of the evening with him. In the same letter Freud also invites Jung to his regular Wednesday Psychological Society event.[44]

In addition, as we have noted, one day the Jungs apparently went on a downtown shopping trip with Minna and one of Freud's daughters. (Based on Martin Freud's recollection, Eissler indicates this was Mathilde Freud, the oldest child.) So why would Freud say he could offer Jung "no real hospitality," Eissler asks. It is obvious the whole family was ready to welcome their guest.[45]

Also, Eissler strongly doubts Jung's statement to Billinsky that while visiting Freud's laboratory he was pulled aside by Minna and asked if they could talk. "This event cannot have taken place the way Jung reported," Eissler maintains: "The mere physical circumstances of Freud's apartment and professional suite suffice to throw doubt on Jung's account." As Gay did before, Eissler points out that Freud had no laboratory, in the ordinary sense of the word, and because Freud was busy during the day (from "eight to eight," as we have seen), a secret meeting between Jung and Minna could only have taken place after eight in the evening.[46] I'm not certain how Eissler reaches this conclusion, but all his arguments will be discussed in detail in Chapter 4.

Moreover, Eissler continues, "Minna Bernays was certainly not in the habit of sauntering through her brother-in-law's office, nor could she have been alone with Jung for any length of time to speak of, either there or in the living quarters."[47] If one were to accept Jung's account, Eissler maintains, one would have to assume "that Minna Bernays had secretly waited on the landing of the second floor for a moment when Freud left his office, then rushed downstairs in order to catch Jung alone."[48]

In addition, Eissler asks, "invalidating factors of external reality aside"—such as the difficulties Minna might have had in getting to meet with Jung alone—how could Minna have divulged such a well-guarded secret to someone twelve years her junior, whom she had met only a few days before? This point is similar to the one made by Elms and Gay. Also, wouldn't Freud have noticed "Jung's bewilderment when his revered authority, the man he idealized, was suddenly thrown off his pedestal, nor Minna's embarrassment and discomfiture for having betrayed, with her confession, a man to whom she owned loyalty and gratitude"?[49]

Further, Eissler argues, Minna must have known how important this visit by Jung was to Freud as he tried to broaden the appeal of psychoanalysis. Would she have "stabbed Freud treacherously in the back" this way?[50]

I believe the question of Minna's motives in sharing her secret with Jung is a good one, and it will be discussed later in this study. This issue has not been given the attention it deserves by scholars working in this area.

Also, Eissler cannot easily reconcile Jung's expressions of "agony" once Minna told him of the affair with the effusive praise Jung heaps on Freud in the letters he sends him after leaving Vienna. A similar point is made by Elms.[51] As you'll remember, in the March 31, 1907, letter to Freud, Jung writes of the "tremendous impression" Freud had on him,[52] and he expresses his hope that Freud might visit him the next summer or fall: "A visit from you would be seventh heaven for me personally."[53]

Eissler points out that this sort of intense admiration continues in Jung's next letter to Freud, dated April 11, 1907. Jung writes: "I have the feeling of having made considerable inner progress since I got to know you personally; it seems to me that one can never quite understand your science unless one knows you in the flesh ... the best and most effective faith is knowledge of your personality."[54]

If one might have thought that these letters merely reflected Jung's enthusiasm immediately following his visit to Freud, Eissler references a letter Jung wrote some six months later (October 28, 1907), which I have already noted, in which his enthusiasm for Freud has not diminished: "I have a boundless admiration for you both as a man and a researcher." This is where Jung adds, "My veneration for you has something of the character of a 'religious' crush."[55] These passages, Eissler argues, are "irreconcilable with an agonizing experience involving discovery of Freud's alleged intimate relationship with Minna Bernays."[56]

Eissler is also critical of Jung's description of what happened during Freud and Jung's voyage to the United States. Here Eissler sees a contradiction which he feels "proves that Minna Bernays never confided in [Jung]."[57] Eissler focuses on that part of the interview where Jung says he and Freud were "together every day for some seven weeks. From the very beginning of our trip we started to analyze each other's dreams."[58] Is it credible, Eissler asks, that Freud could have "analyzed Jung's dreams over such a long period of time without noticing that Jung harbored an agonizing secret about his private life?" Freud was a keen interpreter of dreams, Eissler points out. Could he have been so consistently deceived by Jung throughout their voyage?[59] Obviously, Eissler thinks not. He argues that Billinsky must have been naive to believe that on the one hand Jung and Freud were analyzing each other's dreams and on the other, as Jung says in the interview, "Freud had no idea that I knew about the triangle [dream] and his intimate relationship with his sister-in-law."[60]

Furthermore, Eissler feels that Jung's claim that Freud invoked his authority when asked for personal details regarding the "triangle" dream "sounds strange from [Freud's] mouth," though Eissler admits that Jung did refer to this incident at least three times—which, oddly enough, seems to argue against what Eissler is trying to prove. The three instances are as follows. (1) In a December 3, 1912, letter, from which we have already quoted, when Jung reminded Freud of the reason "our analysis ... came to a stop [was] your remark that you 'could not submit to analysis *without losing your authority*'" (emphasis Jung's).[61] (2) In Jung's 1925 seminar in Zürich, when Jung notes that after asking Freud for details about "a dream on an important theme which I cannot mention" Freud looked at him "with a peculiar expression of suspicion in his eyes and said: 'I could tell you more but I can't risk my authority.'"[62] And (3) in Jung's autobiography, *Memories, Dreams, Reflections,* where Jung recalls: "Freud had a dream—I would not think it right to air the problem it involved. I interpreted it as best I could, but added that a great deal more could be said about it if he would supply me with some additional details from his private life. Freud's response to these words was a curious look—a look of the utmost suspicion. Then he said, 'But I cannot risk my authority!'"[63]

Eissler maintains that to fully understand the Billinsky interview and what Eissler feels are the bizarre things Jung says therein, one needs to understand both the psychotic episode Jung went through following his break with Freud (Eissler sees four distinct phases to that) as well as Jung's serious childhood psychopathology. With regard to the latter, Eissler maintains that Jung's conflicts with father figures "were bound to appear in one way or another in Jung's relationship to Freud."[64] Later in his essay Eissler adds: "Freud the atheist, the materialist, the positivist and whatnot had to be inferior to the God-fearing pastor's son [i.e., Jung]. ... But in one respect Freud was undeniably superior to Jung: his sexual record was lily-white"— hence, Eissler seems to imply, Jung's motivation for wanting to blemish it.[65] Eissler argues, "if [Jung] could not emulate Freud as a past lover, present faithful husband and exemplary paterfamilias, at least he could destroy that image of Freud by claiming that Freud had maintained an extramarital affair from early on and, worse yet, an incestuous one."[66]

"Minna Bernays never confided the secret of an intimate relationship with her brother-in-law to Jung," Eissler says in his conclusion to his lengthy polemic; "This much is unquestionable."[67] Like Gay, however, Eissler does hedge his bets—somewhat. "If further research," he writes, "should unearth proof of an intimate relationship between Freud and Minna Bernays, this would necessitate a revision of the ideas that have been held about Freud."[68] I assume Eissler means his ideas as well.

On a related subject, Eissler touches upon the missing Freud/Minna letters Gay had mentioned, and we learn new information. Eissler says Anna Freud made him custodian of the restricted letters (the unrestricted ones Gay had already reported on in his 1989 *New York Times* article, as we have seen), and Eissler released the remaining letters for publication to German scholar Albrecht Hirschmüller. We shall be discussing Hirschmüller's ideas about a Freud/Minna affair later in this chapter. "There seems to be no question that some letters from this correspondence are missing," Eissler says. Eissler indicates that Ernst Freud, Freud's son, told him that Minna had requested the destruction of the letters Freud wrote her, though he didn't know whether this request also applied to her letters to him. Eissler also points out the Freud family had been negligent in the care of the letters. He remembers: "Some of them—and I recall that a few of these were addressed to Minna Bernays—were kept in an unlocked closet in a corridor of Anna Freud's house. Thus, there were opportunities for loss."[69]

"MUCH ADO ABOUT NOTHING"

More recent studies also question whether Freud had an affair with his sister-in-law. In his essay, "The Sigmund Freud/Minna Bernays Romance: Fact or Fiction?"[70] Zvi Lothane begins by assessing the importance of Franz Maciejewski's discovery that Freud had registered himself and Minna as man and wife at the Schweizerhaus Inn. Although important, Lothane does not see Maciejewski's discovery as a smoking gun: "even highly probable does not mean proven," he asserts. He wonders whether Freud signed the logbook that way as part of a legal stratagem, given Swiss cohabitation laws at the time which forbad couples who were not married from renting a double room.[71]

Lothane then turns to the Billinsky interview. He questions Jung's assertion that his knowledge of the Minna affair was a very important factor in his break with Freud. You'll recall, Jung had told Billinsky that Freud's refusal to provide intimate details associated with the "triangle" dream— Freud's evocation of "authority" over "truth," according to Jung—was one of the main reasons for his break with Freud.[72] Lothane challenges Jung, maintaining he did "not break with Freud over Minna," but for several other, unrelated reasons, including Jung's "reinterpretation of Freud's libido as a nonsexual energy." Also, Jung's "disagreements about interpreting the Schreber case, where Jung sided with Bleuler against Freud."

Daniel Paul Schreber, a Saxon jurist who also suffered from paranoia and who wrote extensively about his illness, was the subject of a paper by Freud, which Jung was at first impressed with but later soured on, again because of Freud's strong emphasis on the role of sexuality as a causal factor in Schreber's illness.[73]

A final reason for the break between Freud and Jung, according to Lothane, was "manifest and latent mutual homosexual emotions."[74]

Lothane also questions the veracity of the messenger—Billinsky—as Eissler had started to do but soon abandoned in his *Three Instances of Injustice*. Lothane references Paul Roazen, who told Lothane he knew Henry Murray at the time Billinsky published his interview, and Murray informed Roazen that "Billinsky got it wrong." Lothane maintains that it was Jung who "was the real womanizer, above all with Toni Wolff, who first met him as his patient."[75] Murray, as we have noted, was at the Harvard Psychological Clinic and was a prominent disciple of Jung's.[76]

With regard to Murray's statement, it is obvious that Lothane had not read Kurt Eissler's essay, where he reveals that the highly-respected Swiss psychiatrist C. A. Meier had confirmed the facts of Billinsky's interview with Jung, since Jung had told Meier basically the same thing, and Meier's integrity, at least in Eissler's eyes, was beyond reproach.[77]

Lothane also raises many of the same issues we have touched upon before: Why would Minna confide in the callow Jung? Why didn't Jung ever throw his knowledge of the affair in Freud's face?[78] In any case, Lothane argues, Minna was too unattractive for Freud to have wanted to sleep with her—a point which, as we have seen, Gay also makes.[79] As evidence of Minna's unattractiveness, Lothane quotes Jung's biographer Deirdre Bair: "Anne Bernays, Freud's grandniece … said she remembered her mother [Freud's sister Anna] saying, 'Sigmund would never have slept with Minna; she was too unattractive.' Bernays adds that her mother was 'hung up on appearance,' and her remark 'demonstrated that she had no clue as to how love/lust works.' As for her own opinion, Bernays holds 'no strong conviction' either way." Anne Bernays adds: "Anthony Storr [a British Jungian] … thought it 'very likely that Billinsky [had] drawn on his fairly active imagination.'"[80]

In a second paper published in 2007, titled, "Sigmund Freud and Minna Bernays: Primal Curiosity, Primal Scenes, Primal Fantasies—and Prevarication,"[81] Lothane takes up again the subject of Maciejewski's discovery of the logbook at the Schweizerhaus Inn. Based on Maciejewski's work, Lothane again admits that it is "probable" that Freud and Minna had sex at the inn, but it is not "proven."[82] Lothane reminds us of several practical questions that might explain why Freud represented himself and Minna as man and wife. Since it seems to have been a busy night at the inn, perhaps single rooms were not available. A double room would also have been cheaper. But in Lothane's mind, perhaps the more important reason for Freud's deception is the one he had mentioned in his earlier article, to wit: "an innkeeper 'providing accommodations' to an unmarried couple could be prosecuted as a pimp." Lothane cites Swiss Cantonal law.[83] Also, Lothane argues, had Freud and Minna registered as Dr. Freud and Miss Bernays, "they might … have attracted unwelcome attention from and gossip by other hotel guests."[84]

Lothane stresses that Freud, unlike public figures who might be voted into office, was under no obligation "to reveal his private life to anybody else, even as we are entitled to investigate it."[85] I am not sure anyone would want to argue with that. Further, Lothane asks, if we assume Freud and Minna did have sex at the Schweizerhaus, did they also have sex at Berggasse, "where Minna's bedroom opened directly into Martha and Sigmund's bedroom"?[86] Obviously, Lothane had not read Gay's 1990 essay, where he informs us that Minna occupied that particular bedroom *only after 1920*.[87] Also, in an apparently unrelated point, Lothane feels that reducing everything to sex detracts from the dignity of the intellectual and spiritual friendship between Freud and Minna.

Lothane then addresses many of the same issues he had in his other article. Perhaps, he argues, Jung's recollections are a "belated repartee of a man with a guilty conscience over his adulterous relationships?"[88]

At the end of the day, what are we to make of this whole sensation about the Maciejewski Schweizerhaus discovery, Lothane asks. "Much ado about nothing," is his reply. He says he does not need to have Freud "lily white," but he prefers "the grand mistakes of a genius to the trite truisms of a mediocrity."[89]

In both of Lothane's 2007 papers there are not-so-subtle references to Jung's advanced age at the time of the Billinsky interview—82—with its obvious implications for the accuracy of Jung's recollections. We will address the issue of Jung's age and the accuracy of his memory in the next chapter.

"JUST ONE NEW DETAIL"

In the same year Zvi Lothane's papers appeared (2007), Albrecht Hirschmüller published an article titled, "Evidence for a Sexual Relationship between Sigmund Feud and Minna Bernays?"[90] You'll recall, Hirschmüller is the editor to whom Kurt Eissler turned over the entire Freud/Minna collection of letters, both restricted and unrestricted, housed at the Freud Archives at the Library of Congress. Eissler had asked Hirschmüller to prepare them for publication, and this is exactly what Hirschmüller did. As we have noted previously, his collection appeared in 2005, in German, under the title, *Sigmund Freud—Minna Bernays: Briefwechsel, 1882-1938*.[91]

After reviewing Franz Maciejewski's paper in light of the newly published Freud/Minna correspondence, Hirschmüller concludes that the letters "show a relationship of mental and personal intimacy, as between siblings, but they do not in any way hint at a love affair, nor do any of the other available historical sources."[92] Also, Hirschmüller points out, Jung's testimony in the Billinsky interview cannot be trusted. He doesn't say why, but later in his article he references Eissler's arguments against the idea that an affair had taken place—arguments, Hirschmüller claims, that have not yet been disproven.[93]

Hirschmüller raises some of the same questions about the hotel log at the Schweizerhaus that Lothane had: "What was the situation Freud and Minna found in Maloja? Was there an option to book separate rooms? Did they share rooms and register as man and wife in the other hotels they stayed in during their journey?"[94]

Hirschmüller claims that Maciejewski "was unable to answer such questions when asked, nor does he appear to have raised them himself." While Hirschmüller identifies two letters which indicate that Freud and Minna sometimes rented two rooms on their holidays—a joint Freud/Minna letter to Martha of August 9–10, 1898,[95] and one from Freud to Martha from Lake Maggiore, dated September 5, 1900[96]—Hirschmüller admits that "those passages are no solid proof how they signed in or in which rooms or beds they in fact slept. Unfortunately, the other hotels either no longer exist or their old logbooks have disappeared."[97] Here Hirschmüller seems to be answering his own question about whether Freud and Minna shared rooms and registered as man and wife in the other hotels they stayed at during their journeys—to wit: the other hotels no longer exist or their old logbooks have disappeared.

Hirschmüller talked to the present owner of the Schweizerhaus, one Jürg Wintsch. From him he learned that at the time Freud and Minna were at the inn it "was quite filled with guests" and the logbook "shows only arrivals not departures … so it is impossible to reconstruct which other rooms would have been available on what day."[98]

Hirschmüller points out that Freud and Minna did not stay for three nights, as Maciejewski claims. Not even for three days. Hirschmüller says the next guest entered room No. 11, which Freud and Minna occupied, on Monday, August 15, so Freud and Minna probably arrived late in the afternoon on Saturday, August 13, and departed on Monday morning, August 15, hardly the "unusually long" time Maciejewski had suggested in his 2006 article.[99] The image of Freud and Minna lingering in a love nest for three days is not supported by the facts, Hirschmüller claims.[100]

Also, Hirschmüller questions whether Freud would have been so callous as to expose his sister-in-law to an unwanted pregnancy. Maciejewski's finding, Hirschmüller concludes, is "just one new detail" and not irrefutable proof, as Maciejewski had argued.[101]

"MORE STRONGLY ATTRACTED TO MEN"

Numerous other scholars have questioned whether an affair between Freud and Minna ever took place. Let me mention some of them briefly in closing.

In her 1988 book, *Freud and Jung: Years of Friendship, Years of Loss*, Linda Donn maintains that even though "Minna was an important part of Freud's life ... it is unlikely [he] ... entered into a physical liaison with his sister-in-law,"[102] while Lisa Appignanesi and John Forrester in their 1992 work, *Freud's Women*,[103] argue that "given the evidence, and the overall picture of Freud's sexual life that can be put together, the story of the affair with Minna will remain simply an interesting rumour."[104]

Similarly Frank McLynn, in his 1996 biography *Carl Gustav Jung*, expresses his doubts—though, like Gay and Eissler had, he also hedges his bets. "The idea of an affair between Freud and Minna Bernays," McLynn writes, "strains credulity to snapping point, which is not to say that the story might not still be true."[105]

Louis Breger, in his 2000 book *Freud: Darkness in the Midst of Vision*,[106] offers both conventional and rather novel reasons as to why there was no affair. The conventional: such a liaison would have been out of character for both Freud and Minna, "who were extremely sexually and emotionally constricted." The novel: "Freud ... was more strongly attracted to men, in any case."[107] And Paul Roazen opines in his 2001 *The Historiography of Psychoanalysis* that the conjecture that Freud was erotically entangled with Minna is "a notion that I have not been able to share." [108] Roazen also expresses skepticism in his 1993 study *Meeting Freud's Family*[109] and his 1976 book *Freud and His Followers*.[110]

PART II

The Affair and the Reality

CHAPTER 4

Sorting Out the Arguments

What are we to make of all these divergent opinions regarding Freud, Minna, and their alleged affair? Let me start by first considering evidence in support of there having been a romantic liaison.

THE ELEMENTS OF PROOF

The most important evidence in this regard is Jung's memory of what Minna told him. Even though many scholars have dismissed Jung's recollections rather casually, they constitute the gold standard. Why do I say this? Because in thinking about how one can "prove" that an affair took place, there are only so many possible sources of evidence. Minna's confession that she had an affair is one of these.

Might there be even stronger evidence that the two had an affair? Yes, but not much stronger. Strongest of all would be if *both* Minna and Freud had told people. That is unlikely in the case of Freud. He was too cautious to do that, but it is possible. The evidence would also be stronger if Minna had told *multiple* people, not only Jung. And perhaps she did. The Freud family was secretive, so we do not know with what friends and relatives Minna might have shared her secret. Perhaps many, perhaps none. We only know what Jung said because *one* of the several people he told about it—namely, Billinsky—got angry when he read that *Time* magazine article and jumped to conclusions, feeling he needed to set the record straight. If Billinsky hadn't reacted in that way, and, as I have pointed out, he reacted to misinformation on the part of the *Time* reporter, we would know next to nothing about a Freud/Minna affair. Luckily for history Billinsky reacted as he did.

C. A. Meier, who admits Jung told him the same thing he told Billinsky, never published anything about the affair, nor did Toni Wolff, who, according to Meier, Jung also told. Even Kurt Eissler's interview with Jung, in which Jung talks about an unmistakable transference (affection) between Minna and Freud, but where he does not mention a confession from Minna or an affair between the two—even this "softer" version of the story was kept secret, as per Eissler's instructions, for some sixty years! We will be discussing Eissler's interview with Jung shortly.

Another possible source of evidence would be a diary or cache of letters or some form of archival evidence that would show they were lovers. While there are numerous letters available, a vastly larger group are not. Unfortunately, most of their correspondence between 1893 and 1910—when, as Peter Gay has pointed out, an affair might have been at its height—are missing.[1] The extant letters show an obvious affection between the two and, I would add, a sense of comfort when they are alone together. But the letters in themselves do not reveal an affair.

Would the missing letters, if discovered, reveal more? It is certainly possible, and should not be discounted. My own sense is that affairs are, by their very nature, secretive, and Freud would have worked hard to ensure that his liaison with Minna remained so. As mentioned, Freud would probably have been discreet in what he wrote Minna and advised her to do the same in her letters to him. Revelations of an affair would have been devastating, particularly because of the special emphasis Freud placed on sexuality in his theories, for which he was already being severely criticized. Remember, at the time people were not only skeptical of Freud, they were sneering at him, even laughing at him. It's hard to imagine today what he was up against in the early years of psychoanalysis.[2] So I wouldn't expect much in the way of revelations even if the missing letters one day are found—though I could be wrong, and the fact that so many letters are missing remains a tantalizing mystery.

To sum up, there are only so many ways one can "prove" an affair took place, and I would argue that a confession by one of the two parties to the affair—in this case, Minna Bernays—is one of the strongest.

CONNECTING THE PIECES

Another factor that, in my mind, strengthens the veracity of what Jung said Minna told him is that he ties it directly to a second incident, two years later, that deals with the same subject. Thus Minna's confession of an affair does not stand by itself, at least in Jung's mind, and I don't think it ought to in ours, either. I am referring, of course, to Jung's trip with Freud to America and the incidents surrounding the "triangle" dream episode, where Freud used his "authority" to put an end to Jung's request for intimate associations.

With Minna's confession in hand, Jung was apparently trying to press Freud to admit his dalliance, and when Freud wouldn't say anything further, Jung felt that Freud was not a true friend—not someone who would share personal information even with his closest ally at the time, which Jung felt he was. So I think not only did Jung feel disappointed by Freud's appeal to "authority," he also felt deeply hurt. I suspect Jung was hoping for more from his friendship with Freud.

Did Jung fabricate the story of Minna's confession, as more than several commentators have implied? It's certainly possible, but I don't think he did, and I don't believe there is evidence to support such an allegation. This subject will be examined again in our concluding chapter.

INSTANCES

Let's briefly look at the various instances when Jung revealed to others in private, and sometimes to the public in published form, what Minna confessed to him, or what happened with the "incontinence" issue or the "triangle" dream episode in America, or at least in one instance all three.[3]

One

There is, of course, Billinsky's 1969 publication of his 1957 interview with Jung. This contains Minna's confession, a reference to Freud's incontinence, and Jung's story of the "triangle" dream episode in America.

Two

A second instance was, as we have seen, the December 3, 1912, letter from Jung to Freud where he reminds Freud that the reason "our analysis ... came to a stop ... [was] ... your remark that you 'could not submit to analysis *without losing your authority*'" (emphasis Jung's).[4]

Three

A third instance involves Jung's confidante, C. A. Meier. Billinsky's recollection of what Minna confessed to Jung (and presumably also the information about Freud's incontinence and the "triangle" dreams episode in America) was, according to Peter Gay and Kurt Eissler—both staunch Freudians—confirmed by Meier, who said that what Billinsky published is exactly what Jung had told him. Eissler vouches for Meier's integrity. Gay indicates that Meier told him this "years before."[5] I assume that means "years before" 1957, the year we know Jung told Billinsky.

Four

A fourth instance is when Jung recounts the "triangle" dream episode with Freud in America in his 1925 lecture in Zürich. I quoted a brief excerpt in Chapter 3. Now Jung's description more fully: "In 1909 Freud and I were both invited to Clark University, and we were together daily for about seven weeks. We analyzed dreams each day. … Freud had a dream on an important theme which I cannot mention." This is apparently the "triangle" dream involving Freud, Martha and Minna. Jung continues: "I analyzed it and said there was more to be said if he would give me some points about his private life. He looked at me with a peculiar expression of suspicion in his eyes and said, 'I could tell you more but I can't risk my authority.' Then I knew further analysis was impossible because he put authority above truth."[6]

Five

Another instance is in Jung's 1961 autobiography, *Memories, Dreams, Reflections*. Jung recalls that in their trip to America Freud had a dream, the subject of which Jung felt it was not right to air. "I interpreted it as best I could," Jung remembers, "but added that a great deal more could be said about it if he would supply me with some additional details from his private life. Freud's response to these words was a curious look—a look of the utmost suspicion. Then he said, 'But I cannot risk my authority!'"[7]

Six

Still another instance, you'll recall, is when Jung tells the American psychologist Saul Rosenzweig about the incontinence incident and the "triangle" dream episode in a 1951 interview.[8] Unfortunately, as mentioned, Rosenzweig did not make his entire interview with Jung available; he only quotes from parts of it in his book. Perhaps Jung told Rosenzweig everything he told Billinsky, but unlike Billinsky, Rosenzweig decided not to reveal the more salacious parts of Jung's story. We just don't know. What Rosenzweig does say is that Jung at first appeared reluctant to talk about the "triangle" dream episode, but then relented and appeared to derive "some special satisfaction from the disclosures he was making about Freud."[9]

Seven

From John Kerr we learn that Jung told several additional people about (I presume) Freud's affair with Minna, but I don't know for certain. You'll remember, one was Toni Wolff, Jung's longtime mistress—or at least this is according to C. A. Meier, whom Kerr quotes. Another person was Harvard psychologist Henry Murray, who revealed what Jung told him in a November 11, 1968, interview with Dr. Gene Nameche, who was conducting interviews for the *Jung Oral History Archive*. A third person was John Phillips, an analyst in training. A final person was the Italian journalist Hugo Charteris. Based on my research, Kerr's description is incorrect. Charteris was a British novelist, not an Italian journalist, although, as I have pointed out above, Charteris's story seems suspect because he reports that Jung told him Freud had revealed the affair, not Minna. It is possible that might have happened; there is certainly no way to disprove it. But it is inconsistent with what Jung told everyone else.

"A WHOLE WORLD TOOK PLACE"

The most recently available instance of Jung discussing the subject is Kurt Eissler's August 29, 1953, interview with him. This is the interview released by the Freud Archives at the Library of Congress in 2013. It is an especially interesting exchange because it was tape-recorded, unlike Jung's discussions with Billinsky and Rosenzweig, in which both men, following their respective interviews, wrote down notes of their conversations. With the Eissler transcript we get every nuance of Jung's thinking and every subtle aspect of the interplay between the two men, even the break halfway through the interview, when Eissler has to put a new tape in the recording machine.

Because the interview was conducted in German and has not been translated into English, minimal attention appears to have been paid to it in the English-speaking world. I have had the sixty-one-page interview professionally translated and would like to correct that situation now.

The more comfortable Jung felt with an interviewer, and the less public the setting, the more he appeared willing to reveal about Freud, Minna, and their relationship. This is probably to be expected. In the 1925 public lecture, Jung limits himself rather severely to a discussion of the "authority" issue with Freud during their trip to America and talks about "a dream on an important theme which I cannot mention."[10] With known Jungians Billinsky and Meier, on the other hand, he reveals everything. With Eissler, a prominent Freudian and head of the Freud Archives, Jung is somewhere in the middle. The same story is there, but you have to read between the lines, and Jung is obviously uncomfortable being interviewed, continually asking for reassurances from Eissler that what he says be kept confidential.

In the interview Jung does not specifically mention an affair, nor does he recount a private meeting with Minna in which she shared her secret with him. But what he does say about Freud, Minna, and Martha is often revealing and perfectly consistent with what we have seen him reveal at other times to other people. Jung offers unmistakable hints of an erotic, improper relationship between Freud and Minna, though when pressed he often avows complete ignorance about what was really happening in Freud's private life.

"Professor," Eissler starts the interview, "I would like to know all that you would like to tell me about Freud. There may [well] be discreet matters there! I am happy to leave the room. Since I'm not writing a biography and actually have no scholarly interest in doing so, [I want] rather, only to make myself an instrument of this collection. I don't know what you think, but I believe that the historical development of depth psychology will one day be of great interest, and your relationship with Freud, and your observations of Freud—whom you knew in such an important phase, such an important era—will, I imagine, interest historians a great deal."

Before Jung can respond, Eissler once again emphasizes how confidential everything will be kept: "And as I said, if it concerns anything discreet, I'm happy to leave the room, if you speak into [the recorder], and I'll seal it in your presence."

My sense is that Eissler is hoping Jung would feel comfortable being interviewed and might, as a result, share as many personal memories of Freud, including "indiscreet" ones, as he can remember.

Still Jung is wary: "I am old now," he says, "and cannot get used to this apparatus."

Eissler asks if the recorder bothers him.

Jung calls it a devilish thing. "I hate broadcasting and all that, you know!?" he says. "It is repugnant to me to the last!"

Eissler persists, appealing to Jung's sense of fairness. "If I were younger," Eissler explains, "I could go home and write down what you have told me. But my memory is not that good ... and it would really be a pity, if ...."

Jung finally agrees, and the interview proceeds with the recorder on.

Jung muses out loud: "—what I experienced with Freud! But how to put it into a few words? So, you know, Freud was a highly complex phenomenon, you know?! A very interesting man, with many light sides and dark sides. And there's of course a colossal amount to say about him, you know?! I was, of course ... I mean, of course, when one is confronted with such a man, one is implicated, you know, and is party to, you know, and all that, you know?! We had a very good friendship, until we just came up against the things that were incompatible. That's how it was—it was a terrible disappointment to him that I turned away from him. And for me it was the same!"

A few minutes later they turn to Freud's incontinence problem that flared up during the trip to America.

Jung explains that Freud told him that whenever he was in a city where there was no toilet nearby, he would get the urge to urinate, and he was frightened that he might not be able to hold his urine. And then Jung explains: "when we came to New York [in 1909] … And we were in the Palisades." (Actually, across the Hudson from the New Jersey Palisades, on Morningside Drive near Columbia University.) "And there were no saloons anywhere, you know?! [laughs] nothing in the neighborhood [where Freud could relieve himself]. And suddenly his phobia is acting up, he couldn't hold water anymore and pissed all over his pant leg. We then had to get ourselves into a taxi … And it was really embarrassing, and he was terribly affected by it and said, See, I'm senile. And so on. And I said, Nonsense! You're not senile! It's just a neurosis!"

Jung says he and Freud argue about whether his incontinence is a neurosis or a physical condition of some kind, a palsy, and Jung convinces Freud that it is caused by a neurosis that could be alleviated through analysis. Freud says he would be happy if it were just a neurosis, and then Jung says: "'I want to analyze you already. I'll get around it somehow!' Said he [Freud], 'I would be delighted!' 'Good! So, give it a try,' I said." So Freud assents. "Now, let's analyze your dreams!" Jung continues. "I analyzed the dreams … and there was very personal content. Very delicate things.[11] And I said to Freud, now comes some very personal material and I must of course set you at liberty, whether you want to speak of them or not. But I am also gladly prepared to take it on. Then he reflected for a long time. And when he was done, he said, 'My dear Jung, I cannot risk my authority!' At that moment, he lost it."

Eissler then hones in. He asks Jung what Freud might have been concealing.

Jung replies defensively: "Those are personal family matters. So I know *nothing!*" (The emphasis is Jung's.)

Eissler persists: "But, I mean, what was your guess?"

Jung suddenly recalls his first visit to Freud in Vienna in 1907. His recollection is almost identical to what he tells Billinsky four years later. So any question that Billinsky might have got it "wrong" in his interview with Jung, as some have alleged, is not true, based on this tape-recorded version, which is obviously unbiased.

Jung remembers: "The first time I came to Vienna I went with my wife, and Freud came to the hotel and brought my wife flowers and welcomed us charmingly, and said that he unfortunately couldn't invite us over, his modest home, etc., and he had nothing other than a somewhat elderly housewife to offer. My wife was terribly shocked. And I, of course, as well! We were then at his place once to eat, and Mrs. Freud was a very nice lady, but utterly extinguished [washed out]. ... Utterly extinguished. But the prominent role was played by the younger sister [Minna] ... who was also at the table."

Eissler asks what sort of person she was.

"Oh, she was an intelligent person," Jung responds, "who also knew about psychology. The wife [knew] nothing [about that]!"

Then Eissler asks: "And you believe Freud was embarrassed by his wife?"

"Yeah," says Jung cautiously, "*I* don't know, *I* don't know, so there!" Again, the emphasis is Jung's. "Freud told me only that he keeps everything away from the family, nothing of his psychology of the family! ... Yes, that was psychology *à compartiment*. And yes, so, I mean, I have a certain, a certain speculation that that stuff was around *that line*, you know!" (Emphasis Jung's.) "So, his family circumstances, um ... So, I don't know anything!"

Eissler keeps up the pressure: "But what is your guess?"

"So, my guess is as follows: this is a definite fact: the younger sister had [showed] a great transference, and Freud, Freud *was not insensible*."

The phrase "*was not insensible*" is spoken in English, and the emphasis is Jung's.

"You believe there was an, an attachment to the younger sister?" Eissler asks point blank.

"Ah," Jung scoffs. "Attachment? I don't know how much?! Yes! But God, one knows, how these things are, right?! In any case, the boy had the advantage. He always told me that in his neurosis: 'Well, now I'm an old man, and, and ... Yeah, if one had a young woman, one could rejuvenate oneself!' So that, that played a big role. There are further indications in *The Interpretation of Dreams*"—Freud's work—"as well."

"Of the relationship to the wife's younger sister?" Eissler asks.

Jung backs off: "Oh, whether there was such a thing, I cannot say! ... But what is certain, is that the sister had a blossoming transference toward Freud. There is, there is absolutely no doubt about that!"

"But how was his relationship toward her?" Eissler inquires further.

"Well that," Jung says cautiously, "that I cannot say! I just cannot say! I, I suppose that everything was most proper, in any case on the surface everything entirely proper."

It is interesting that Jung says "on the surface" everything is proper, but what about under the surface? He does not elaborate.

Then Eissler returns to the "triangle" dream interpretation in America and asks: "But, Professor, you would assume that you came closer to this topic in the analysis in New York? And he then broke it off?"

Jung: "Then he broke it off!"

Eissler: "Because he …"

Jung: "Well, he had there, every man has intimate stuff!"

Eissler: "Yes."

Jung: "He reflected twice, whether [to do so], before he spoke of it."

Eissler: "Yes."

Jung: "Every man has his secrets."

It seems obvious that the "secrets" Jung is referring to involve Freud's relationship with Minna.

Later in the interview, they return to the subject of the "other woman," in the context of trying to understand why, in Jung's view, Freud often seemed emotionally disturbed in some way—cranky, dogmatic, autocratic, inflexible.

Eissler asks what sort of event might have caused such moods, and Jung hypothesizes: "Well, it could be a disappointment in love, you know, or it could be precisely that he found himself in the conflict that is so common in marriage, you know, the young woman, the other woman …"

An obvious reference to Minna? It appears so.

Then still later they return to the subject of Jung's first visit to Vienna and his conversations there with Freud.

"Can you recall how long you remained in Vienna that time?" Eissler asks.

"Yes," Jung responds, "we were in Vienna for fourteen days.[12] On the first day we spoke together for thirteen uninterrupted hours," Jung adds proudly.

"No way!" Eissler counters.

"Yes, yes! For thirteen hours! I probed him, to the very last detail."

"And what …"

"It was very interesting! Very interesting!" Jung's enthusiasm increases.

"What was the impression that first day?" Eissler asks.

"Well, I pushed forward to his limits, until we got to, to his science of positivism. And there came the philosophical limits, which he greatly regretted."

Eissler: "Thirteen hours?!"

"We spoke for thirteen hours!"

"And you saw each other daily during that time?"

"We, yes, I can say, I was with him every evening. We got along perfectly …"

Later in the interview there is a pause. Eissler needs to change the tape in the recording machine. Eissler and Jung must have started talking about

Jung's 1907 visit to Vienna again while the tape was being changed, for the new tape abruptly begins with Jung's recollections of his wife's reactions to what was perceived to be Freud's disparaging remarks about Martha.

Jung starts: "That, that really did not please her!"—meaning Jung's wife. "I … yeah, she [Emma Jung] was, as you know, people were so negatively opposed to him back then, and my wife did not exactly have positive feelings for him. And then, then I had to placate her because, you know, the marriage of the wife … really aggrieved her. That Freud spoke like that about his wife, yeah! That was substantially more awkward. He was *embarrassed.*" Emphasis Jung's.

Then Eissler asks Jung about how long after his visit to Vienna Freud returned the courtesy by coming to Zürich, and whether he came alone.

"He came alone," Jung responded. "He always traveled alone; he always left his wife at home."

Martha the dispensable!

"The second time, too?" Eissler asks, a bit incredulous.

"Yes, yes! Yes, yes!" Jung replies emphatically.

A little later in the conversation, Jung refers to Minna, Martha, Freud and the so-called transference problem once more, this time with tantalizing hints of an affair.

Jung says: "tentative supposition, namely that, that I thought, the transference of his younger sister-in-law, his sister-in-law, that it did not leave him unimpressed. … It's also difficult, you know, when one is so close to someone with such a transference. She was a pretty person, and mentally very lively, and entirely *au courant* in her ideas. She did some secretarial duties for him as well. It's easily possible, you know, that something went wrong there! You find hints in *The Interpretation of Dreams* of something that went wrong. There are also a number of very interesting. … Or it's there in promises, in misreadings." (Interpretations?) "Well, in any case it's somewhere, it's somewhere, I remember that precisely. There's a case where, where such a situation comes up, where a possible pregnancy, you know? But, as I said … this may all be silly supposition! I really don't know anything! But that, that there was transference on the part of his sister-in-law is certain, that is dead certain, any blind person would see that. And the wife alongside, totally washed out, ego-disturbed, ego-disturbed."

Ego-disturbed? Meaning, I suppose, having a weak ego; being passive.

So here again, four years before Jung spoke to Billinsky, Jung describes Minna, as opposed to Martha, as the attractive woman in Freud's life—pretty, very lively, entirely *au courant*. For fans of Swales, please note that Jung hints that a possible pregnancy may be interpreted from Freud's writings (*The Interpretation of Dreams*), though it may be a "silly supposition" on his part after all, he admits.

As the interview progresses, it is obvious Jung can still not get out of his mind the thrill of his first meeting with Freud. This time Eissler brings the subject up: "But for example this encounter between you and Freud, it's truly something historically unique and ..."

"Yes," Jung says, "there you are by all means right! ... We were ourselves amazed, when we realized at one A.M. that we had been speaking with one another for an uninterrupted thirteen hours ...."

Eissler comments, "So much must have taken place [in that time]."

And Jung replies poignantly, with a memorable line: "Yes, a whole world took place! ... Everything, even that which came later! On both sides! It was all there! He got his big shock from me, and I got my big shock from me [laughs], a part of me, of my unconscious! And it was all already there! But it never happened to me otherwise, that I could talk with someone for an uninterrupted thirteen hours! One had absolutely no sense of fatigue ...."

At one point in the interview, Eissler seems to sense that Jung has not opened up as much as he would have liked—whether by 1953 Eissler had heard what Jung told others about a Freud/Minna affair is not clear, but his probing questions seem to indicate as much. In any case, Eissler asks if another interview might be possible the following year. Eissler says he is convinced that Jung has much more to say. Eissler once again strongly emphasizes how everything Jung says will be kept strictly confidential, because Jung keeps raising the issue. Eissler tries to reassure him in the strongest possible terms: "Professor," he says to Jung, "if any indiscretion happens with the archive I will have to kill myself, because so many people have trusted me, it would be just terrible if even the smallest indiscretion took place. ... That would be truly awful!"

Well, we now know that Eissler kept his word—for all of sixty years!

Two final points about Eissler's interview with Jung. There is a story that Jung relates rather joyfully, it seems, for it is one in which the positivist Freud is confronted with the occult. In a sense, it is a ghost story and as such, a victory for the spiritualist Jung.

Jung recalls: "He [Freud] told me that he had had a case of a woman who had Graves' disease. Not severely ill, but distinctly so. And she had a twin sister, but he didn't know that. And she died. But he knew that she had died, you know?! And one day comes her twin sister. She had Graves' disease as well. She comes into the room, and he said he almost died of shock. He had thought it was her ghost! You know, he knew that she's dead, then she comes in, because he didn't know there's a twin sister."

Eissler says, "Yes."

Jung: "And, and then he had a really strong reaction after the fact. It was very powerful for me. It showed me that he is at a deep level very prone..."

Eissler: "... to believing in ghosts!"

"Yes," Jung says triumphantly.

This story also stresses the serious differences between the two men in terms of ideology—Jung's continued emphasis on spirituality and the occult versus the positivist cynicism (or realism) of Freud.

The second point concerns Jung's feelings toward Freud, as evidenced in the interview. Setting all the criticisms that Jung directs at Freud to one side—and admittedly there are many in the interview—what comes across most powerfully is the incredible love (I know of no other way to describe it) Jung has for Freud, not necessarily of a homoerotic sort, though that might have been part of it, but a love based on adoration, of knowing someone so intelligent and insightful that his very presence could take Jung's breath away. This is coupled with a deep regret that, for whatever reasons, the two men could not have remained close friends and collaborators. Never again would Jung meet a man with whom he could converse for thirteen straight hours, and that loss he sorely feels.[13]

ADDING BELIEVABILITY

The evidence provided by Franz Maciejewski and Peter Rudnytsky is important, not because their combined contribution constitutes anything close to a smoking gun, but because what they offer adds *believability* to Jung's story.

I think when Maciejewski asserts that his discovery of Freud's Schweizerhaus notation, *Dr. Sigm. Freud u[nd] Frau/Wien*, indicates that by "any reasonable standard of proof, Sigmund Freud and his wife's sister Minna Bernays had a liaison,"[14] he overstates the case, yet the importance of Maciejewski's finding cannot be underestimated. There may have been many reasons why Freud would have written what he did in the hotel registration log, and we will get into those suggestions later in this chapter, but *the most likely one* is that he wanted to hide the fact that he was having an affair with his sister-in-law.

Rudnytsky's contribution is to show that there is independently verifiable evidence from Sándor Ferenczi (a witness) that confirms one important part of what Jung tells Billinsky—about the incontinence event on Riverside Drive and Freud's invocation of "authority" when pressed by Jung to provide personal details concerning the "triangle" dream.

As mentioned, because one part of Jung's recollection of what Billinsky said can be independently verified does not mean that the whole story, including Minna's confession of an affair, is true, but it does add *believability* to Jung's overall recollection. As I asked earlier, why would Jung lie in one part of his story and tell the truth in the other?

THE LIMITS OF AFTER-THE-FACT, INTERPRETIVE ACCOUNTS

I am leery of after-the-fact, post-Billinsky interpretations that suddenly find "evidence" of Freud's affair with Minna in various of Freud's writings and letters. If it's so obvious, why wasn't it also obvious before Billinsky published his interview? I refer here to the studies of Swales and O'Brien.

I have another concern with regard to these sorts of analyses. Because of the nature of their arguments, with numerous assumptions and inferences, their work can often be more easily picked apart, or at the very least misunderstood. I know I have had trouble following Swales's subtle arguments and hoped for some sort of chart or roadmap which would enable me to see more clearly how all his various assumptions and inferences are linked together. I realize that with considerable work the reader can do that himself, but I believe that having such guides available would make Swales's hypotheses easier to understand.

Gay's criticism of Swales for offering "confident conjectures as demonstrated fact" and employing what Gay describes as the Siegfried Bernfeld method—reading Freud's texts "as disguised autobiographical revelations"—is well taken. You'll recall Gay admits this method can be useful, but also fears it can be risky, especially when Swales selectively applies some of his arguments.[15] Gay's criticism is not too dissimilar from Elms's, and I think both must give us pause regarding the validity of Swales's arguments.

With regard to O'Brien, I find baffling his argument that while the manifest content of Freud's June 4, 1896, letter to Fliess does not appear to concern an affair, upon closer examination it in fact does. I think O'Brien has a high evidentiary hurdle to overcome for his argument to be at all compelling. And his "contextual" analysis, which is based on Freud and Minna being alone in Vienna at a time when Martha was away, seems to me a bit tenuous.

On the principle that weak arguments tend to undermine strong ones trying to prove the same thing, doubters of the veracity of Jung's recollections of a Freud/Minna affair benefit from analyses such as Swales and O'Brien's, because they can lump all the pro-affair arguments together, quickly skipping over Jung's recollections of Minna's confession. The net result is that those skeptical of an affair gain an unfair argumentative advantage.

In my own version of Occam's Razor (and I know there are many variants), it seems to me that the best arguments are those that involve the least number of assumptions. And my particular argument involves only one major assumption—that Jung did not lie. I cannot say the same for the arguments of Swales and O'Brien.

A MOST DANGEROUS METHOD

John Kerr's major contribution to the Minna question is the information he provides, which indicates that Billinsky was not the only one that Jung told about a Freud/Minna affair—so if Jung did lie, he did so with remarkable consistency. Kerr mentions as other recipients of Jung's story: C. A. Meier, Toni Wolff, Henry Murray, John Phillips, and an Italian journalist (really a British novelist) by the name of Hugo Charteris, whose description of his interview with Jung is contained in Vincent Brome's *Jung: Man and Myth*.[16]

I have already expressed concern about Charteris's recollection, because he indicates that Jung told him *Freud* said he slept with Minna, which differs from every other account of Jung's story, where Minna is the one who reveals the affair. Also, although Kerr references Brome as the source for his information about Charteris, I have checked, and Brome does not describe him as an Italian journalist; he calls him a novelist.[17] So I wonder from what other source Kerr might have gotten his information about Charteris. There is no other source mentioned. Also, Kerr says Jung was seventy-one years of age when he had his interview with Billinsky but he was actually eighty-two.[18] If Jung were only seventy-one, I suspect there would be fewer concerns raised about the accuracy of his memory—but perhaps not.

Kerr also mentions contemporaneous rumors of an affair, which he attributes to Dr. Oskar Rie, Freud's family physician. Remember: "For children, Freud went with Martha; for pleasure, he took Minna." I think this is important information. It does not necessarily mean Freud had an affair with Minna, but it certainly suggests the level of affection and comfort Freud felt with his sister-in-law.

THE "MINNA WARS"

I believe Barry Silverstein has raised evocative questions, including the possibility that Freud felt it permissible to have an affair with Minna, given Freud's deep sexual frustration, alienation from Martha, and growing attraction to Minna at the time of their trip alone together in 1898.[19] Silverstein reminds us of Freud's July 8, 1915, letter to James J. Putnam, where he seems to allow for such "permissible" behavior.[20]

Silverstein finds support for his ideas in several of Freud's works and letters in which he appears to believe in the notion of a superior human being—someone who is not bound by standard moral constraints and hence can do anything he wants, sexual or otherwise. We know that Freud read Nietzsche as a young student and had purchased the latter's collected works in early 1900, though he seems to have been both influenced and repelled by Nietzsche, at least according to Peter Gay.[21] I am not sure I agree with Gay with regard to Freud being "repelled" by Nietzsche. In any case, in Chapter 5 we will look carefully at Freud and the idea of a "superior" class and his disdain for those less fortunately endowed, an attitude which Minna seems to have shared.

Silverstein also points to Esti Freud's conversations with Paul Roazen. Remember, while Esti doesn't necessarily think there was an affair, she also does not rule one out and thinks that Minna "made a play" for Freud. Her views provide new insight into the sort of person Minna might have been— more sexually aggressive and predatory than might have been imagined. After all, Minna did become the center of Freud's life at Berggasse, pushing Martha to one side. By all accounts, she was definitely a force to be reckoned with, the kind of strong, dominating woman Freud seemed to admire. And although Martha apparently did not mind that Minna became Freud's confidante and muse—or at least this has become part of the Freud family myth—my own theory is that she probably did mind. What wife wouldn't?

Silverstein also raises another important point. If there was an affair, why would Freud have done something so risky? Silverstein believes that if we assume Freud acted as a rational person, his behavior is indeed rather puzzling. But did Freud always act in a coherent way? Can we expect a man dealing with powerful, pent-up sexual feelings to always be in control of his emotions? Silverstein doubts it, and I do as well. I know it might sound trite, but I think it's true when they say that love makes people do strange things, even apparently "out-of-character" things.

I cannot accept Daniel Burston's argument that Maciejewski's discovery of Freud's handwritten notation in the Schweizerhaus Inn registration book makes "outright denial" that Freud and Minna did have an affair "no longer an option,"[22] though it certainly adds credibility to the idea that an affair took place. But it does not completely rule out other possible explanations. It merely makes the argument that there was no affair more difficult to defend. I think Burston's other point is more compelling: that the 1975 publication of the Freud/Jung letters[23] reveals how "deeply estranged from one another" Freud and Martha were.[24] Burston aligns himself with Erich Fromm on this question. Fromm criticizes the idealized notion of Freud and his life promoted by Freudian orthodoxy.[25]

The main culprits in this last point are Ernest Jones and later Kurt Eissler, both of whom paint an idyllic portrait of family life at the Freud household. Eissler writes in *Three Instances of Injustice*: "Everyone who had contact with the Freuds ... [remembers] the family's striking harmony, geniality and cheerful spirits."[26] I agree with both Burston and Fromm that, on the contrary, there was considerable tension in Freud's marriage and Freud's life was far from ideal. In fact, it seems to have been quite wretched at times. More on this later.

In sum, these are more than several scholars who support the idea that Freud and Minna were lovers, and their arguments seem to be on solid ground. I have noted the exceptions. Let me now turn to those who strongly question that an affair took place, by far the largest number who have examined the issue.

"SHEER NONSENSE"

Ernest Jones doesn't mention an affair explicitly (Billinsky's public revelations are more than a decade off), but he does talk about various "legends" concerning Freud and Minna, and dismisses the idea of any sort of "sexual attraction" between the two—that, he says, is "sheer nonsense."[27] He also makes a special point of criticizing Helen Walker Puner's 1947 biography of Freud, which rejects the idealized notion of Freud's marriage.[28] As we have seen, he even criticizes her for things she does not say.

I believe Jones has done more to promote a naïve, romanticized vision of Freud's personal life—the puritanical, almost chaste Freud, Martha assuredly the only woman in his love life, the remarkable harmony within the Freud family, even between Martha and Minna—than any single person, with the possible exception of Kurt Eissler. I think such a portrait would be fine if we did not live in an age where, as adults, we know how dysfunctional even the most apparently serene families can be.

In Chapters 5 and 6 I will provide a more three-dimensional, albeit less idyllic portrait of Freud and his family life as a counterweight to what I consider Jones's overly blissful view—and Eissler's as well.

"NOT A TATTER OF EVIDENCE"

It's hard for me to take seriously Ronald Clark's claim in his 1980 biography of Freud that there is not "a tatter of evidence" that Freud had strong sexual interests and that "the known context of his life makes it distinctly improbable" that he and Minna had an affair.[29] We will see in Chapter 5 just how sexually interested (in both men and women) Freud was and that the dismissively termed "tatter of evidence" is actually more like a mound. Also, I am not certain what Clark means by "the known context" of Freud's life. Do we really know what this context was? Can we ever be certain what a family's life is behind closed doors?[30] I suspect it is not out of the ordinary for peoples' lives to be different from what they seem to be from the outside. Perhaps private lives being different *is* the norm.

A little later in this chapter, when we consider Peter Gay's comments, I will examine in greater depth this "context" issue—the idea prevalent among many doubting that an affair took place, that it just doesn't seem consistent with what we know about them that Freud and Minna might have been lovers.

Clark also claims the rumor has Jung being approached by both Minna and Martha in 1907. As far as I am aware, there is no evidence to support this assertion.

SOUNDS UNNATURAL

Elms's article in *Psychology Today* raises many of the same issues other doubters of a Freud/Minna affair have pointed to and as such provides a good microcosm of those arguments. That Elms might find Jung's account of Minna's confession unnatural is not unreasonable. But remember the circumstances of Billinsky's interview. He did not tape-record his conversation with Jung, as Eissler had. He wrote notes soon after his meeting with Jung. Also, we now know from Peter Rudnytsky that Billinsky published a "sanitized" version of his notes. Billinsky's son, Dr. John M. Billinsky, Jr., as I've indicated, has confirmed the same to me.[31] So perhaps some of what Elms sees as unnatural language or a lack of clarity in Jung's language can be attributed to Billinsky's attempt to soften the language—though I, for one, don't find Jung's language unclear or unnatural even in the "sanitized" version.

Why did Billinsky try to tone down the language in the published version? We don't know for certain, and his son did not address that issue when I communicated with him, but my guess would be that he realized he was sitting on explosive and rather embarrassing information about Freud and he wanted to keep that embarrassment to a minimum.[32] Remember, Billinsky kept quiet about Jung's revelations for twelve years before being driven into publication by the 1969 *Time* article.

THE CALLOW JUNG

While it is true, as Elms points out, Jung was a decade younger than Minna—he wonders why Minna would have confided in man so junior to her in years—Jung was not a complete stranger to her at the time, as Elms maintains. If he was a stranger, he was also a complete stranger to Freud. We know that is not the case because Freud had been communicating with Jung for about a year at that time (1907). As I indicated in Chapter 1, they began exchanging letters in April 1906,[33] and Freud knew that even before then Jung had been using Freud's ideas in some of his own papers and had been proselytizing on behalf of psychoanalysis at the Burghölzli.[34] In addition, Freud had been communicating with Jung's boss at the Burghölzli, Eugen Bleuler, since 1904.[35] If Minna, as Jung says, knew everything about what Freud was doing, she must have known about Freud's correspondence with this rising young star and how important he was to Freud for the future of psychoanalysis.

So Jung was not a stranger, an unknown person visiting Freud at Berggasse in 1907 to discuss psychoanalysis. He was the bright light on the horizon, the future incarnate, someone whom Freud hoped might save psychoanalysis for the larger world, far beyond the small cabal of physicians and others in Vienna who were, at that time, Freud's sole supporters.

THE POWER OF PERSONALITY

In addition, Jung had a powerful personality—he was dynamic, brilliant, filled with charm and enthusiasm.[36] He was also a man known to have an eye for the ladies, an inveterate flirt.[37] And he thought Minna was not only bright but "very good looking." I can see Jung flirting with Minna and gaining her confidence in a way that made her feel comfortable enough to share with him her shocking secret.

Why would Minna want to tell Jung about her relationship with Freud? What were her motives? Obviously she possessed information that could ruin Freud's marriage and set his efforts at bringing psychoanalysis into the mainstream of medical life back decades. These are particularly germane questions which we will look at in detail later in this study.

HOW MUCH TIME?

I challenge Elms's point about Jung being someone Minna spent very little time with during his 1907 visit to Freud—the assumption being that Jung did not have much free time available that week. Yet if we look carefully at his schedule, we can see there was ample opportunity for Jung to meet with Minna. In fact, he could have met with her more than once.

How much time would Jung have needed to hear what Minna had to say? Ten minutes probably would have sufficed, so we are not looking for a large block of time in order to make plausible the idea that Jung talked to her. And how much free time did Jung have during his week's stay in Vienna? The answer is, quite a lot. You'll recall that particular week was not the best time for Jung to visit, at least from Freud's point of view. He was busy with patients Monday through Saturday. He had suggested Easter weekend as a better time, since he would have both Sunday and Monday off. Let's look at the details.

The Jungs arrived on Saturday, March 2, and Freud went to their hotel to greet them. I think it reasonable to black out March 2 as a time Jung and Minna might have talked, since there was little free time that day and Jung hadn't yet met Minna. On Sunday, March 3, Jung, his wife Emma, and Ludwig Binswanger went to Berggasse to meet Freud and his family for lunch. Martha, Minna, and apparently some of the children were there, since Freud's son Martin remembers Jung's visit.[38] That was the day Jung was immediately impressed with Minna and saw Martha in quite a different light—as someone not having much of a role in Freud's life, as a person who looked "utterly extinguished [wiped out]."[39] That is also the day Jung spent thirteen hours in continuous conversation with Freud, apparently a magical experience for both men and one which Jung proudly remembered almost fifty years later, in his interview with Eissler. So let's black out Sunday as well.

The other days of the week, the days when Freud was working "from eight to eight," as he put it in his February 21 letter to Jung,[40] Jung had free, with the following exceptions: he attended Freud's Wednesday Psychological Society meeting that week, followed by conversations with Freud; he went "shopping" with Minna and one or more of the Freud daughters (probably Mathilde, based on Martin Freud's recollection)[41] for one day, or at least one afternoon; and he joined Freud for lunch on several days and at least several evenings for dinner as well.

The rest of the week Jung had free, approximately half the time he was in Vienna. So he had plenty of opportunity to talk to Minna and do other things as well.

JUNG THE HYPOCRITE?

Elms also finds it odd that following Jung's 1907 visit his first letter to his new friend would be filled with enthusiasm for Freud, especially given what he had heard from Minna.[42] This is a point which Eissler makes over and over again, referencing, as we have seen, several enthusiastic letters Jung sent to Freud following his first visit.[43]

The question is, what alternative did Jung have? Although he may have been shocked by what Minna told him and felt "agony" at the news—remember, he heard not only that Freud was having an affair but that the person he was having it with was his own sister-in-law—he was also deeply impressed with Freud, the first "great man" he had ever encountered, and no doubt saw great promise for his own career in working with him, much as Freud saw the value for the future of psychoanalysis in having Jung as his heir and successor.

I think the tone of Jung's letters to Freud in the wake of his visit was also a matter of common courtesy. It is plausible that Jung could at the same time feel great admiration for Freud as an innovator and disgust at what he knew about his new friend's affair with Minna, and not mention the latter to Freud. After all, what would he say? *Herr Professor, I think your talent is great, but your morals leave much to be desired?* That would have been unlikely. Jung was too ambitious to do anything to jeopardize his budding relationship with Freud, at least at that time, and confronting him about Minna might have done just that.

TELLING OTHERS

Elms also finds it strange that while Jung was apparently at that time deeply involved in a love affair with one of his patients (Sabina Spielrein), he never mentioned a word of Freud's alleged affair to her. The brilliant Spielrein had originally been a patient of Jung's, one of the first he analyzed using Freud's psychoanalytic techniques.[44] She then studied medicine at Zürich (with Bleuler and Jung as her dissertation advisors), and joined the Vienna Psychoanalytic Society in 1911. She began a correspondence with Freud in 1909, writing him about her concerns regarding her relationship with Jung. She undoubtedly had a strong transference to Jung, and although her feelings toward him were powerful, Jung seemed ambivalent toward her. Whether there actually was a love affair between the two is apparently a matter of some contention.[45]

Since 1977, various materials related to Sabina Spielrein have been discovered, including diaries, letters (some from Jung), and hospital charts, but the record is still fragmentary, so we cannot be certain that other materials do not exist, or might have existed at one time, which could indicate that Jung did share knowledge about the Freud/Minna affair with Spielrein.[46]

If Jung did not confide in her, why not? We can ask the same question with regard to Jung's wife Emma. In both cases, perhaps he did, and we simply don't know it. No extant evidence exists. We do know from what C. A. Meier said that Jung did tell his mistress Toni Wolff, but that was only later.[47] Perhaps Jung saw his relationship with Spielrein as volatile at best, dangerous at worst. He might have thought she was still unstable, and feared that if he told her she might tell Freud, with whom she was communicating, and he didn't want her to do that. It's hard to determine why Jung might tell one person and not another, but not telling Spielrein about the affair cannot be considered "evidence" that there was no such affair. That is too much to ask.

"OBVIOUS BIAS"

I find disturbing Elms's casual dismissal of Jung's account of what Minna told him simply because of what he calls Jung's "obvious bias against Freud, plus his own history of repeated affairs with female patients." If Elms wants us to believe that, he needs to show how Jung's bias against Freud, which he undoubtedly had (though the relationship was often very complicated), led to his lying about Freud and how Jung's history of repeated affairs with female patients, if Elms could document these affairs, did the same.

It is clear that Jung disagreed with Freud on important aspects of psychoanalytic theory, and a love/hate relationship with him developed, but I don't see any evidence these disagreements led Jung to lie about Freud—simply make up stories. Nor do I see any evidence of Freud lying about Jung because of the differences he had with him. Neither Jung nor Freud was shy about their bitterness toward each other and how they each felt betrayed by the other. They demeaned each other on a regular basis, privately in letters and sometimes quite openly in published writings, so I don't think either man had any special need to contrive tales in order to attack the other. Each seemed to have enough ammunition for repeated attacks without resorting to fiction.[48]

"ELABORATE SUPPOSITIONS"

I agree with Elms when he says Peter Swales's arguments rely on "elaborate suppositions, confidently asserted," where "suppositions of guilt … [are] no more probable than suppositions of innocence." Elms's point about Swales's use of Freud's *aliquis* example is also well taken. You'll recall that Swales maintains that the young man in the *aliquis* anecdote from Chapter 2 of *The Psychopathology of Everyday Life* is actually a poorly camouflaged version of Sigmund Freud, and that the young man's concern about his Italian girlfriend becoming pregnant (missing her period) is really Freud's own concern about Minna's supposed pregnancy.

Yet the parallel breaks down, Elms argues, in one important respect: the young man expressed a desire to inflict vengeance on his oppressors (those preventing the Jewish people from achieving their full potential), and Freud interpreted this as a wish for descendants. As Elms points out, Freud already had plenty of those—three boys and three girls—already sharpening their knives. I think the parallel breaks down with regard to the Italian girlfriend as well, unless Freud also had one of those.

Swales maintains that it is odd Freud would encounter so well-educated a person as the young man in Freud's *aliquis* story on his holidays, especially one who was familiar with several of Freud's works. Yet in Martin Freud's biography of his father, he indicates that he often socialized with many well-educated, middle-class people while on holiday.[49] Some of the people might have been as well educated as he. In Freud's September 14, 1900, letter to Wilhelm Fliess, where he details the places he visited on his summer holiday that year, he reports running into a Society of Professors meeting at the Hotel du Lac in Riva. Although Freud did not want to get too close to them because he was at the time travelling alone with Minna, he must have attended one of their meetings, because he was able to describe those who attended: "Sigm. Mayer (from Prague), whose assistant I was to have been, Tschermak, Jodl, Felsenreich from Vienna, Dimmer from Graz, Hildebrand from Innsbruck."[50]

SCANT ATTENTION

I am of two minds with regard to Peter Gay's contribution to the debate over the alleged affair between Freud and Minna. On the one hand, I find Gay's biography of Freud brilliant—together with the mass of information that Jones's three-volume work contains, Gay's insights provide a firm foundation for a deep understanding of Freud, his life and work, like no other biography of Freud before, and without the hagiography that is so obvious (and irritating) in Jones's work. Gay's portrayal of the main characters in Freud's life is illuminating, and this includes his portrait of Minna as an indispensable part of Freud's household; a permanent fixture by the mid-1890s; a woman to whom Freud wrote "intimate and affectionate" letters; and to whom he signed his letters "Your Brother Sigmund."[51]

On the other hand, when Gay turns to "the rumor, launched by Carl G. Jung, that Freud had an affair with Minna Bernays" and says it "lacks convincing evidence," he seems on much less solid ground and does not bring the full weight of his considerable intellect to the issue. And he does not appear to give the matter more than passing attention, relegating a discussion of it to a bibliographical essay toward the end of his book and to two brief footnotes in his biography, one in a section titled, "Hysterics, Projects, and Embarrassments," the other, "Jung: The Enemy."[52]

JUNG THE UNRELIABLE REPORTER

While Gay describes Jung as an unreliable reporter, as Jung's "contradictory autobiographical comments suggest," Gay does not specify what those contradictory autobiographical comments are, so I am at a loss either to agree with or potentially contest Gay's observations. If he has evidence that Jung was known to simply make things up out of whole cloth, he needs to indicate what that evidence is.

We know that Jung, from time to time, did make mistakes in remembering the past, and this is especially true with regard to details. I have found several errors of this sort. In his 1925 Zürich lecture he writes: "Through this book on dementia praecox I came to Freud." Jung had sent Freud a copy of the book in December 1906. Jung then goes on: "We met in 1906. The first day I met him it was at one o'clock in the afternoon, and we talked steadily for thirteen hours."[53] Well, he didn't meet Freud in 1906; it was 1907. And if he met Freud at one o'clock and then talked thirteen hours straight, they would have finished their conversation at two A.M., not one A.M. A small point, but nonetheless an error.

Also, Jung mentions in his interview with Eissler that he spent fourteen days with Freud during his first visit to Berggasse and that in New York that they "were in the Palisades" when Freud "couldn't hold his water any longer and pissed all over his pants leg." We know Jung spent only about a week with Freud, though he was probably away from home for about fourteen days or so. It was Binswanger who, like Jung, was greatly impressed with Freud,[54] who stayed an extra week in Vienna. And the incontinence episode did not occur "in the Palisades," which are in New Jersey, but across the Hudson River from them, on the New York side of the Hudson.

These are obvious errors of memory, but are they really lies? Do they indicate that Jung would simply make up whole stories? There is no evidence to suggest that he did.

ABOARD SHIP

Also, while Gay says Freud's refusal to interpret one of his own ("triangle") dreams "aboard ship ... may be true enough," since Jung repeated it "'more than once' and even once directly to Freud (the December 3, 1912, letter, as we saw), and "Freud never denied it," in all other respects, Gay has his doubts. At least Gay is willing to admit that the second part of the story that Jung told Billinsky "may be true enough." The evidence? Jung repeated it "more than once" and once even to Freud. As we have seen, Jung also repeated the story of Minna's confession "more than once," though, apparently, never to Freud. I wonder whether in Gay's thinking the repetition of a story adds believability to it. I think it probably does, and that fact should be weighed when assessing the veracity of Jung's story about a Freud/Minna affair.

But the "triangle" dream episode did not occur "aboard ship," as Gay says, though we know, according to Billinsky's interview, Freud and Jung began interpreting each other's dreams almost immediately upon departure.[55] Interpreting dreams seems to have been a form of recreation for the two men. What we do know is that the episode Jung mentions took place following the embarrassing incontinence incident on Riverside Drive outside of Columbia University *after* the men had arrived in New York, and that Jung's memory of this is confirmed independently by Sándor Ferenczi, who was there with Freud and Jung.

Gay does not take up the incontinence issue, even to mention it in passing. I find that disappointing, because it is integral to the "triangle" dream interpretation episode that follows. The most important part of Jung's interview with Billinsky is what Minna tells him in 1907—her confession. But the other, which confirms the first in Jung's mind, and in mine as well, is the story of Freud's incontinence. As you'll recall, this leads to Jung's offer to help alleviate Freud's urinary problem through analysis, and this in turn results in Jung's interpretation of Freud's "triangle" dream and the latter's refusal to provide information from his personal life which might have helped Jung interpret it. Gay does at least mention the link between Freud's refusal to provide details concerning the dream and Jung's assertion of Freud's infidelity.[56]

RED HERRINGS: FREUD'S "LABORATORY"

I find Gay's point about Jung's reference to Freud's "laboratory" a red herring. Gay does admit that Freud had a consulting room next to his study, and maybe that is what Jung meant, but still the expression "remains a strange one," Gay says. But is it really that strange? We know that Jung had a laboratory where he conducted word association experiments at the Burghölzli, so that is the place where Jung did his work.[57] It seems that he is simply using the same term to describe the place where Freud did his work. It might have been inaccurate to describe it that way, but given Jung's own laboratory it is not a strange use of the word. But obviously Gay wants it to be "strange" because he wants Jung to appear odd and unreliable when it comes to what he said Minna told him about her affair with Freud.

In perusing Hirschmüller's collection of Freud/Minna letters, I have come across an interesting passage in an April 28,1887, letter which Freud writes to Minna. I think this passage will shed light on the "laboratory" issue that seems so important to many who believe Jung's use of the term somehow sheds doubt on the accuracy of what he told Billinsky. The letter in question is one where Freud affectionately addresses Minna as "Minn-ich." He is reporting to her about how things are going at home in Vienna, and at one point he writes: *Ich wiege 78 Kilo und arbeite den ganzen Tag mit voller Lust, meine Nerven sind brav, und seitdem ich mein Hauslabora-torium habe, fühle ich mich auch für die wissenschaftliche Zukunft ruhiger.*[58] In English: "I weigh 78 kilos and work all day with gusto, my nerves are good, and since I've had my laboratory in the house, I feel calmer about my scientific future as well." So even Freud calls the place where he works his "laboratory"!

RED HERRINGS: MINNA'S APPEARANCE

The issue that Gay raises, along with others, about Minna's appearance is one I also find a red herring. Remember, Gay tells us that after the death of Minna's fiancé Ignaz Schönberg in 1886, "Minna Bernays apparently resigned herself to spinsterhood. She grew heavier, more jowly, becom-ing exceedingly plain; she looked older than her sister Martha, though she was in fact four years younger."[59] While Minna may have been to Freud's taste, Gay writes, "it seems highly implausible that Jung, who had an eye for feminine beauty and was himself sexually quite active during these years, beyond the bounds of marriage, would really have found her so."[60] Also, Gay advises us, Dr. Max Schur, who was Freud's physician and attended him during his last illness and who, Gay admits, knew Minna Bernays "only in relatively advanced age, found her quite unattractive." This is according to an interview Gay had with Helen Schur, Max Schur's wife, on June 3, 1986.

Of course, what Jung thought of Minna's appearance—he describes her as "very good looking" in the Billinsky interview and "a pretty person" in Jung's earlier interview with Eissler—or what Dr. Schur thought of her looks as an older woman is interesting but not relevant. The question is, what did Freud think?

There is no evidence that I have seen, either in available letters or fam-ily reminiscences, to suggest that Freud thought Minna unattractive. In Hirschmüller's book in which the extant Freud/Minna letters are collected, he reproduces several photographs of Minna. A few I had not seen before. There is one portrait of Martha and Minna together in 1883, and they look almost identical.[61] Thus, if Minna was an ugly duckling, so was Martha. Another portrait is from circa 1883, of Minna alone. She certainly does not look unattractive.[62] A portrait of Minna from circa 1884 shows her look-ing almost exactly like Martha and as thin as a rail.[63] These photographs

were taken years before she became, in Gay's words, "jowly." A circa 1910
portrait does show her heavier and more matronly, but not unattractive.[64]
Others may view these photographs differently. I leave it to you, the reader,
to judge.

Paul Roazen, in *Freud and his Followers*, reports that an "old neighbor
of the Freuds thought Minna was prettier than Martha."[65] Was it because
Martha looked so "utterly extinguished," as Jung describes her to Eissler?

Of course there are many reasons why Freud might have found Minna
attractive: it could have been her wit, her vivaciousness, her sardonic view
on life, her energy, her robustness. Or it might have been something as simple as her possibly being sexually adventuresome and willing to do things
which Martha might have found disgusting. There is no way to know. Yet
for someone as seemingly unattractive as Minna is supposed to be, Freud
seems to have spent a lot of time with her. We will see later in this study
that Freud was very proud of her and delighted in introducing her to his
friends and even used the word "beautiful" in describing her.[66]

One thing is obvious: Minna had some sort of feminine qualities that
drew men to her. Three men of superior intellect and capability found her
attractive: Ignaz Schönberg (who fell in love with her), Sigmund Freud
(who seemed to thoroughly enjoy her company and who I believe had an
affair with her) and C. G. Jung (who was taken with her "very good looking" appearance and intellectual powers immediately upon first meeting
her). I think it is dangerous as well as misleading to underestimate how
attractive Minna might have been to men.

"VIRTUALLY IMPOSSIBLE TO VISUALIZE THE SCENE"

Gay also raises Elms's point about Jung being a stranger to Minna and
then adds that he was "alien to her in religion and culture and professional
interests," though Gay does admit that perhaps that is just the sort of person
she might have wanted to confide in—someone who was soon to depart.
Still, Gay concludes, "I find it virtually impossible to visualize the scene" in
which Jung and Minna met to discuss the affair.

I have already dealt with the Jung-as-stranger issue when discussing
Elms's ideas. Let me comment briefly on Gay's several additional points.
While Jung was certainly alien to Minna in terms of religion, I disagree that
he was also alien to her in culture and professional interests. With regard to
the latter, Jung seemed to sense immediately that Minna was Freud's confidante: "she not only knew enough about psychoanalysis but also about
everything that Freud was doing."[67] So "professionally," Minna was probably as up to date as anyone close to Freud. And culturally, she could not

have been that different from Jung, in the sense that she was well read, intelligent, and perhaps most importantly, Viennese.

It is interesting that when Jung first came to Vienna, he was a bit overwhelmed with how advanced Viennese society and culture were compared to his own in Switzerland, and he expressed an immediate discomfort with the disparity. Deidre Bair writes in her biography of Jung:

> Vienna was a "reasonably small" city but one so "rich in culture and creativity" that the "intelligentsia produced innovations that became identified throughout the European culture sphere." It was as different from Zürich as the proverbial night from day, and everything about Vienna melded into a barrage of overwhelming sensations [for Jung]. He was a man in his thirties who had no experience with the kinds of conversation one had in the cultural salon or the coffeehouse.[68]

So Minna might have actually been more advanced than Jung culturally, and perhaps that's another reason why he found her attractive. On the other hand, that may also be a reason Minna might not have felt threatened sharing with him some of her most cherished secrets.

MISSING LETTERS

As we have seen, in 1989, a year after his biography of Freud appeared, Gay published an article titled, "Sigmund and Minna? The Biographer as Voyeur," in *The New York Times* book review.[69] You'll recall, the occasion was the opening of the Library of Congress's file of letters that Freud and Minna exchanged over the years. While Gay does not see passionate passages in the letters, he does admit that "the absence of erotic material in these letters could offer no conclusive demonstration one way or the other."

What troubles Gay, and me as well, is that the collection is fragmentary. The gap he points to—of some seventeen years—is between Freud's letter to Minna of April 27, 1893,[70] and her letter to him of July 25, 1910.[71] According to the organizing system used by the Freud Archives, letters 95 to 160 are missing, he claims. And Gay admits that the period 1893 to 1910 "were the very years when an affair between Freud and his sister-in-law would have taken place, if it did."

Hirschmüller, in the introduction to his collection of Freud/Minna letters, contests Gay's explanation. Hirschmüller suggests that only letters after the turn of the century were numbered, and hence the material is "much more completely preserved" than had previously been thought, though he admits "that letters that once existed between Sigmund and Minna have been lost ... that the surviving remaining material is not complete ... and it is certain that many more letters were written beyond those that exist today."[72] How many more, he does not say.

Gay contends, you'll remember, that even if those now missing letters did show up—and he assumes they probably no longer exist—he does not believe they would reveal that an affair between Freud and Minna took place.

The information Gay provides about the history of the Freud/Minna correspondence is illuminating and important, especially where he tells us how Anna Freud turned over a "substantial cache" of documents to the Library of Congress in 1972, but she "could not bear to part with certain letters," namely, those between herself and her father and those between Freud and Minna. Apparently many of these letters eventually reached the Library of Congress, but some did not.

I want to jump ahead a bit to Eissler's essay for a moment, because he also provides information concerning the Freud/Minna letters. We will address Eissler's attempt to refute the veracity of Jung's recollections a little later in this chapter.

Eissler tells us that more "than 70 letters from Freud to Minna Bernays, and 80 of her letters to him, are deposited in the Library of Congress." He also clarifies that what Peter Gay had examined in his 1989 *New York Times* article were only the unrestricted letters, which means there is also a group of restricted ones. Apparently, Anna Freud made Eissler the custodian of this second group of letters, which he turned over to Albrecht Hirschmül-ler for editing and publication. But even in this group there are letters missing. I would estimate that there are more letters missing than are extant.[73]

Why are so many missing? You'll recall, Eissler says that Freud's son Ernst told him that Minna had requested that Freud's letters to her be destroyed. Whether that also meant hers to him, he was not certain. That, he believes, is the main reason for the loss of the letters, and I agree. But Minna's request was not carried out, at least not completely, for some letters remain. You'll also recall that Eissler blames the Freud family for being "negligent" in the care of the letters, keeping some of them, including a few addressed to Minna, in an unlocked closet in Anna Freud's home (the 20 Maresfield Gardens address in London where Freud lived before his death in 1939), so "there were many opportunities for loss."[74] Hirschmüller has his own ideas about how the letters may have been lost.[75]

Hirschmüller's collection of letters was published in 2005, with the restricted letters included. Earlier, Christfried Tögel's book of travel letters, *Sigmund Freud, Unser Herz zeigt nach dem Süden, Reisebriefe 1895–1923*, was published in 2002, also with some restricted letters included. Based on both these collections I believe that Gay's 1989 assessment of the letters needs to be updated and corrected. While Gay says that letters between April, 27, 1893 (Freud's letter to Minna), and July 25, 1910 (Minna's letter to Freud), are missing, the publications by Tögel and Hirschmüller now fill in that gap—somewhat. Having looked carefully through both collections, I think we can now be more precise with regard to what letters are missing. And while some additional ones have been found and published within the gap identified by Gay, there are still other gaps where letters are missing, in addition to the one identified by Gay. I focus only on those letters written after Freud's letter to Minna of April 27, 1893, a period when an affair seems most likely to have happened.

In 1898, there are three letters written jointly to Martha (August 6, 10, and 12).[76] Freud begins the letter; Minna then adds on. There is also one joint postcard sent on August 5 of that year.[77] Freud and Minna were on holiday and were writing Martha about their trip. The first communication that involves only Freud and Minna is a Freud postcard of September 7, 1898.[78] *So five years pass between Freud's letter to Minna of April 27, 1893, and his postcard to her of September 7, 1898.* Not to have communicated for such a long period seems strange, given that Freud was an inveterate letter writer, seemingly writing at least one letter a day to someone, so I assume that there are a number of letters and/or postcards missing from this period. Writing letters was Freud's way of communicating. Even when the telephone came into vogue and he had one installed at Berggasse, he hated it and tried to use it as little as possible.[79]

Freud writes one more postcard to Minna (on September 9, 1898),[80] and then *there are no more letters or postcards for a period of an additional four years,* from September 9, 1898, to August 26, 1902. Again, it would have been unusual that they would not have written to each other at all during such a long period, so I assume once more that additional letters and postcards between the two are missing.

There are a total of five postcards that Freud sends to Minna in 1902 (August 26, 27, 28 [I], 28 [II], and 29).[81] In addition, there are two postcards Freud sends addressed to both Minna and Martha (September 1[I and II]), and one letter addressed to the whole family (September 3).[82] *There is then another gap—this time three years.* The next communication of any kind are postcards dated September 4 through 13, 1905,[83] but again these are primarily joint postcards, from Freud and Minna to others (most to Martha, one to Anna Freud, one to Rosa Freud), not any directly between Freud and Minna. For the next direct communication between Minna and Freud, we have to jump to July 18, 1910, when we find one from Minna to Freud,[84] so there is *a period of eight years* when there is no

written communication between Freud and Minna—Freud's postcard to
Minna of August 29, 1902, and Minna's letter to Freud of July 18, 1910. *This
is an enormous gap.*

There are a number of letters and/or postcards (fifteen, to be exact) written primarily from Minna to Freud for the remaining months of 1910. This
year may give us a good sense of how often they actually wrote to each
other. There is then *another three-year gap,* and twelve letters/postcards
are written from Minna to Freud in 1913. One postcard is sent by Minna
to Freud in 1917, *another four-year gap.* Not another letter or postcard is
sent until May 28, 1922, *a five-year gap,* though there is an envelope with
inscription sent by Freud to Minna on June 18, 1920. There are three more
letters between Minna and Freud in 1922 (May 28, June 10, and June 23),
and then nothing until 1930, Minna's May 8, 1930 letter to Freud—*another
eight-year gap.*[85] This last gap, though large, is of less concern, assuming
that any affair between them would have subsided as they grew older, but
there is no guarantee that that is true.

The Hirschmüller and Tögel volumes both contain the September 7 and
9, 1898, postcards from Minna to Freud,[86] but only Tögel has the several
1902 postcards from Freud to Minna—those of August 26, 27, 28 (I), 28
(II), and 29.[87]

In sum, I count a total of approximately *thirty-seven years when letters
and/or postcards between Freud and Minna are missing*: a five-year gap
between April 27, 1893, and September 7, 1898; a four-year gap between
September 9, 1898, and August 26, 1902; and an eight-year gap between
August 29, 1902, and July 18, 1910. This is the most crucial time period.
Then additional gaps of three years (1910 to 1913), four years (1913 to
1917), and five years (1917 to 1922). And finally an eight-year gap between
their letters of June 23, 1922, and May 8, 1930. And, of course, there are
presumably many additional letters missing during those years for which
we actually do have extant letters and postcards.

If we make a conservative assumption that Freud wrote about 20 letters
(or postcards) to Minna a year, then I estimate there are some 740 letters
(and postcards) missing! That means we only have in hand a small percentage of all the correspondence between the two. To have so many missing means that someone probably consciously destroyed them, whether
for nefarious reasons or not, so it seems Eissler may be correct when he
says that Minna asked that most of the letters be destroyed. Who actually
destroyed the letters is another question. Hirschmüller, on the other hand,
does not believe many letters were destroyed.[88]

We also need to ask why Minna wanted Freud's letters to her destroyed—
and perhaps hers to him as well—as Eissler tells us. The answer could be

as simple as that she did not want her private correspondence open to the public for inspection, and, in any case, there was nothing in the letters to raise any suspicions. Alternatively, she could have wished her correspondence destroyed because she did not want to leave even a hint of how close she and Freud were, and the missing letters might have raised questions. The letters that we do have reveal that they were very close. Of course the other possibility is that Minna or some other person destroyed Freud's letters to her (and her letters to him) for fear they might reveal an affair between the two. Sadly, we will never know the answer to these questions unless miraculously some or all of the missing letters show up one day. I, for one, will not hold my breath.

REPRISE: TWO KEY FOOTNOTES

In 1990, Gay reprised his *New York Times* essay as a chapter in his book *Reading Freud: Explorations and Entertainments*, this time expanding his essay a bit and adding references. I have identified two footnotes he added which I see as being of special interest in our investigation. You'll remember, one informs us that "C. A. Meier, a longtime intimate of Jung and an eminent professor of psychiatry in Zürich, has confirmed the accuracy of Billinsky's recollection: Jung had told Meier precisely the same thing years before. (Personal communication, February 15, 1989)."[89] That information is important because it not only bolsters Billinsky's credibility as messenger (his accuracy) but also shows that Jung told at least two people the same thing, and hence it also bolsters Jung's credibility as a consistent storyteller.

Also important is the fact that C. A. Meier says he was told precisely the same thing "years before." I say that because implicit in much of the criticism of Jung's recollection of what Minna told him has been the idea that Jung was an old man at the time of the Billinsky interview (eighty-two years of age) and perhaps he didn't know what he was talking about, or couldn't accurately remember. After all, it was some fifty years after Minna's supposed confession of 1907. But if Jung told C. A. Meier "years before" then obviously he was younger than eighty-two years of age when his conversation with Meier occurred. How much younger, we do not know.

I have looked into the question of Jung's mental capacities at the age of eighty-two and discovered an interview he gave to Dr. Richard I. Evans, who at the time was in the Department of Psychology at the University of Houston. The interesting thing about this interview is that it was also conducted in 1957, when Jung was eighty-two, and it was filmed and is publicly available online: http://www.youtube.com/watch?v=-kdF-qV6PpE. There is also a printed version of the interview, as I indicated in Chapter 1.

The interview, which was edited, took place over a four-day period, August 5 to 8, 1957, in Zürich. This was approximately three months after Billinsky's interview of May 10, 1957. The edited version lasts one hour and seventeen minutes, but one need not watch the entire interview, for Jung shares his memories of Freud in the first few minutes. Although Jung discusses his differences with Freud, he is also very complimentary of him, calling *The Interpretation of Dreams* a "masterpiece." In this filmed interview of August 1957, Jung appears alert, insightful, knowledgeable, charming, and funny. And his English is remarkably fluent. But readers can judge for themselves.

In the second note, as you'll recall, Gay refers to a diagram contained in the book *Berggasse 19: Sigmund Feud's Home and Offices, Vienna 1938*. Here Gay provides a critical new piece of information. To have an affair you need not only willing partners, but opportunities for those two people to see each other, to be alone together. Remember, the diagram (circa 1938) shows the only entrance to Minna's bedroom being through the room shared by Martha and Freud. As I mentioned, this arrangement had always puzzled me. How could Freud have had an affair with Minna with Martha right there, or at least knowing who was going in and out of her own and her sister's bedroom? Or was there a *ménage à trois*? That seemed unlikely. I then reasoned that Freud and Minna could only become intimate during their several holidays alone together. This would mean that at best their lovemaking occurred only occasionally.

Gay's information that Minna only occupied the bedroom off of Freud's beginning in 1920, while before that it was probably Anna's bedroom, changes the whole equation. Now the *opportunities* for intimate contact between Freud and Minna increase exponentially. I do not know where Minna's bedroom was prior to 1920, but as long as Freud did not have to go through the bedroom which he shared with Martha to get to Minna's, he would have numerous opportunities in the evening to "see" Minna before joining Martha in their own bedroom. And remember, Freud stayed up till all hours of the night, almost never getting to bed before two or three in the morning.[90] So Freud arriving late for bed each evening would have seemed normal to Martha.

"VERY POSSIBLE THAT THEY SLEPT TOGETHER"

Following the appearance of Franz Maciejewski's 2006 discovery of Freud's log entry in the Schweizerhaus registration book, Gay seems to have softened his position on the "Minna" issue a bit, becoming more open to the possibility of an affair between her and Freud. As we have seen, Gay is quoted by Ralph Blumenthal, the author of the December 12, 2006, article in *The New York Times* on the Maciejewski discovery, as saying that the discovery "makes it very possible that they slept together. It doesn't make him or psychoanalysis more or less correct." I suspect that, like me, Gay does not see Maciejewski's discovery as a smoking gun, but something that makes an affair between Freud and Minna much more likely—or, to put it in Gay's words, much more possible.

KURT EISSLER: GOING FOR THE JUGULAR

Although Kurt Eissler's comments on the Freud/Minna affair are maddeningly long and often rambling, I respect what he is trying to do. He goes right for the jugular. He seems to know that in order to demolish the idea of an affair, one of two things must be shown: that Billinsky was a bad messenger and got it wrong in terms of what Jung told him; or that Jung lied, misunderstood, fantasized, couldn't remember, or did something to throw doubt on the veracity of what he told Billinsky. Some of Eissler's arguments have merit; the majority do not. Several I find paper thin. He first tackles Billinsky.

Oddly enough, if you'll remember, Eissler first excoriates and then exonerates Jung's passionate messenger. He has serious doubts about Billinsky's credibility: so much of what Jung says seems "contradictory, improbable and even bizarre" that Eissler feels Billinsky's interview must have been an "invention." Yet Eissler counters his own argument by admitting that C. A. Meier, Jung's confidant whom Eissler had talked to, had assured Eissler that Jung had given him the exact same account, and that assurance is good enough for Eissler. Billinsky's credibility remains intact.

"DISRESPECTFUL, INDEED VULGAR"

Now it is Jung's turn. First Eissler attacks Jung's description of what Freud said when he first met his new Swiss visitors. As you'll recall, Freud had gone to the hotel where the Jungs were staying and brought some flowers for Frau Jung. He was very considerate and, according to Jung, remarked, "'I am sorry that I can give you no real hospitality; I have nothing at home but an elderly wife.'" Jung then added, "When my wife heard him say that, she looked perturbed and embarrassed."[91]

Such a description lacks authenticity, Eissler argues. It was not only tactless but also out of character: "No one else ever heard Freud make such a disrespectful, indeed vulgar, remark about his wife," Eissler says.[92]

I agree that Freud's remark may have been tactless, or at the very least awkward, but how does Eissler know that no one else ever heard Freud make such a remark? I find that quite an amazing statement, as if every remark Freud ever made about his wife is known and has been documented. And why is it really out of character? We will be examining in detail Freud's relationship with his wife in Chapter 6, and I think you will see that it would not be out of the ordinary for Freud to say and think such a thing about Martha, given the tension in their marriage and the anger each seems to have felt toward the other. Unlike most of Freud's colleagues' wives, Martha was never a substantial person in her own right. She defined herself, and was defined by Freud, in terms of how she could help him, a situation which Freud initially found attractive—the fragile, passive Victorian woman slavishly protecting and supporting her god-like husband—but eventually a role of which Freud apparently grew weary.

"NO REAL HOSPITALITY"

Also, Eissler finds puzzling Freud's statement that he could provide the Jungs "no real hospitality." But I do not find that puzzling at all. Remember, Freud had warned Jung that coming when he had planned was not the best time for Freud. He would be busy with patients during the day, and would only have Sunday, March 3, completely free. Whereas if Jung and his party had visited during Easter Freud would have had both Sunday and Monday off. Also, I don't think that Freud thought Martha was up to entertaining the Jungs in a way they might find interesting. Probably this would be because she was too busy with other things, including a large family with many children, but possibly also because of who she was: she was not Minna, not *au courant* with regard to everything Freud was thinking and doing. In the Eissler interview, you'll recall, Jung sensed that Freud felt embarrassed by Martha: "That Freud spoke like that about his wife, yeah! ... He was *embarrassed!*" The emphasis is Jung's. Compared to Jung's wife, who became an analyst in her own right,[93] or A. A. Brill's wife, who was a physician,[94] Martha lacked professional credentials. In addition, I think Freud was being polite and suitably humble; he could never show Jung and company the hospitality they really deserved. It was his way of showing how highly he regarded them while at the same time setting realistic expectations given the time constraints he faced.

"THIS EVENT CANNOT HAVE TAKEN PLACE"

Eissler next takes up Jung's statement about visiting Freud's "laboratory," when Minna pulled him aside and asked to talk to him. Remember Eissler's argument: "This event cannot have taken place the way Jung reported. The mere physical circumstances of Freud's apartment and professional suite suffice to throw doubt on Jung's account."[95] Because Freud was busy during the day, Eissler maintains that the secret meeting between Jung and Minna must have taken place after eight P.M., following Freud's work day.

Yet how Eissler can come to this conclusion is baffling to me, but more on this in a moment. Eissler's argument continues: "Minna Bernays was certainly not in the habit of sauntering through her brother-in-law's office, nor could she have been alone with Jung for any length of time to speak of, either there or in the living quarters." If one were to accept Jung's account, Eissler concludes, one would have to assume "that Minna Bernays had secretly waited on the landing of the second floor for a moment when Freud left his office, then rushed downstairs in order to catch Jung alone."[96]

I don't know where to begin with these arguments. They might be the strangest that Eissler offers. Why does Eissler assume that because Freud was busy during the day with patients, Jung could only have met with Minna after 8 P.M., when presumably Freud was done with his work? Wouldn't it have been safer and smarter for Jung and Minna to meet *while* Freud was seeing his patients? After all, Freud's office suite consisted of three rooms, not one: a waiting room, a consulting room (where Freud saw patients and had his famous couch), and a study, where Freud did his work and which Jung apparently thought of as Freud's "laboratory." While Freud was seeing patients in one room, Jung and Minna had access to the other two. The waiting room, admittedly, might not have been an appropriate place to meet because of a possible lack of privacy—patients coming in and out. But what about the study, which was Freud's "laboratory," where he did his work? And it is specifically in Freud's "laboratory" where Jung tells Billinsky that Minna first asked to talk to him on the subject of the affair. It is not clear that the study (or "laboratory") is where Jung and Minna eventually talked. But it is clear that is where she first approached him.

In 1892 Freud had rented another flat at Berggasse, on the ground floor directly below his existing flat. The new flat contained his office suite—patients' waiting room, consulting room, and study ("laboratory"). However, Ernest Jones informs us, this arrangement only lasted until 1907,[97] when the Freud family flat was expanded in size—on the same floor. Yet if we look at the diagram of Freud's flat in 1938, the same three-room arrangement is replicated: separate patients' waiting room, consulting room, and study ("laboratory").[98] Thus in either configuration (pre- or post-1907), Freud's study would have been available to Jung and Minna while Freud was seeing patients in his consulting room. And there were numerous hours each day that week when that was possible.

Also, it is not clear to me why Eissler assumes that Minna was "not in the habit of sauntering through her brother-in-law's office." Eissler seems to be assuming that Minna would never have been allowed in Freud's "laboratory" and hence could never have met Jung there. But why would Eissler assume that? The opposite seems more plausible—that Minna had free rein, or at least something approaching that when it came to Freud's suite of offices. After all, she served as Freud's secretary, as well as his close confidante, so I can imagine she was able to "saunter" wherever she pleased and whenever she might want, within certain reasonable limits.

And Eissler's contention that Minna could never have been "alone with Jung for any length of time to speak of, either there"—in the "laboratory"—"or in the living quarters," is not borne out by Minna's role in Freud's life at the time and all the free time Jung had available that week, precisely because Freud was busy and could not show Jung the "hospitality" he would have liked. I think when Freud talked about "hospitality," he was really referring to how much personal time he would be able to spend with Jung.

It would have been awkward and dangerous for Minna and Jung to meet in the Freud "living quarters," for that's where Martha held sway, but Jung doesn't say that. He says Freud's laboratory. Perhaps Jung was waiting there to see Freud between patients and Minna ran into him. Or perhaps Minna and Jung were waiting there together to see Freud between patients and that is when they talked. I don't know. But they certainly had the opportunity to talk—perhaps more than once.

FREUD THE MIND-READER

Eissler raises the issue of the disparity in age between Jung and Minna and asks the same question Elms and Gay had about why Minna would have sought the younger man's advice—a matter we have already covered in some detail. Eissler also raises a question about Freud's mind-reading talents. He asks: Wouldn't Freud have noticed "Jung's bewilderment when his revered authority, the man he idealized, was suddenly thrown off his pedestal, nor Minna's embarrassment and discomfiture for having betrayed, with her confession, a man to whom she owned loyalty and gratitude"?[99]

With regard to Freud noticing Jung's bewilderment, we need to remember that Freud had a specific goal in mind with regard to Jung's visit that week, and that was to enlist him in the cause of psychoanalysis. I think everything else was secondary. How Freud could have sensed Jung's bewilderment (actually, Jung said he felt *agony* at Minna's confession, not bewilderment) and somehow relate that to Jung knowing that Freud was having an affair with Minna is not clear to me, since Freud knew nothing of

Minna's confession to Jung. Brilliant is one thing; superhuman is another. Freud realized from his year-long correspondence with Jung that while the latter had expressed strong support for psychoanalysis and was showing that support in terms of his proselytizing activities, Jung also had reservations about some of Freud's ideas, especially regarding the latter's strong emphasis on sexuality. Jung also had doubts about the efficacy of psychoanalytic therapy.[100] Any sort of feelings of bewilderment Freud might have picked up from Jung—and I am not saying that he did—he could easily have attributed to Jung's ambivalent feelings about psychoanalysis at the time.

With regard to Minna feeling embarrassed and discomforted by what she told Jung, I believe that Freud was focused mainly on Jung during that week and what this young psychiatrist might mean for the future of psychoanalysis, rather than how Minna might have been feeling at the time. Also, why does Eissler assume Minna felt only embarrassed and discomforted? Although she tells Jung she felt guilty, maybe her strongest feeling was relief for having finally shared her secret with someone, like Jung, who seemed understanding and empathetic. Perhaps Minna felt more anger than embarrassment at the time, but that is a subject for a later chapter. So too is a discussion of Eissler's other point about Minna—to wit: knowing how important Jung's visit was to Freud as the latter tried to expand the acceptance of psychoanalysis, how could she have done what she did? You'll remember, Eissler asks, "Is it likely that at such a critical moment she would have stabbed Freud treacherously in the back and endangered one of his most promising and cherished expectations?"[101]

Maybe she didn't think she was "[stabbing] Freud treacherously in the back," but was focused rather on her own pent-up emotions. But I believe Eissler is asking an important question—Minna's motives for sharing her secret with Jung—which we will explore later in this study.

JUNG THE HYPOCRITE, PART II?

Also, Eissler argues, how can we reconcile Jung's feelings of "agony" when he learned about the affair from Minna with the effusive praise Jung heaped on Freud in letters he sent him after leaving Vienna? This is essentially the point that Elms makes earlier and which we have already discussed at length.[102] Let me just add this. Most professional people react the way Jung did—in other words, make the distinction between how they might personally feel about someone, even someone they may dislike, and the best way to act toward that person so as not to offend. Freud did this himself. For example, although he disliked Eugen Bleuler, then head of the prestigious Burghölzli and Jung's boss, he kept his personal feelings to himself. He knew that Bleuler was an important figure in European psychiatry, and he sought to stay on the man's good side. He limited his negative feelings to letters he sent to confidants. Gay writes in his biography that Freud "continued to cultivate Bleuler and at the same time to denounce him in letters to his intimates. 'Bleuler,' Freud confided to Ferenczi, 'is insufferable.'"[103]

PROOF THAT MINNA NEVER CONFIDED IN JUNG

In Freud and Jung's voyage to America in 1909, Eissler sees a contradiction which he feels "proves that Minna Bernays never confided in [Jung]."[104] You'll remember that Eissler maintains that since Freud and Jung were together for so long (seven weeks) and from the beginning began to analyze each other's dreams, would it be credible that Freud could have "analyzed Jung's dreams over such a long period of time without noticing that Jung harbored an agonizing secret about his [Freud's] private life?" Could Freud have been so "consistently deceived by Jung throughout their voyage?" Eissler asks.[105] After all, Eissler points out, Freud was a keen interpreter of dreams.[106]

I think the answer to this is yes, it is credible that Freud did not know. Or if he did, which I think unlikely, perhaps he did want to say anything. We don't know all the dreams the two men discussed during their trip—or perhaps even many of them. It seems that prior to leaving on the journey, Freud was most concerned with what he felt were Jung's death wishes toward him. As we have seen, this came to a head in Bremen, when Jung's persistent focus on corpses discovered in bogs near that city led Freud to faint, at least according to Jung's account.[107] If Freud was looking for anything in Jung's dreams during their seven weeks together, I suspect it would have been confirmation that Jung wanted to overthrow him, or at least contest his authority, and not something about what Jung might have heard from Minna about an infidelity, since Freud had no idea that Minna might have confided in Jung.

Also, Freud's skills at dream interpretation might not have been as powerful as Eissler seems to think. In his *Memories, Dreams, Reflections*, Jung recalls that during their visit to America Freud struggled to interpret Jung's dreams. "We were together every day, and analyzed each other's dreams," Jung remembers. "At the time I had a number of important ones, but Freud could make nothing of them. I did not regard that as any reflection upon him, for it sometimes happens to the best analyst that he is unable to unlock the riddle of a dream."[108]

SOUNDS STRANGE FROM FREUD'S MOUTH

We know that Freud and Jung discussed Freud's "triangle" dream—so called by Jung—while in America. Yet the story of Freud invoking his authority when asked for personal details regarding the dream "sounds strange from his mouth," Eissler contends, though he does admit that Jung did refer to this incident at least three times: once in a December 3, 1912, letter to Freud; a second time in his 1925 Seminar in Zürich; and a third time in Jung's 1961 autobiography, *Memories, Dreams, Reflections*. Details regarding these references have already been provided. These instances would seem to argue against the very point Eissler is attempting to prove— to wit, that the words about authority sound strange coming from Freud's mouth since, at least in one instance (the December 3, 1912, letter), Freud made no attempt to refute what Jung said, even though he could easily have done so.

A PSYCHOLOGICALLY DYSFUNCTIONAL JUNG

You'll recall, Eissler also argues that in order to understand the Billinsky interview and what Eissler feels are the rather bizarre things Jung says therein, one needs to consider both the psychotic episode Jung went through following his break with Freud as well as Jung's serious childhood psychopathology. Eissler goes into excruciating detail with regard to both of these in order to prove that Jung's obvious conflicts with a father figure "were bound to appear in one way or another in his relationship to Freud."[109]

"Freud the atheist, the materialist, the positivist and whatnot had to be inferior to the God-fearing pastor's son [i.e., Jung]," Eissler argues. Remember Eissler's conclusion? If Jung could not emulate Freud as an exemplary father and husband, he could at least destroy the "image of Freud by claiming that Freud had maintained an extramarital affair from early on and, worse yet, an incestuous one."[110]

Not being a trained clinician—my field is the history and philosophy of science—I am not certain how to deal with accusations based on Eissler's analysis of Jung's personality. Undoubtedly, Jung did experience something approaching a psychotic episode (or nervous breakdown) following his break with Freud,[111] and his childhood development could at best be described as strange, if not actually pathological. Yet I find it difficult to believe that Jung's psychological makeup might have led to his inventing a story about Freud and Minna as a means of blemishing Freud's reputation. As mentioned previously, Jung didn't really need to make up anything about Freud in order to criticize him quite severely. Jung was always candid and open about their disagreements. And if Jung really wanted to hurt Freud, he could easily have published the story of Minna's confession himself or urged others to do so, and it doesn't appear that Jung ever tried to do either of those things.

In fact, Jung seems to have done just the opposite: making certain that what he said about Freud and Minna never got out. It is unclear what he told Billinsky about publically releasing the contents of their interview. Billinsky did sit on the interview for twelve years and only published it after Jung's death, so I think it's safe to assume Jung had not urged him to publish it. I suspect Billinsky would have said something to that effect if Jung had. On the other hand, we do know how concerned Jung was that his 1953 interview with Eissler would ever see the light of day. Eissler, you'll remember, had to reassure Jung that their conversations would not be published, that Eissler would rather kill himself than have that happen. My suspicion is that Jung probably asked for similar assurances from others he had confided in, including Billinsky.

Although it is not unreasonable to assume that Jung might have taken pleasure in seeing Freud embarrassed, I suspect he never thought anything would publically get out about the affair. And if Billinsky hadn't panicked, nothing would have. The vague rumors that had existed before about Freud and Minna would only have continued to be just that: vague and unsubstantiated. Every other person with whom Jung appears to have shared his story of Minna's confession—C. A. Meier and Toni Wolff at a minimum, but perhaps several others[112]—never published a word about it, so if Jung did want to get back at Freud and embarrass him terribly, he certainly chose the wrong people to confide in, with the obvious exception of Billinsky.

The truth is that Jung was always discreet in dealing with the subject in public, even when talking about the "triangle" dream episode, which he knew was directly connected to the affair. Remember both in his 1925 Zürich lecture and later in his autobiography (*Memories, Dreams, Reflections*) he mentions Freud's "authority" problem, his unwillingness to provide personal details about his "triangle" dream, yet Jung consciously refrains from mentioning the subject of Freud's dream.

"THIS MUCH IS UNQUESTIONABLE"

After spending over seventy printed pages arguing why one should not believe Jung's recollections of what Minna told him—and most of these arguments, as I have indicated, I do not find compelling—Eissler asserts that he has proved "that Minna Bernays never confided the secret of an intimate relationship with her brother-in-law to Jung. This much is unquestionable."[113] How Eissler can come to this conclusion is something I do not fully understand.

In the end, as we have noted, like Gay before him, Eissler does hedge his bets—somewhat. "If further research," he concludes, "should unearth proof of an intimate relationship between Freud and Minna Bernays, this would necessitate a revision of the ideas that have been held about Freud."[114] Eissler seems to be writing here almost in the third person, not wanting to associate himself too directly with such "revisionist" conclusions.

"MUCH ADO ABOUT NOTHING"

As we have seen, Zvi Lothane published two papers in 2007 dealing with the Freud/Minna affair.[115] He argues that while it is "probable" that Freud had an affair with Minna, it has certainly not been "proven"; there is no smoking gun. Many of the points Lothane makes in these papers we have already covered: Why would Minna confide in the callow Jung? Why didn't Jung confront Freud with his knowledge of the affair? Wasn't Minna too unattractive for Freud to have wanted to sleep with her? Did Billinsky get the whole story wrong? And so on.

Lothane does raise several new questions regarding Maciejewski's Schweizerhaus logbook discovery and its possible significance. Perhaps, Lothane speculates, Freud could have misrepresented Minna as his wife as part of a stratagem to get around Swiss cohabitation laws which forbade couples who were not married from renting a double room—"an innkeeper 'providing accommodations' to an unmarried couple could be prosecuted as a pimp," and Lothane cites Cantonal law to that effect. Also, had Freud and Minna registered as Dr. Freud and Fräulein Bernays, "they might … have attracted unwelcome attention from and gossip by other hotel guests."[116] In addition, Lothane reminds us that at the time the inn seems to have been busy, so perhaps single rooms were not available. Maybe Freud and Minna were forced to share a room. Also, he speculates, wouldn't a double room have been cheaper?

In the end, Lothane asks, what is the net effect of Maciejewski's Schweizerhaus discovery? "Much ado about nothing," is his reply. And if there was an affair? So be it. Freud need not be lily white. Lothane prefers the "the grand mistakes of a genius to the trite truisms of a mediocrity."[117]

Certainly Freud's contribution to the history of psychiatry is not dependent on his being morally "perfect," so I agree with Lothane on his last point. I have more concern with some of his other thoughts. With regard to the Schweizerhaus stay, Lothane does not indicate whether the sort of

Cantonal law he cites was one of those all too common in many countries—
a prohibition on the books but one that was rarely enforced. In other words,
a law about which hotel proprietors habitually looked the other way. After
all, how do you enforce such a law? Did Switzerland have inspectors checking every registration book in every hotel? The bottom line: Was this prohibition really something Freud had to worry about? That is the important
question, and I suspect the answer is no.

Also, if the hotel clerk had any concerns, couldn't Freud have told him
that the woman he was going to share a room with was his sister-in-law (in
other words, a relative) and that cohabitation prohibitions need not apply
under those "familial" circumstances? If that was the only room available
at the hotel, as Lothane suggests, wouldn't Freud's argument for sharing a
room with his sister-in-law have carried even more weight?

Lothane's theory that Freud signing in as Dr. Freud and Fräulein Minna
Bernays "might have attracted unwelcome attention from and gossip by
other hotel guests" doesn't make much sense. How often do guests scruti-
nize a hotel's registration book? And Freud could have signed the log book
Dr. Sigmund Freud and Sister-in-Law and presumably have forestalled any
suspicion.

Although a single room would likely have been cheaper than renting
two rooms, and in that regard Lothane is correct, what evidence do we
have that Freud was attempting to economize on this trip? If he were, he
would not have stayed at the Schweizerhaus in the first place, because it
was one of the most expensive hotels in Maloja.[118] It is interesting, as I
pointed out before, that in an August 13, 1898, postcard to Martha, Freud
described the Schweizerhaus as "a modest Swiss house,"[119] yet Maciejewski
describes it as rather venerable and grand. Based on my understanding of
Freud's tendencies with regard to holiday arrangements, as evidenced in
his letters as well as remarks by his son Martin on the same subject, if Freud
had to economize during the summer holidays he would settle the family
into the nearby Bellevue resort in the Alpine foothills overlooking Vienna,
or a similarly nearby resort, and keep his wandering beyond that location
to a minimum. How far Freud travelled depended on how successful his
practice had been in any given year.[120]

A question that Lothane does not address with regard to Freud and
Minna's stay at the Schweizerhaus is the matter of reservations. Had Freud
made a reservation for their stay there? After all, it was the holiday season—in fact, a weekend during the holiday season—and most of the hotels
in tourist locations were filled or at least near capacity. If they had made
a reservation, it would be interesting to know in whose name the reservation was made—Dr. and Frau Freud? And if advance reservations were

required, why hadn't Freud booked two rooms before the trip so he and Minna would not have had to share a room?

Freud was an experienced traveler, and Martin Freud tells us that his father was the one who usually researched where and for how long he and those traveling with him would stay. "The selection of a family summer holiday resort was always father's duty," Martin Freud writes, "and he took this very seriously indeed: it became, in fact, a fine art in later years when he acted as a kind of pioneer, ranging about the mountains until he found what he believed would be popular with the family."[121] Booking two rooms in advance would have been easy enough to do and would have been sensible, especially if he did not want to share a room with Minna. But perhaps he *did* want to share a room with her.

With regard to accommodations, there is some evidence that Freud did "wing it" on many trips. For example, Maciejewski says Freud's stay at the Schweizerhaus was the result of Freud and Minna altering their original plan to travel as far as Chiavenna, Italy, the implication being that their stay at the Schweizerhaus was a bit impromptu—or at least their stay for more than one night might have been a spur-of-the-moment decision.[122] Also, in a letter to Martha dated August 10, 1898, Freud writes about trying to get rooms for himself and Minna on the run in Le Prese: "We arrive, no vacancies. Two attic-cubbyholes, where the telegraph operators otherwise sleep … and then comes the *maître d'hôtel* to inform us that some reserved rooms had not been occupied and we could relocate, executive rooms with a view of the lake, one with a balcony."[123] Maybe flexibility of movement is what Freud wanted and the need for reservations would have tied him down. Or, most likely, he did both: at some places where it was hard to get a room he made reservations; at others he simply took his chances. It is obvious from Freud's August 10, 1898, letter that reservations could be made, since he mentions that several reserved rooms were not filled and that is how he and Minna finally got accommodations that evening.

I am also concerned about another point Lothane makes on a different but related subject: the issue of the reason for the eventual break between Jung and Freud. You'll recall, Lothane questions Jung's assertion that his knowledge of the Minna affair and the fact that Freud's placed "authority" over "truth" when it came to providing intimate details associated with the "triangle" dream in America was one of the main reasons for his break with Freud. Lothane asserts that Jung "did not break with Freud over Minna" but for several other, unrelated reasons, which Lothane then details.[124]

I think if Jung felt the Freud/Minna affair and Freud's reluctance to share personal information about a dream that may have been related to that subject was one of the main reasons for his break with Freud, then we need to take him at his word, though I agree with Lothane that there were many other, primarily ideological disagreements that contributed to the two men going their separate ways. It seems Jung was already primed to become independent from Freud even as the two talked cooperation and collaboration at Berggasse as early as 1907. Their views of the world were simply too different, and though they saw how each man's research could buttress the work of the other—and hence they understood the value of working together—their different theories about the etiology of neurotic symptoms and the psychological makeup of people appear to have prevented any long-term collaboration.

INTIMACY BUT NO LOVE AFFAIR

In his 2007 article, "Evidence for a Sexual Relationship between Sigmund Feud and Minna Bernays?"[125] Albrecht Hirschmüller, editor of the largest collection of Freud/Minna correspondence,[126] argues that he cannot find any indication of an affair between Freud and Minna. The letters show, he says, "a relationship of mental and personal intimacy, as between siblings, but they do not in any way hint at a love affair, nor do any of the other available historical sources."[127]

The latter part of Hirschmüller's statement I find rather sweeping, given Billinsky's published interview with Jung in which Minna's confession is revealed. Does not Hirschmüller consider the interview an historical source? Perhaps not, because he also indicates doubt about the authenticity of Jung's testimony, though he doesn't say why.

In addition, Hirschmüller doesn't mention that the vast majority of letters from Minna to Freud, as well his to her, are missing. I will grant, as previously indicated, that the extant letters do not provide evidence of an affair, yet the cache of letters between 1893 and 1910, when an affair would have been most likely, is, as we've seen, fragmentary at best.

At least Hirschmüller admits that the letters offer a picture of "mental and personal intimacy." As I have maintained, that intimacy is displayed in a sense of happiness—it's hard to describe it any other way—that the two feel when they are alone together.

In the August 10, 1898, joint letter from Freud and Minna to Martha, we also get a sense of the affection that Freud feels toward Minna. He writes admiringly of her stamina: "Yesterday's tour was tiring," he informs Martha, "at least for me; Minna cannot be worn out by any exertion." Just the sort of travelling companion Freud desired! And Minna, in her own addendum to the same letter, tells Martha of how her husband admires how she looks. "Today we relaxed completely," she writes, "I'm finally parading around in a flannel dress and full jewelry, and Sigi of course finds me ever the height of elegance, whether the others do as well I don't know."[128] Whether Minna is saying this sarcastically or not, I do not know, but there is still an obvious playfulness and warmth in her tone. The "ever" in her description of how Sigmund finds her is interesting in that it may suggest he often thought of her in those terms—not Minna the spinster, but Minna the "elegant" one. So much for the ugly duckling sister-in-law.

We have already discussed whether having in hand the full set of letters (or at least a large majority of them) might constitute the "smoking gun" everyone is anxiously seeking. It is difficult to know. Freud was too smart to expose his love for Minna to possibly probing eyes in letters he might write. He certainly could not afford to be careless. But what about Minna? After all, she was the one who actually revealed the affair, if we are to believe Jung, and I am one who is so inclined. She was obviously less cautious than Freud. Perhaps that's why she asked that all his letters to her, and perhaps her letters to him, be destroyed.

"JUST ONE NEW DETAIL"

Like Lothane, Hirschmüller in the same article casts a doubtful eye on Maciejewski's discovery at the Schweizerhaus inn. "What was the situation Freud and Minna found in Maloja?" he asks. "Was there an option to book separate rooms? Did they share rooms and register as man and wife in the other hotels they stayed in during their journey?"[129] This last question is a good one and almost immediately, on the same page, Hirschmüller answers it himself, to wit: "Unfortunately, the other hotels either no longer exist or their old log books have disappeared."[130]

As we have noted, Hirschmüller talked to the present owner of the Schweizerhaus, one Jürg Wintsch. From him, you'll remember, Hirschmüller learned that at the time Freud and Minna were at the inn it "was … filled with guests,"[131] apparently at the height of the tourist season. This would suggest that reservations would have been needed. On the other hand, it might also suggest, if they had no reservations, why they might have been forced to accept a single room.

Hirschmüller argues that Freud and Minna did not stay for three nights, as Maciejewski had claimed. Not even for three days. Hirschmüller presents evidence from the registration book to support his contention that the next guest entered room No. 11, which Freud and Minna occupied, on Monday, August 15, so Freud and Minna probably arrived late in the afternoon on Saturday, August 13, and must have departed on Monday morning, August 15, so it was hardly an "unusually long" stay, as Maciejewski had maintained. The image of Freud and Minna lingering in a love nest for three days is not supported by the facts, according to Hirschmüller.[132]

But might not the image of Freud and Minna "lingering in a love nest" for two days, or for that weekend, be supported by the facts? Maciejewski points out that Freud was "indefatigably peripatetic,"[133] and Minna wrote that Freud loved "to sleep every night in a different bed."[134] So can we assume even spending two days at one location might be considered unusual, or at least somewhat out of the ordinary? I don't know the answer to that question, but I think it needs to be explored. In Chapter 6 on Freud and Minna, we will see that sometimes Freud and Minna spent more than several days at one location when on holiday together.

With regard to Hirschmüller's information that sometimes Freud and Minna wrote of having rented two rooms, the evidence from this seems inconclusive. One reference, according to Hirschmüller, can be found in a letter from Freud and Minna to Martha, dated August 9–10, 1898, sent from Le Prese.[135] I found the letter and it is actually dated August 10. Hirschmüller says the other is a letter Freud sent Martha from Lago Maggiore, dated September 1900.[136] There is no September 1900 letter sent by Freud from Lago Maggiore (either in Hirschmüller's collection or Tögel's) There is one dated September 5, 1900, sent from Riva (which is 252 kilometers from Lake Maggiore), and in this letter Freud talks about "two rooms."[137] This must be the second letter Hirschmüller is referring to. But, of course, Hirschmüller muses, "those passages [in the letters] are no solid proof how they signed in or in which rooms or beds they in fact slept."

I would add that they also do not tell us if they were telling the truth when they talked about having stayed in two rooms, as opposed to one. It would not have been out of the question to have dissembled with regard to the number of rooms they occupied. Rather, it would have been a convenient way to keep their affair a secret. And why the need to even say they are staying in two rooms? Shouldn't that be obvious? I find that suspicious. Perhaps it was to show Martha that they were not sharing the same room in order to make her feel more comfortable about their being alone together for so long on these various holidays.

In any case, Hirschmüller concludes, Maciejewski's discovery is "just one new detail," not irrefutable proof, as Maciejewski maintains.[138] As noted before, Maciejewski's discovery is certainly no "smoking gun," but it surely adds plausibility to what Jung remembers Minna telling him. That Freud signed into the Schweizerhaus as husband and wife in order to hide an affair with Minna *is the most plausible explanation* for what he did, but certainly not the only one. Maciejewski's discovery may be "just one new detail," but it is an important new detail.

CALLOUS

Finally, Hirschmüller wonders out loud whether Freud would have been so callous as to expose his sister-in-law to an unwanted pregnancy? I say the completely rational Freud would not have done so, but an emotional Freud, the Freud in love...? That may have been a completely different matter. This is basically Barry Silverstein's point.

"MORE ATTRACTED TO MEN"

As we have seen, there are many scholars, journalists, biographers, and other commentators who have also questioned whether a Freud/Minna affair ever occurred—doubters of an affair, as previously indicated, far out-number believers in this regard, including Linda Donn, in her 1988 *Freud and Jung: Years of Friendship, Years of Loss*;[139] Lisa Appignanesi and John Forrester in their 1992 work *Freud's Women*;[140] Frank McLynn in his 1996 biography of Jung;[141] Louis Breger in his 2000 *Freud: Darkness in the Midst of Vision*;[142] and Paul Roazen in his 2001 *The Historiography of Psychoanalysis*,[143] 1993 *Meeting Freud's Family*,[144] and 1976 *Freud and his Followers*.[145]

All the arguments they present have been dealt with before except two offered by Louis Breger. You'll recall, he maintains that such a liaison would have been out of character for both Freud and Minna, "who were extremely sexually and emotionally constricted."

Freud and Minna as "sexually and emotionally constricted" people? It is certainly the accepted story, but is it true? We will examine Freud's relationships with both Minna and Martha in Chapters 5 and 6, in an attempt to answer that question. In any case, Breger argues, an affair is unlikely because "Freud ... was more strongly attracted to men."[146]

I agree that Freud was strongly attracted to men. He seems to have developed "crushes" on certain male friends from time to time, extremely intelligent, highly cultured handsome men, particularly Ernst von Fleischl-Marxow and Wilhelm Fliess. And also Jung. But unlike Breger, I don't think he was more strongly attracted to them than to women. A full assessment of Freud's powerful sexual self will be discussed in detail in Chapter 5.

A SMOKING GUN

Many scholars who have done research in this area seem anxious to find a "smoking gun" that would "prove" that there was an affair, but to those I would say, you need not look further. The "smoking gun" has been in front of you all along. It's Jung's recollections of what Minna told him about Freud's intentions toward her, as well as Jung's description of the related "triangle" dream episode in America. Kurt Eissler, whose orthodox Freudian credentials cannot be questioned, seemed to sense this, and that is probably why a goodly portion of his book *Three Instances of Injustice* is an attempt to discredit Jung: attack his character, question his mental stability, doubt his memory, and look skeptically at the veracity of what he told Billinsky. With Jung discredited, the foundation for the idea of an affair disappears. With Jung's credibility intact, an affair appears likely.

I have not found Eissler's arguments, and those of other skeptics of an affair, compelling enough to discredit Jung, and until someone can come up with stronger arguments or new information emerges, I stand steadfastly in the camp of those who believe Jung told the truth.

In the next two chapters, one on Freud and Minna, the other on Freud and Martha, we will see how the dynamics of those two relationships make the idea of an affair between Freud and Minna all the more plausible. I think the key to understanding an affair is to understand Freud's relationship with these two women, the two most important females in his life, after his mother.

PART III

FREUD'S WOMEN

CHAPTER 5

FREUD AND MINNA

The most important fact to remember regarding the relationship between Freud and Minna was that it began with deep affection—Freud's letters to Minna while he was still engaged to Martha have been described by both Freudians and non-Freudians as intimate, passionate, almost amorous[1]— and that the relationship remained that way until his death.

"SHE GHOSTS THROUGH THE HOUSE"

Of all the Freud family, it was said that Minna was the most upset at her brother-in-law's passing. Paul Roazen writes in *Freud and His Followers*: "Of the three women closest to Freud at the time of his death—Anna, Martha, and Minna—[Ernest] Jones believed it was the last, already in poor health, who took the blow the hardest."[2]

After Freud's death on September 23, 1939, Minna became depressed and began to withdraw. On October 2 of that year, Freud's daughter-in-law Lucie Freud writes: "Aunt Minna's health is a new cause of worry. I fear she is again very close to one of her terrible illnesses. She has become—not to fault her—unbearable lately. It seems that her serious illness has disturbed her emotional life (always her Achilles' heel). She is entirely unaffected by all that has happened and is happening. Her body is well maintained, her memory for all poems fantastic, her spirited and mischievous remarks are still audible. But her personality is frozen masklike, she ghosts through the house like the Statue, uncloudedly cheerful and thoroughly unbearable. Her death would be a blessing for herself and for all, including Mama."[3]

It is interesting that Lucie Freud talks about Minna's emotional life as her Achilles' heel. We will have an opportunity to examine Minna's emotional state vis-à-vis Freud later in this chapter.

THROUGH A GLASS DARKLY

What do we actually know about Minna? Her personality? Her desires? Her predilections? In some ways we can only see her through a glass darkly, a person who played a central role in Freud's personal and intellectual life during the most creative and important years of his career but whose character is defined primarily by assorted family memories and a group of letters often dealing primarily with practical matters, at least those letters which have survived. As historians, we are slaves to a paucity of archival information.

Of certain things we can be reasonably confident. She was literary and intellectual. She was said, even as a child, to have had a book in one hand, a duster in the other as she went through her daily chores.[4] She was also confrontational, acerbic, outspoken, strong, spontaneous, and, as we have seen, full of energy, a characteristic Freud appreciated.[5]

"A BEAUTIFUL SISTER-IN-LAW"

Freud found his sister-in-law physically attractive, unlike the opinion of many contemporary Freud scholars who had never met Minna and could only judge her from old photographs, several taken when she was a middle-aged or elderly woman.[6] In a May 7, 1886, letter to Minna, Freud says he considers himself lucky to have "such a beautiful sister-in-law ... my wish would be that you would come and visit me in my palace." He then adds significantly, "if you were not my sister-in-law, you could even stay with me."[7]

Eager to have Minna visit Vienna, Freud writes in an April 14, 1886, letter that he would be happy to "show you off proudly to everyone as my sister-in-law," [8] and in a July 5, 1886, letter he admits, "I hope you know how dear you are to me."[9]

LOOK ALIKES

We have already seen, in the August 10, 1898, letter Minna and Freud write to Martha, while they were again alone on holiday, Minna's testimony as to how much Freud liked the way she dressed: "Today we relaxed completely. I'm finally parading around in a flannel dress and full jewelry, and Sigi of course finds me ever the height of elegance."[10] It does not seem he was alone in his appreciation of Minna's attractive looks. Remember the old neighbor of the Freuds from Vienna who thought Minna was prettier than Martha?[11] Even Freud thought Martha and Minna looked alike, so if Minna was an ugly duckling, so was Martha, which we know she was not. "I appreciate all the more how people mix you up," Freud writes Martha on August 6, 1898; "She [Minna] is very similar to you."[12]

FIRST BONDS

Like Freud, Minna could sometimes become wild and passionate.[13] And unlike Martha, she confronted her dominating mother directly, a fact Ernest Jones sees as creating a bond between her and her brother-in-law. "Minna ... was quite frank in her criticisms of her mother," Jones writes, "it was the first bond between her and Freud."[14]

Freud also found Minna an amusing and stimulating companion, in conversations, walks, travels, and during evening games of Tarock. He thought of her as one of the two "mothers" in his family—and, by extension, I would say, two "wives."[15] He addressed her affectionately in letters as "Dear little sister" (*Liebes Schwesterchen*)[16] or "Dear Minning" (*Liebes Minning*)[17] or "Dear Minnie" (*Liebes Minnie*).[18] She addressed Freud as "My beloved Sigi" (*Mein geliebter Sigi!*) or "Beloved Old Man!" (*Geliebter Alter!*).[19] The latter affectionate appellation was also used by Martha when she addressed her husband.[20] And Freud would sign his letters to Minna, "Your Brother Sigmund" (*Dein Bruder Sigmund*)[21] or "With fond regards, Your brother Sigmund."[22]

Minna was closer to Freud than Martha was, on most matters. She sometimes answered Freud's phone by saying, "Frau Professor Freud,"[23] and often played host to Freud's guests and students—especially to those who were important enough that Freud felt they should receive some attention but whom he really did not want to or have time to see. In this sense, Minna played the important role of lightning rod for Freud, allowing him to devote himself to things he felt were more important.[24]

TOO CLOSE

Their relationship was perceived as too close by some, becoming a source of envy in the family, especially to young Anna Freud, who wanted her father for herself. In *Martha Freud: A Biography* Katja Behling points

out the prominent role that Minna assumed in the Freud family and its
impact on Anna Freud: "As the last-born child, [Anna] felt she was given
a rather raw deal, with neither Martha nor Minna taking full responsibility for her needs. Further, from Anna's point of view the new situation"—
Minna becoming a fixture in the Freud family—"meant that along with
her mother there was another woman who was the possible object of her
father's affections, in other words another person with whom she was com-
peting for her father's love."[25] Elizabeth Young-Bruehl, in her biography of
Anna Freud, makes a similar point, when she describes Anna as being "so
jealous of her Tante Minna."[26]

INDISPENSABLE

By the mid-1890s we see Minna as an indispensable part of Freud's life
and an unwavering supporter of his ideas. As Jung told Billinsky, she knew
"about everything that Freud was doing,"[27] and according to Deidre Bair,
Minna was the only one who dared mention those things at mealtime.
Bair indicates she was also the only member of the family who could tease
Freud and make jokes or puns about his work, and she was able to do so
with impunity.[28] Bair does not provide a source for this information, and
I have not come across it elsewhere, though it is consistent with Minna's
strong personality and acknowledged assertiveness.

THE ONLY TWO

As we have seen, Freud felt that in the early years Minna and his medical colleague from Berlin, Wilhelm Fliess, were the only two people who
believed in him.[29] And in a May 21, 1894, letter to Fliess, we'll recall, Freud
mentions Minna as "my closest confidante."[30] Eventually, when Freud's
friendship with Fliess came to an end, soon after the turn of the century,
she was the *only* one who unqualifiedly supported Freud, and she did so
for several years, until the emergence of Swiss support (Bleuler and Jung)
in the mid to late 1900s.

Freud did have his Wednesday Psychological Society, which began
meeting in his apartment in 1902 and served as a sounding board for
many of his ideas, though its composition was heterogeneous (those
from other professions as well as physicians) and its character was not
intimate—at least not in the sense of Freud's close relationships with
Fliess and Minna.[31]

While Minna understood most of Freud's ideas, she did not understand
all of them—as Peter Gay has pointed out, not every subtlety—and Freud

did not tell her everything he was doing.[32] But I think we can conclude that if she was not the ultimate intellectual interlocutor for Freud, she was certainly the ultimate kindred spirit.[33]

Following the death of her brilliant fiancé, the Sanskrit scholar Ignaz Schönberg, Minna found an emotional as well as a physical home with Freud, for she saw Freud and Ignaz as branches of the same tree, descendants of the same irreverent soul, and that was why she was able to fit so seamlessly into Freud's intellectual and emotional worlds.

CIRCLES

Minna entered into Freud's life in April 1882, at the same time he met Martha and apparently at the same place: Freud's parents' apartment. The Bernays women were visiting Freud's sisters.[34] Minna was then only seventeen and was already engaged to Schönberg,[35] who was a friend of Freud's—perhaps a source of jealousy for Martha, who was four years older than Minna.[36]

Although basically a solitary person, most comfortable alone in his study with his books (even as a student, as we will see, he sought refuge from the outside world and his family in a small room in his parents' apartment), Freud also had a strong need for human contact, a desire to talk to people, bounce ideas around. As a result, throughout his life he tended to form groups or circles of friends. They could be small in size, consisting of Freud and one other person (Freud and Breuer, Freud and Fliess, Freud and Jung), or they could be larger, such as the Wednesday Psychological Society, whose membership eventually grew to more than a dozen. Later, he formed the so-called Committee, composed of fervent Freud supporters seeking to safeguard psychoanalytic orthodoxy from heretical desertions. Comprised of Karl Abraham, Max Eitingon, Sàndor Ferenczi, Ernest Jones, Otto Rank, and Hanns Sachs, and led by Freud, it was also called the Seven Rings, so named for the rings containing semiprecious stones of Greco-Roman origin which Freud gave to each of its members.[37]

The earliest Freudian circle, and perhaps the most important from his point of view, consisted of Freud, Martha, Minna, and Schönberg. And Freud consciously called it that—a circle. Concerned about the health of Schönberg and his advancing tuberculosis, Freud writes Minna on Sunday, October 12, 1884: "We want to hope that after this stay [in Italy, to help cure Schönberg's tuberculosis], or perhaps after a second one, [Schönberg] will remain a high-spirited member of our circle."[38] On February 7, 1886, soon after Schönberg's death, Freud writes Minna from Paris, attempting to persuade her to come live with him and Martha in Vienna, to ensure that their little group would stay together. He implores: "live for awhile quietly with the two of us who are closest to you now ... what a long life is still ahead of us and what remarkable things worthy of experiencing might still be the lot of our small circle."[39]

In a sense, Freud thought of Minna not only as an individual but also as part of this intimate, cherished group. Although Freud was engaged to Martha at the time and deeply in love with her, he seems to have thought of his future life as one that included Minna. When a couple is married, they are usually the center of things, and their friends are satellites circling about them. Not so with Freud. It was always the four of them that mattered. The quartet. And when Schönberg tragically died, the circle did not die with him. It just became smaller, three people instead of four, and Freud assumed Schönberg's role vis-à-vis Minna.

CRISSCROSS

"They looked forward to being a happy quartet together," Ernest Jones has written. "Freud once remarked that two of them were thoroughly good people, Martha and Schönberg, and two were wild passionate people, not so good, Minna and himself; two who were adaptable and two who wanted their own way."[40] Freud commented: "That is why we get on better in a crisscross arrangement; why two similar people like Minna and myself don't suit each other specially; why the two good-natured ones don't attract each other."[41]

What sort of woman would Freud like? Not a "robust woman who in case of need can single-handed throw her husband and servants out of doors." That was never his ideal, however much there is to be said for the value of strong, healthy women. "What I have always found attractive is someone delicate whom I could take care of," Freud avers. In other words, someone like Martha.[42]

MUTUAL ATTRACTION

Of course, at the time, Freud did not have a choice. When he met Martha, Minna was already engaged. Over time he appears to have had second thoughts regarding the "opposites attract" dictum. In any case, right from the beginning he seemed attracted to Minna. Remember what he wrote her: "If you were not my sister-in-law you could live here with me."[43] Both Ernest Jones ("he found [Minna] a stimulating and amusing companion") and Peter Gay ("he had written Minna intimate and affectionate letters") readily admit that Freud was strongly drawn to her.[44] So strong an attachment developed that, as we have seen, he actively recruited Minna to come stay with Martha and him in Vienna soon after the death of Minna's fiancé.[45]

Minna was also attracted to Freud—right from the beginning. Jones tells the story of Freud and Martha in their courting days strolling down the Prater together, with Mama Bernays as chaperone. Freud asks Martha many questions about herself. So many, in fact, that when she gets home she tells Minna about it and asks: "What do you make of it?" Minna's reply is significant: "It is very kind of Herr Doctor to take so much interest in *us*," she proclaims. The emphasis is Minna's.[46] With the passing years, Minna's opinion apparently did not change. We have already seen Elfi Freud accuse Minna of making "a play" for Freud."[47]

AN ABIDING INTEREST

There are many reasons why Minna and her brother-in-law grew close. One was Minna's unqualified support for Freud. Another was that Minna had an abiding interest in what Freud was doing in terms of his research and recognized its importance. Early on, Freud had shared information about his work with Martha: "Martha can tell you about my other work anytime," he writes Minna on October 29, 1884.[48] In a footnote Hirsch-müller indicates that Freud had reported to Martha about his research into cocaine and ecgonine and about a paper on electricity.[49] But that early sharing of information between husband and wife did not last, perhaps because of Martha's growing interest in home and children and the rise to prominence of Minna as Freud's devoted assistant. Freud found it easier to talk to Minna not only about his work but, as we shall see, about many other things as well.

The subjects Freud and Minna discussed were various. With regard to Freud's research on the anesthetic qualities of cocaine, for example, he writes Minna in the same letter (October 29, 1884): "The cocaine affair has certainly brought in a great deal of honor, but the lion's share has gone to others."[50] The principal "other" in this case is Dr. Karl Koller, Freud's friend and colleague, to whom Freud had first suggested the application of cocaine as an anesthetic in ophthalmologic surgery.[51] It is obvious from this letter that Freud had previously discussed his work on cocaine with Minna.

In an April 27, 1893, letter to Minna, Freud reveals his new focus on dreams. Having been banished from his bedroom, as Peter Gay puts it, while Martha was recovering from the birth of their daughter Sophie,[52] Freud's tone is self-deprecating: "I am now using my sleep in the library to write down my dreams, which will in ten years amount to a nice piece of work and a good chunk of toilette-money."[53] This is the first mention of Freud's work on the *Interpretation of Dreams* project. Gay notes, "Not even his letters to his intimate Wilhelm Fliess have anything as early as this on the study that would eventuate in his classic 'Interpretation of Dreams' not ten but six years later."[54]

Zvi Lothane has commented on the depth of the intellectual relationship that developed between Minna and Freud, which he calls a "rare friendship," and points out her "intellectual status as Freud's muse and confidante in matters professional." He adds: "In [Freud's] letters to Minna ... [he] writes to her about his book on aphasia; discusses his treatment of patient Anna von Lieben; and has Minna check the proofs of his translation of Bernheim's book on hypnosis."[55] Peter Gay paints a similar picture of close intellectual cooperation. He writes that Minna "had been [Freud's] confidante in psychoanalytic maters far more than his wife. ... In short, Freud confided in Minna Bernays—about many things, much of the time," though he did not "initiate her into all his intimate medical concerns."[56]

With regard to Freud's book *On Aphasia* mentioned above, Freud shares with Minna his growing anger with Josef Breuer, his erstwhile friend and collaborator, one in a long line of relationships with men which began with great promise but ended in bitterness and acrimony. In a July 13, 1891, letter to Minna he writes of his "deep disappointment" at Breuer's initial reaction to the book. "Breuer's reception of it was such a strange one," a frustrated and bewildered Freud laments; "he hardly thanked me for it, was very embarrassed, made only derogatory comments on it, couldn't recollect any of its good points, and in the end tried to soften the blow by saying that it was very well written. I believe his thoughts were miles away."[57]

PERSONAL CONFIDANTE

Freud also often confided in Minna with regard to personal matters, hoping to enlist her help, especially regarding his desire to see his then-fiancée Martha, who at the time was ensconced in Wandsbek, Germany, where Frau Bernays had moved back, along with her two daughters. Here we see Freud using Minna as a secret ally, an indication of how intimate their relationship had become. He hoped to thwart the plans of his future brother-in-law, Eli Bernays, who was scheduled to go to Wandsbek, which would, in Freud's estimation, delay his seeing Martha even longer. Freud writes to Minna on August 22, 1882 (the first letter to her that has survived): "Why am I turning to you and what do I want from you, little sister? I must turn to you, because you are in every respect the closest [to me] … Don't worry; he [Minna's fiancé Schönberg] will not be angry if he hears that I have written you … what is it that I want? That you tell me whether there might be a chance of thwarting the plan [of Eli going to Wandsbek] … If you can no longer prevent Eli's trip, I ask at least for assurance that Martha not stay away past the middle of September … Answer me dutifully … and be less afraid of me in general; we will, after all, be dependent on each other … while Martha and Schönberg are absent, and we should make a tolerable relationship out of it, after all? Right? … I must be flattering you, ultimately, that I have such confidence in your influence."[58]

Jones tells us that Freud eventually travelled to Wandsbek and met secretly with Martha "in the marketplace in Hamburg." In order to make certain that Martha's relatives were unaware of his presence (he stayed in a nearby hotel), and especially Martha's brother, Eli Bernays, Freud concocted various ruses to ensure that Eli would not catch on to what he was up to.[59]

Freud also sought Minna's help in getting Schönberg to see reason and put his health above his desire to advance his career. Freud confides to Minna in an October 12, 1884, letter: "I don't trust myself with this task, but you will be able to manage it if you really urge him. I want to support you in your effort [to get him to take care of himself]. He is going to balk because it's linked with giving up his current chances, which he considers his only chances [for a career]. The [Sanskrit] lexicon will not wait for him. But that's none of our business; he must get healthy first. … The question presents itself—when should I notify his people? Should we ask him and do so only if he agrees? I think, rather, that we should broach the subject without asking him. I want to leave the decision up to you."[60]

Also, as Gay points out in his biography, Freud and Minna felt close enough to each other to exchange letters in secret. We have already seen him write in a letter dated April 28, 1887: "Dear Minning, my effort to appear as an affectionate son-in-law, in addition to my lack of time, has led to the cessation of our private correspondence." Gay points out that Freud wanted to resume it, especially since he sensed that she was in a bad mood for which he does not "want to be even partly responsible." Again he inquired about the possibility of her visiting Vienna, which both he and Martha desired. Freud is quite honest about their "selfish" goal: "We firmly intend to keep you with us until you establish your own household or after you, following our previous discussions, begin studying at the university at Thirty." And so, he urged, "dear child, don't be grumpy. Come to us and let us consider together, how we can move Mama [Frau Bernays] here." Gay comments, "These were not matters the two could discuss openly, since

Frau Bernays, exacting and pious, would feel uncomfortable in the secular Freud household."[61]

TRAVELS ALONE TOGETHER

The more than several holiday trips Freud and Minna took alone together indicate just how comfortable they felt with one another. A few of these trips were for a day or two, or perhaps a long weekend. Others lasted as long as a month. While Freud only made sparing use of the many holidays in the calendar of Catholic Vienna, he did take long summer vacations, usually lasting a full three months, from the end of June until the end of September. The first part he spent with his family, in an Austrian Alpine resort, such as Aussee, or, if funds were scarce, in nearby resorts such as Bellevue in the Alpine foothills overlooking Vienna. Following time with his family, he then would go on excursions without them, often to Italy, usually with one other traveler, sometimes his brother Alexander, sometimes Ferenczi, sometimes Minna.[62] There is one instance I have found where Freud went off on an excursion with a stranger.[63] While Freud liked to travel, he obviously did not like to travel alone.

1897

According to Ernest Jones's biography of Freud, the first trip that Freud and Minna took alone was in the middle of July 1897. He met Minna in Salzburg, and together they made a short walking tour to Untersberg and Heilbrunn. Freud then accompanied Minna to where her mother was staying in nearby Bad Reichenhall (which is actually in Germany, near the Bavarian Alps). On this trip he then returned to Vienna—Minna presumably remaining with her mother in Reichenhall—in order to make arrangements for his father's gravestone.

Near the end of July he joined the family, who were staying at Aussee, and then left at the beginning of September for what Jones describes as an "astonishing tour," lasting a little over two weeks, accompanied by his brother Alexander and a Dr. Gattl, who was both Freud's student and his patient. Minna did not accompany him. Cities visited included Venice, Pisa, Leghorn, Siena, San Gimignano, Poggibonsi, Chiusi, Orvieto, Bolsena, Spoleto, Assisi, Perugia, Arezzo, and Florence.[64] Freud was always on the run and could cover large geographical areas in a matter of days—by train, coach, boat, and even walking. Staying more than one night at any given place along his route was the exception rather than the rule.

Jones does not indicate how many days Freud and Minna were together in Salzburg and environs in 1897, or whether the couple stayed the night (or nights). It might have been a one-day visit. On the other hand, since Untersberg is some twenty-five kilometers from Salzburg, and it is another ten kilometers from there to Reichenhall, I expect it was more than just a day's journey by foot, but I could be wrong. Freud was an energetic hiker, and, unlike Martha, Minna could keep up with him—most of the time.

1898

The same trip, though perhaps a day or two longer, was repeated the next year, 1898. In the middle of June, Jones informs us, Freud made a weekend trip to Salzburg, where he met Minna and took her to Bad Reichenhall once again, to see her mother.[65] Since it was a weekend trip, we can assume that they stayed overnight—someplace. Where, we don't know.

But Freud and Minna were not done travelling together that summer. Later, in early August, he met her in Munich and they embarked on a rather extensive excursion. They travelled to Kufstein and Innsbruck, then Landeck, Trafoi, up the Stelvio Pass, and over to Bormio in Italy. Then they took the train to Tirano, made a long tramp up the valley to a little village called Le Prese on the shores of Lake Poschiavo. Then up the Bernina Pass to Pontresina in the Engadine, where they walked on a glacier for five hours. From there to Maloja (where they stayed at the Schweizerhaus Inn) and back, and then they returned to Aussee to join the rest of the family.[66]

In addition to the information provided by Jones, for this second trip in the summer of 1898 we have a letter to Martha, jointly written by Freud and Minna, that describes their experiences. This is the August 10, 1898, letter they send from Le Prese.

Freud's section (he always began these joint letters) is pretty much matter-of-fact in terms of the places visited. He grouches about a "vile" pub from which he removed himself "in anger," yet he also admits to Martha that "we have seen such great beauty." But in the second half of the letter, Minna's part, she is absolutely gushing: "I must tell you something," Minna writes to Martha

> but you won't believe it. Your husband was eating at the *table d'hôte*, he liked it a great deal, and we will do the same in the evening. It is entirely as if he were a new man, has befriended the spa doctor, speaks to everyone and takes even more pleasure in nobility and comfort than do I. You can roughly imagine how nice it is here, for Sigi to have freely decided to spend a day, until now we have been

traveling frantically fast because we wanted to stay in Pontresina for two days, but it was too magical here, elegance and comfort in one, and the surroundings are a true fairytale. Heavenly weather as well, sunny and cool. ... The last three night camps, Finstermünz, Prad, and Bormio, would have been nothing for you, dear heart, everything is overcrowded and one must be dead-grateful to be admitted at all, so we are indulging ourselves all the more here. Hasn't Mama said repeatedly, Minna will definitely collapse along the way? I can assure her, however, that it is not so and I have not felt this way in years and am handling it all fine. ... The most splendid day was perhaps Monday ... it is beautiful beyond any description and then here, the most beautiful we've seen. ... The Stelvio Pass starts already on the way to Trafoi, an hours-long serpentine ascent, we naturally got off a lot, and Sigi picked the most heavenly flowers, which I saved. At 4 we were at the peak (2800 m.), the snow still lies in great mounds and the glacier is within one's reach, at the same time the pass is so sublime that I went in my torn yellow shoes.[67]

I can almost imagine Minna trying to catch her breath as she writes this description, so obvious was her excitement.

1900

In August of 1900 Freud and Minna begin another long holiday together, as one part of a six-week excursion Freud took that year while the family was ensconced at Bellevue. I have already described this trip in Chapter 2.[68] This is the holiday that Freud wrote Fliess about on September 14, 1900, soon after returning to Vienna. Because it is an important trip, let me briefly summarize.

The holiday starts with Freud and Martha traveling to Trafoi in the South Tyrol, then Sulden, Merano, and Mendola. In Mendola they meet Dr. Lustgarten, and other Viennese acquaintances. Martha goes home, Freud continues with Lustgarten to Venice, where Freud meets his sister Rosa and his brother-in-law Heinrich. The group then travels to Berghof on Lake Ossiach, where Freud runs into his sister Anna Bernays. A day later Freud's brother Alexander arrives.

On August 26 Minna arrives as well. She and Freud take off alone—to Trentino, to visit the "dreamlike" Castello Toblino, then to Lavarone and Lake Garda, where they stay for five days at Riva. Five days! That's a long stay! They then sail from Pallanza to Stresa and spend the night, and the next day Freud drops Minna off in Merano for her cure. Freud then returns to Vienna via Milan and Genoa, arriving September 10, having spent approximately two weeks with Minna. This is the trip that is the focus of Swales's analysis.

As you'll recall, Freud's letter is interesting because of the tone of joy it exhibits after Minna arrives to join him. After outlining for Fliess the various places visited on his excursion, Freud continues: "Finally—we have now reached August 26—came the relief. I mean Minna, with whom I drove through the Puster Valley to Trentino, making several short stops along the way." As they travelled further south, he tells Fliess, he begins "to feel really comfortable." They visit "the extraordinarily beautiful Castel Toblino" and traverse "a spectacular mountain road." On a high plateau they find "the most magnificent forest of conifers and undreamed of solitude." They stay at Riva for five days, where they are "divinely accommodated and fed, luxuriating without regrets, and untroubled." He drops Minna off at Merano and finally arrives back in Vienna "feeling outrageously merry and well."[69]

Note the "undreamed of solitude" Freud and Minna experience together, the "luxuriating without regrets, and untroubled." The tone of his letter to Fliess is very different from the one Freud sends Martha on August 10, 1898, about the same holiday. When compared to Minna's portion of that same letter, Freud's was very businesslike and analytical. It's as if Freud could feel free to reveal the true happiness he was experiencing travelling with Minna when writing to Fliess, whereas with Martha, for obvious reasons, Freud needed to tamp down his enthusiasm.

Some of this enthusiasm, however, does come out in a letter he sends Martha from Lake Garda on September 5, 1900, during the same trip. This letter also indicates the awkwardness Freud felt travelling alone with Minna, or at least the feeling of awkwardness he wants to communicate to Martha. "Let me tell you quickly of the beautiful day on Lake Garda," he writes her. "It was the right thing [to do], coming here. It is paradisiacally beautiful, I promise you Lago Maggiore for next year."

The sense here is that since he is seeing so much beauty at Lake Garda he feels he has to make it up to Martha by showing her as much beauty next year and taking her to Lago Maggiore: "I promise you Lake Maggiore for next year."

Freud continues:

It is not hot, i.e. the sun doesn't hurt but feels good, in fact, there is a delicious noon breeze, the evening chill is more abundant than in Grinzing. A lot of dust on the country road but with that comes the full certainty of the weather. After spending the first night in a noisy and airless hotel in the center of the small town, the next morning we found the most divine *logis* in the *dependence* of another hotel 20 minutes outside Riva, two rooms, the front one with a view of the lake, electric lighting on demand, a search-light from the lake to the bed, a garden—or rather, park—around, across from that of Lovrana, and in a [hotel] located nearby, meals at the "Tabel des Todes" [it is unclear what this refers to] more substantial and good, lighter and more appetizing, than I have ever encountered.

Notice that Freud makes a point of mentioning "two rooms … one with a view of the lake." Does that mean that sometimes (or even often), given the helter-skelter fashion in which he often travelled (*lit-à-lit*) that he and Minna had to share one room? Just as in Maloja, where we have documentary evidence that they did? It is not clear.

More of the letter: "That Minna is thereby thriving is clear," Freud writes. "Picture postcards will follow. It was too beautiful will have to wait for a verbal description … The company in the hotel consists of the nicest people, among them many university professors and councilors"—as we have seen, he mentions several prominent ones.[70] "As a non-professor and afflicted with the wrong woman," he adds, "I am keeping my distance as much as possible."[71]

The *wrong woman*? He obviously means Minna. Based on Tögel's notes to this letter, it appears he knew most of these professors from Vienna, and one can assume that they might also have met Martha at some time. He obviously wanted to avoid having to explain to these "nicest people" who Minna was. Thus it seems that even Freud felt it was unusual for a married man to be travelling with his unmarried sister-in-law. But he's smart. He keeps his "distance."

1902

In 1902, at the end of August, Freud travels to Naples for his holiday/ excursion and hopes to go to Sicily as well, this time accompanied by his brother Alexander. The only mention of Minna that summer is that Freud and his brother meet her in Venice on their way back from their holiday, and the three then travel back to Vienna together. During Freud's holiday with Alexander that summer he writes five postcards to Minna along the way. One from Rosenheim on August 26, another from Bozen on August 27, a third from Trento on August 28, another from Venedig (Venice), also on August 28, and a fifth from Bologna on August 29.[72] In themselves these postcards do not contain material of any significance. I mention them to point out how prolific a letter-writer Freud was—and more particularly, how often he wrote to Minna.

1903

In the summer of 1903 Freud's travelling companion is Minna, and the holiday is for two weeks. The first is spent in Munich and Nuremberg; the second, Minna having become ill, at Merano, a favorite resort of the Freud family women.[73] I have not been able to find any further details regarding this trip.

1905

In the summer of 1905, Freud and Minna embark upon an extensive excursion, one which lasts over three weeks. On September 3, they leave the family at Alt-Aussee and spend the night at the Hotel Europa in Innsbruck. The next day they go to Bozen and Rovereto. On the fifth they explore Verona and push on to Milan. From there they sail up Lake Como and stay at the Villa Serbelloni in Bellagio. They rest there during the day, and then on to Lugano that evening. The following day they double back to Bellagio and reach Pallanza on Lake Maggiore.

Jones tell us this last excursion involved four journeys: two by train and two by boat. During their trip they had a view of two "magic islands," the Isola Madre and the Isola Bella. In a postcard to Martha from Isola dei Pescatori, Freud mentions that Minna, though not in the best of health, stood the tiring journey pretty well.[74]

On September 10 they go to Stresa. They spend two days there in the Hotel Alpino. Off again, they go to Bergamo, and once more to Milan. Then to Genoa for an eight-day stay at the Hotel Continental—an unusually long stay in one place for Freud—and then back to Vienna, where Freud begins work again on September 26.[75]

Martha was kept abreast of the trip by an almost daily flow of postcards. Usually Minna would add a few words. One postcard is from Innsbruck, dated September 4; another the same day from Bozen (also one to Anna Freud from Bozen on September 4); one from Verona on September 5. On September 7 Freud writes his sister Rosa from Bellagio; again on September 7 Freud writes to Martha from Bellagio. On September 8, yet another one to Martha from Bellagio, and on September 9 one from Isola dei Pescatori. Two on September 10: one from Pallanza, the other from Baveno (written by Minna only). One on September 11 from Stresa (the Hotel Alpino), and another from Mailand (Milan) on September 12. Two from Genoa (Genua) on September 13, one a picture postcard. On September 17 Freud writes a letter to his brother Alexander from Rapallo. Finally one to Martha from Genoa again, this time on September 19. All of these are contained in Tögel.[76] Almost all the postcards are also reproduced in Hirschmüller.[77]

Again, I point this out as an indication of just how often Freud wrote. Hanns Sachs asked members of the Freud family how their father was able to write so many letters. Sachs was referring to letters written at Berggasse concerning psychoanalysis and related subjects. They told him they didn't know how he did it, either: "He goes to his study and after an hour he brings us ten letters to be mailed."[78] This makes it all the more incredible that for some years (thirty-seven to be exact) we have no letters or postcards at all from Freud and Minna to each other.

1907

In 1906 the Freud family enjoyed their holiday in Lavarone so much that in 1907 they returned.[79] On September 12, 1907, Freud leaves for Bozen, Minna joining the train at the junction of Franzensfeste. They are alone again. The rest of the family had gone to Thalhof, Payerbach-Reichenau, to await Freud's return. From Bozen Freud writes to say he had not yet made any plans. "He always preferred traveling as freely as possible," Ernest Jones points out.[80]

He and Minna leave for Rome but only get as far as Florence. On September 16, he shows Minna Florence and Fiesole, and then she goes on to Merano for a recuperative stay, spending the night first in Verona. Freud goes on to Orvieto, and the following day he reaches Rome. He is traveling alone, hoping to get some writing done in Rome.[81] There is the usual stream of postcards and letters back to Martha and family during this trip as well.[82] He stays in Rome until at least September 25.[83]

While in Rome Freud visits the Jewish catacombs and sees candlesticks which, he says, "I believe are called Menorah." Jones notes that Freud's remark indicates how unfamiliar he was with synagogues[84]—I would add, with Jewish tradition in general. Martha would have known immediately what these strange-looking candlesticks were.

1908

After spending two weeks in London during the first part of September 1908 and then going to see Jung in Zürich, where they enjoyed each other's company, Freud felt he needed a few days of pure rest in the sun.[85] Who does he seek to do that with? Minna, of course. On the evening of

September 21 he takes the overnight train for Milan, where he changes for Besenzano. He arrives there at noon and meets up with her. They spend a few days on Lago di Garda. Salò, Jones tells us, on the west side of the lake, was the spot chosen. That was Tuesday morning. On Friday they go by motorboat across the lake to San Vigilio. On the way home they spend a half day at Bozen, and they reach Vienna on Tuesday morning, September 29. The two spend a little over a week together.

As usual, Freud sends several letters/postcards (five to be exact) to Martha and the children from Salò during the excursion. One, dated September 25, was a long letter to Martha, to which Minna added an addendum. In this letter Freud speaks of his comfort in just doing nothing for a few days. He writes: "after the superabundance of this summer's experiences I am in need of a few days' comfort without any activity. For this Salò and the hotel are just right. It is very comfortable without oppressing one with elegance. … Yesterday and today we [he and Minna] confined ourselves to taking walks, which makes one feel very well for no particular reason."[86]

May I suggest one? He and Minna are alone.

1913

The next indication that I can find of Freud and Minna travelling together is 1913. That year was a particularly difficult one for Freud. It included his final break with Jung, which occurred in September at the Munich psychoanalytic congress.[87] In an effort to rejuvenate his spirits, Freud and Minna travel to Rome, she joining his train at Bologna. In Rome they spent "seventeen delicious days," as he described them, from September 10 to 27. Minna was somewhat under the weather, and her ability to sightsee was limited, so Freud was able to get a great deal of work done.[88]

The reference to "seventeen delicious days" is interesting. What might have made these days feel "delicious" to Freud? To finally be away from the immense tension of the Munich congress and the problems with Jung must have been a relief. And Freud loved Rome. Perhaps of equal importance is the fact that he was alone with Minna, his favorite travelling companion, once again.

In a September 15, 1913, letter to Freud, Ferenczi hints at the comforting presence of Minna on this particular trip. Ferenczi writes, "I hope that you will recover completely in Rome and in the company of your travel companion [Minna], to whom I send kind regards." Freud responded on September 22 from Rome: "Cordial greetings from our great travel enterprise. All is going well." And on the picture side of the postcard Minna adds: "Kind regards, Minna Bernays."[89]

Rome seems to have been the perfect medicine to alleviate Freud's dark mood. In a letter to Karl Abraham dated September 21, 1913, Freud writes from Rome's Eden Hotel: "I have quickly recovered my spirits and zest for work in the incomparably beautiful Rome. ... My sister-in-law, who warmly returns your and your wife's greetings, sees to it that the actual task of exploring Rome is kept within moderate bounds. She herself has taken all the inevitable exertions unexpectedly well in her stride and it is pleasant to watch her feeling more at home and growing more enthusiastic about Rome every day."[90] It was pleasant to Freud, one can surmise, because Rome was Freud's favorite city.

It is interesting that two of Freud's key disciples at the time—Sàndor Ferenczi and Karl Abraham—know Minna well enough to send her greetings. Even Abraham's wife sends her greetings. An indication of how intimately connected Minna was to Freud at the time.

1919, 1921, 1923

Skip now to 1919. More and more in these years, Freud and Minna are ill and use their holiday time for convalescence. I have found documentation for three holidays, if you can call them that, where Freud and Minna spend more than several weeks alone together. On July 15, 1919, Freud leaves Vienna with Minna for Bad Gastein (Villa Wassing), both in need of a "cure" there. Martha, recuperating in a sanatorium near Salzburg from a case of pneumonia, is unable to join them.[91] On July 15, 1921, Freud and Minna again go to Bad Gastein, and once again to the Villa Wassing. Martha is spending the holiday at Aussee in the Salzkammergut.[92] And on June 30, 1923, Freud and Minna leave for "their usual 'cure' at Bad Gastein," as Jones puts it. Does that mean such a "cure" had become a regular summer institution by that time? I don't know, but it seems so. On August 1, 1923, Freud and Minna join the rest of the family at the Hotel du Lac in Lavarone.[93]

Given this record of travel together, I was surprised to read in Peter Gay's biography of Freud the following description:

When summer came, after months of his fatiguing analytic hours, the Freuds—the parents, the six children, and Aunt Minna—would settle in a quiet hotel in the mountains at Bad Gastein in Austria, or at Berchtesgaden in Bavaria, there to spend weeks together hunting mushrooms, gathering strawberries, going fishing, and taking hardy walks. For the last part of the summer—August and early September—Freud would go off with his brother Alexander, or a favored colleague like Sándor Ferenczi, to explore Italy.[94]

No mention at all of Minna as Freud's companion for the second half of the summer? The record of joint Freud/Minna travel during that time certainly belies that notion.[95]

In sifting through the various letters and other materials pertaining to travel by Freud and Minna in an effort to determine just how many times they went on holiday together—unfortunately for the English-reading audience, much of this material is still only in German—I count nine distinct trips between 1897 and 1913, two separate ones in 1898 alone. There were in addition three lengthy month-long "cures" they spent together during the summers of 1919, 1921, and 1923, for a grand total of twelve. *These are the minimum number of trips* I have been able to document. I suspect the record is incomplete. I know that there could not have been less, but there might well have been more. With the possible exception of 1914 through 1918, the years of World War I, I assume that in 1899, 1901, 1904, 1906, 1909, 1910, 1911, 1912, 1920, and 1922 Freud and Minna could also have travelled together, since summer holidays had become a Freud family institution, as had Freud going off on excursions by himself with one other person during the second half of those holidays. I don't have any documentary evidence that Freud and Minna didn't go off by themselves again; but I also don't have any documentary evidence that they did. Since evidence is always on the scarce side in the world of Freud scholarship, and materials are often restricted, other information may exist, which could shed light on this issue. This topic seems ripe for further research.

ALONE AT BERGGASSE

In addition to Freud and Minna travelling alone on holidays, there were also times when they were by themselves at Berggasse, either while Martha was visiting her increasingly ill mother in Hamburg (Wandsbek) or when Martha was simply away on holiday with the children. During the summer, Martha and the children usually left Vienna about a month before Freud did.[96] "Tomorrow I am sending the hen and the five little chicks to Reichenau," Freud writes to Wilhelm Fliess on May 21, 1894, "and during the sad loneliness that follows—my sister-in-law Minna, otherwise my closest confidante, will depart two weeks later—I shall more often carry out my resolution at least to write to you."[97] So here we learn that Freud and Minna are spending at least two weeks together while Martha is away.

But, as previously noted, it was not necessary for Martha to be away from Berggasse for Freud and Minna to be alone together. Freud could also visit Minna while Martha was at home. With Minna having her own bedroom far away from Freud's, he could visit her whenever he pleased and not surprise Martha when he arrived late for bed, because he always arrived late for bed.

SO MUCH ALIKE

As mentioned before, I suspect that after a few years of marriage, Freud came to rethink his "crisscross" formula—that in his case, at least, opposites don't always attract. Or don't attract for long.[98] Remember Helen Walker Puner's comment? "Early in their marriage [Freud] came to regard his wife with the same analytic detachment he regarded a neurotic symptom."[99] His attitude toward Martha had changed. She was no longer the focus of his ardor. Minna, someone very much like himself, came to supplant Martha in Freud's eyes. He had abandoned the "crisscross" dictum, though he seems to have done so unconsciously. Freud and Minna simply had too much in common to be put off by one another for long.

Sense of Humor

One important quality Freud shared with Minna was a sardonic, often biting sense of humor. For example, while Martha showed great solicitude in finding Christmas presents for all the servants and even the servants' relatives, Minna thought her sister could go too far at times. "We draw a line at the niece of our milkman,"[100] she sarcastically remarked. When the question of Freud possibly emigrating to America came up, Minna ironically observed that Freud should stay in Austria until his fame reached America, whereupon so many American patients would flock to him that he would be saved the trouble of emigrating.[101]

It is ironic that what she said in jest turned out to be true in fact. American patients did flock to Freud as his reputation spread worldwide after World War I.

In the summer of 1910 Freud and his family were on holiday, and Minna was in Vienna and in charge of Berggasse. She writes Freud informing him about some repair work that has been done to the apartment. She complains, "We had Jewish electricians who were naturally too refined to remove the filth they had left."[102] When Martin Freud was released from a

World War I prisoner-of-war camp, enabling him to reunite with his wife Esti—whom, as we have seen, Minna did not like—Minna quips, "He is betaking himself from one imprisonment to another."[103]

Sometimes her humor verges on the unashamedly bitter. She writes to Freud on July 23, 1910, from Bistrai in Austrian Silesia, where she is staying with the three Freud daughters: "Otherwise our life here is always the same," she laments, "if you imagine the mugginess of Reichenhall and the humidity of Old-Aussee you have roughly the climate of Bistrai, of course without the beauty of those two places. It is really a hideously desolate hick town ... with many people who unfailingly turn one's stomach."[104]

Freud could match Minna's sarcasm word for word. In his memoir of Freud, Hanns Sachs relates several instances of Freud's biting humor. When the Austrian internal revenue service doubted his tax returns, complaining "since it is well known that your fame attracts patients who are able to pay high fees from foreign countries," Freud comments, "I note with pleasure this first official recognition which my work has found in Austria."[105] In response to a German professor who was intent on establishing a noise league in order to suppress all useless noise, Freud observes, "He wants to make all the noise himself."[106] And when an old friend, once a powerful figure in Austrian politics, visited Berggasse, Freud afterward blithely comments, "Aged lion, well on his way to becoming a couch-cover."[107]

So attuned were Freud and Minna to the same octave of sardonic humor, at times it is hard to distinguish, if one did not know, who might be the author of which blistering epigram.

Intellectual and Cultural Interests

Another similarity between brother- and sister-in-law was an intellectual interest in just about everything—especially literature in the case of Minna, antiquities in the case of Freud—and a deep, probative intelligence to go along with those interests. While Minna was not as intelligent nor as creative as Freud—very few people were—she had her own powerful intellect and capacity for knowledge. As we have seen, she knew, and was interested in, Freud's work on psychoanalysis, which we know he greatly appreciated.[108]

"Aunt Minna was an extraordinarily smart and well-read person, " Hirschmüller writes in the introduction to his collection of the Freud/Minna letters, "she had a wonderful memory. She could later quote what she had read. She spoke fluent English and could read French at the very least. She had an absolutely confident and well-founded opinion about literary matters ... [and she] knew a great deal about psychoanalysis."[109]

Hanns Sachs sees her as continuing the powerful tradition of Bernays
family intellectual pursuits and scholarship. Sachs notes:

> One of ... [her] ancestors ... was the [Chief] Rabbi Bernays in
> Hamburg who is mentioned repeatedly in Heinrich Heine's letters
> as a man of high intelligence (*Geistreicher Mann*). Another Bernays,
> presumably a great-uncle, was in still closer contact with the great
> poet. He was editor of a radical German language newspaper in
> Paris in the early forties [1840s], called the *Vorwärts*, in which
> Heine published some of his poems. The poet sent "greetings to
> Bernays" in a letter to no less a person than Karl Marx who was
> also a contributor to the *Vorwärts*. Professor Jacob Bernays of the
> University of Heidelberg, a famous scholar whose works are still
> highly esteemed and used by classical philologists, was ... [her]
> uncle. This tradition was kept alive by Tante Minna, who was an
> extraordinarily well-read person with a great gift for discriminat-
> ing, and sometimes, sharp criticism. She and I soon found out that
> we were both great admirers of the same author, Theodor Fontane,
> and became friendly, exchanging books—especially the collections
> of his letters—and quotations.[110]

Fontane was an important nineteenth-century German novelist.[111]

In addition to his classical education at the *Gymnasium* and his
medical studies at the University of Vienna, Freud seemed interested
in just about everything and everybody. The breadth of his knowledge
was enormous. Some of his favorite authors and artists: Balzac, Sarah
Bernhardt, Goethe, Heinrich Heine, Copernicus, Darwin, Anatole
France, Donatello, Da Vinci, Michelangelo, William James, Nietzsche,
Agatha Christie and Dorothy Sayers (their murder mysteries), Émile
Zola, Shakespeare (especially *Hamlet, Richard III, Macbeth,* and *The
Merchant of Venice*), Kipling, Mark Twain, Cervantes, Molière, Lessing,
Schiller. ... The list goes on.[112]

And he maintained an extensive collection of ancient antiquities. Hanns
Sachs comments:

> Freud read a great many books and scientific articles on subjects
> in which he felt an interest. ... Greece attracted him, but still more
> the Near Orient; Egypt, Babylonia, Assyria, and Phoenicia. He fol-
> lowed the reports of new excavations and his collecting spirit was
> roused by each new discovery. ... In the years of his growing fame his
> collection grew rapidly too; many valuable and interesting objects

from all parts of the world were added as gifts or by purchase. An Egyptian statuette came to him directly from the tomb of Tutankamen. ... The full impression of the vast size that the collection had attained ... I could not wholly appreciate until I saw it in the summer of 1939 in London.[113]

The only cultural area in which Freud did not show much interest was music, though he did like Bizet's *Carmen*[114]—interestingly, a story about illicit love no less, and seduction! Freud also was skilled in many foreign languages. In addition to German, he had mastered English and French and could read Italian and Spanish fluently. He had been proficient in Latin and Greek in school, but did not use either very much as an adult.[115] The fact that he was able to conduct psychoanalytic sessions with American patients in English is an indication of how comfortable he was in languages other than his own. As noted earlier, foreign patients were always a welcome source of income for him.[116]

I can imagine Minna and Freud over an evening game of Tarock, having lively discussions on an almost limitless variety of subjects, many of which were of continuing interest to both of them.[117]

Extraterritoriality—Above the *Hoi Polloi*

Perhaps the most important bond between the two was the same superior outlook on life, a disdain for those with less intellect and less curiosity than themselves: what they might have thought of as people of limited intellectual capability as well as lower social standing.

Martin Freud remembers his father's attitude during one summer holiday:

Father was not a bit unsocial: he liked company and it was usual to see him at summer resorts in animated conversation walking up and down with newly won friends. These were educated people, not highbrow—leading men in commerce or industry and perhaps an odd newspaper editor, an artist or politician. But Schloss Bellevue [in the Alpine foothills in the suburbs of Vienna] was rather different, because you had here people of the *petite bourgeoisie* ... they spoke, in effect, a different language. He had moved with ease in the Paris salon of the world-famous Jean Martin Charcot; but he tended to feel utterly lost and at a loose end with the people who had taken rooms or apartments at Bellevue. They had no common ground for any sort of conversation.[118]

There is evidence that on these summer holidays Freud invariably sought out upper-middle-class people, some as highly educated and intellectual as he; people he did have common ground upon which he could converse. We have already seen Minna report back to Martha from Le Prese in August 1898 that Sigmund "has befriended the spa doctor, speaks to everyone and takes even more pleasure in nobility and comfort than I do." In the same letter, Freud confirms Minna's report: "Made the acquaintance of the spa doctor who is a Florentine and lived in the Hôtel de France twenty years ago. Conversations in French and Italian."[119]

Two years later, Freud and Minna are again on holiday together, this time in Riva. You'll recall, he writes Martha a letter in which he proudly announces, "The company in the hotel consists of the nicest people, among them many university professors and councilors." He then adds the names of these esteemed people. The list is the same as the one he provides Fliess in his letter from September 14, 1900, with the exception that he does not include Hildebrand from Innsbruck in his letter to Martha.[120] All the men mentioned were acquaintances of Freud. These were the sorts of people with whom he felt most comfortable.

One final example. Staying as a family in the Hotel Ammerwald in a densely wooded area on the Austrian-Bavarian border in 1909, Martin Freud recalls: "We became friendly with a South German family, about the same size as our own, headed by a father who was the manager of an important industrial concern in Düsseldorf. Father got along well with this gentleman, who was evidently a well-educated and intelligent man, and the two were often seen walking together in the pleasant grounds of the hotel in animated conversation."[121]

As with Freud at Bellevue, Minna did not feel comfortable with people outside her intellectual and social "class." In another letter to Freud from Bistrai, this one dated July 18, 1910, she informs him that the management of the spa has "had to place people in the surrounding houses, but among all these people there is not a single one with whom one could exchange a word; not that language alone would be an obstacle, most of them know German or French, but they are so disagreeable, the nervous of the lowest classes, who are incidentally to none more distasteful than to the doctor himself, who curses each new arrival."[122]

Minna never felt comfortable in what she must have considered the "backward" social climate of Vienna, at least when compared to vibrant Hamburg, her birthplace. Hanns Sachs writes: "Hamburg and Vienna are generally considered as antipodes in their 'social climates,'" though the Bernays family had moved to Vienna when Minna was only four years old.[123] An indication of her disdain for Vienna was the fact that even after residing there for over forty years she never gave up (nor did Martha) her "purest" North German accent, for which Hamburg was famous.[124]

It needs to be remembered that Freud chose to marry a *German* woman—Martha—who though, like Minna, was raised in Vienna from a young age, still spoke and acted like a German woman throughout her life. Although more than one great man emerged from Vienna at the time, it was a city where the middle classes, while large and firmly entrenched economically, had "few and narrow intellectual interests," Sachs tells us. "An *intellectual* middle class was almost nonexistent."[125] Emphasis mine.

Freud and Minna's disdain for, and dissociation from, Philistine Vienna went even deeper, according to Sachs. "The segregation [of the Freud family] from Vienna was not only accentuated by the language," he notes, "but also, in an unobtrusive way, by many little mannerisms and habits, so that the household gave an impression of extraterritoriality, like an island that is easily accessible from the mainland, but still an island."[126]

The often-described aloofness of both Freud and Minna's personalities added to this sense of being apart. They were in Vienna but were not actually connected to it, and this lack of connection fostered a sense of superiority on their part. In Minna's case, this attitude actually extended to members of her own family. Hirschmüller writes:

> Visitors to the [Freud] house experience her [Minna] as well read, shrewd, and funny, but also as aloof and arrogant. ... Toward the women of the Freud family, his [Freud's] mother and sisters, she was rather reserved. Their exuberance got on her nerves. In contrast, these women would have said of her she was "tightly wound," by which they would have meant tidiness, pedantry, and social reservedness. Aunt Minna had a very sharp tongue, was a little cold ... was always very good and nice to ... [her niece Judith Bernays Heller, Eli Bernays's daughter]. ... On the other hand, she could approach others somewhat condescendingly. Her impressive stature facilitated that. ... Eli actually could not stand her, and her [Judith's] mother always picked on Minna.[127]

Minna apparently did not care how other people in the family thought of her, as long as Sigmund liked her, and there doesn't seem to have been any wavering in that regard—all the way to his dying day.[128] Anyway, these other people didn't count. For Minna they were not on the same level—intellectually—as she and Sigmund. This attitude revealed not only Minna's snobbery but perhaps also accurately characterized her fellow family members.

Freud, too, was considered by most people who knew him well to be aloof and rather cold. Hanns Sachs, though one of the elite Seven Rings group, and whose loyalty to Freud could not be questioned, was never able to get close to him, mainly because Freud would never let him. Sachs recalls:

> I simply could not believe that he was made of the same clay as others. Some special substance had been infused into him and gave the finished product a higher grade of perfection. This meant a gulf between us which I did not try to cross. Although he called me his friend, I did not feel that I was; fundamentally he remained as remote as when I first met him in the lecture hall [at the University of Vienna, where for many years Freud gave weekly lectures]. I had moments of criticism and rebellion, but there was no time when I did not see this gulf that separated my nature from his. ... I have no doubt that Freud too thought of himself as being "not in the roll of common men." He never said anything which could be taken as a hint of his high opinion of himself ... [however] nor did he ever modestly disclaim his superiority.[129]

Minna and Freud lived in a world far above the *hoi polloi*. It was populated by intelligent, analytically adept, creative souls. That was what made psychoanalysis so attractive to a certain group of people—thoughtful, intelligent, insightful. When Freud learned that Jung's patient Sabina Spielrein was well educated, he wrote to his friend in an October 27, 1906, letter: "I am glad to hear that your Russian girl is a student; uneducated persons are at present too inaccessible for our purposes."[130] Yet even these people could not always meet Freud's high standards for intellectual performance. Sachs recalls one instance when Freud's patients did not respond to his therapy as he had hoped. He called them "the fools" (*die Narren*), apparently more out of frustration than disdain.[131]

What does all this have to do with Freud and Minna having an affair? Plenty. I equate extraterritoriality in the broadest sense of the term with living under one's own rules. Residing in a country but not feeling bound by its laws. Remember Barry Silverstein's arguments? Freud was toying with the concept of the superior human being. As such, he could have sex with Minna because he felt it was *permissible* to do so. He and Minna were special people, not bound by accepted moral constraints, and hence they felt able to do whatever they pleased, because *they* made the rules, not society, which, in large part, both looked down upon.[132]

Paul Roazen writes about this attitude with regard to Freud and his daughter Anna, though it could just as easily be said of Freud and Minna: "There is little doubt in my mind," Roazen notes, "that both Freud and Anna saw themselves as a part of a small elite, beyond the everyday standards of good and evil which might apply to lesser mortals. Analysis itself was seen as a technique suitable for superior beings, and Freud hoped to evolve out of this a higher form of ethical existence."[133] Whether Freud consciously sought to do so is questionable in my mind, but his ideas and behavior seemed headed in that direction.

We know Freud had disdain for the bourgeois classes that made up the largest part of Vienna society, especially the "amiable insincerity" which was so prominent a feature of Vienna at the time. This was the Viennese tradition of fawning obsequiousness which gave everyone a title one or two levels above the one they actually deserved. Hanns Sachs remembers: "In 'my' coffee house I was addressed as 'Herr Doctor' as long as I was a student, but on the day of my graduation I became 'Herr von Sachs.'"[134]

SEXUAL LIBERATION

Freud also looked down upon bourgeois Victorian morals with regard to sexual practices. Here he took "pride in his iconoclasm, his efforts to subvert middle-class pieties," as Peter Gay has put it.[135] Recall that Freud wrote to James J. Putnam in 1915 about standing for a much freer sexual life, though he admitted he had made little use of such freedom except insofar as he was convinced of what was permissible for him.[136]

Is Freud referring here to his having sex with Minna as something that might have been "permissible" to him? One certainly can reasonably infer that. And if he says he has made "little use" of such sexual freedom, does that imply that he had actually made *some* use of it?

Even ten years before he wrote his famous letter to Putnam, Peter Gay points out, Freud had proposed, in response to a series of questions concerning reform of the divorce law in the Austro-Hungarian empire, ideas promoting sexual liberation and had condemned the indissolubility of marriage.[137] Freud also raised concerns about the damaging effects of sexual abstinence.

In answer to a question about whether simultaneous or successive polygamy would be incompatible with our concept of culture, Freud responds: "I can very well imagine that at least successive polygamy could be made consistent with the demands of our civilization. This would in part merely sanction already existing conditions." And when asked whether morality would be better served if existing sexual relationships were legalized,

Freud responds: "Perhaps the only practical way in which to encourage morality would be the legalization of relations between the sexes outside of marriage, according a greater measure of sexual freedom and curtailing restrictions on that freedom."

To a question about whether marriage should be legally indissoluble, even after an actual breakup, Freud's answer is firm: "Indissolubility of marriage contradicts important ethical and hygienic principles and empirical psychological experience." And when asked about the effects of sustained sexual abstinence, Freud's answer is quite revelatory:

> Many physicians even today choose to underestimate the powerful sex instinct. ... It is my opinion that [sexual abstinence] is only possible for a small minority of people with an especially fortunate makeup to be sexually abstinent without damage. ... For the great majority ... sexual abstinence over a large part of life is almost impossible. ... The physical damage from persistent sexual continence may be described as a disposition to various forms of nervousness. ... The individual expends his psychic energies in the never ending struggle against temptation and thereby becomes impoverished of those qualities which he needs for the mastery of his social responsibilities: self-confidence, energy, and daring.[138]

So successive polygamy, or a man having one wife after another, is all right; sex "outside of marriage" is moral and should be legalized; marriage is not indissoluble; and sustained sexual abstinence is "almost impossible" and can actually be damaging given inherent temptations. While Freud might have provided numerous hints that his marriage to Martha had become celibate at an early stage, it is obvious that he believed sustained sexual abstinence was almost impossible to achieve and was unhealthy in any case. How to solve that? Perhaps an affair outside of marriage? He does not comment.

Freud's views were quite revolutionary for the time and were part of his elitist, "extraterritorial" notions of what was acceptable behavior for him and people of his kind.

Freud's determination to live by his own, more libertarian rules, which were invariably at odds with those accepted by society at the time, sounds very Nietzschean. The concept of the *Übermensch*, the superman, would seem to fit. But I am not certain things are that simple. As mentioned in the last chapter, we know that Freud had read Nietzsche as a young student and that he had spent a good deal of money to purchase Nietzsche's collected works in 1900, at a time when he didn't have much money, so we can take that as a measure of his strong interest. In a letter to Wilhelm Fliess dated February 1, 1900, he informs his Berlin colleague how he thought he might use Nietzsche some day: "I have just acquired [the collected works of] Nietzsche, in whom I hope to find words for much that remains mute in me, but have not opened him yet. Too lazy for the time being."[139] Yet Freud seems to see a close connection between his clinical observations and Nietzsche's philosophical insights.

Gay interprets Freud's "too lazy" admission as an indication of his desire to treat Nietzsche's writings "as texts to be resisted far more than to be studied."[140] It is not clear how, or if, Nietzsche actually influenced Freud, and how Freud might have resisted Nietzsche even if he wanted to. One can presume that as a student Freud had already absorbed many of Nietzsche's ideas. The important point here is that, whether influenced or not, Freud *acted* as if Nietzsche had had a major impact on him, because he came to see himself in very Nietzschean terms—the sort of person who could in fact fit the *Übermensch* model.[141]

UNRELENTING PRESSURE

In attempting to understand the broad range of factors which may have caused Freud and Minna to become romantically involved, I think it would be instructive to try to see the world as they saw it at the time, get a sense of how they felt about their lives, what their needs were, why they might have found each other attractive. In modern colloquial terms, see where they were "at" in their lives. I am especially interested in the period between 1893 and 1910, a stretch of years when an affair between the two would most likely have taken place.[142]

Financial Stress

One of the most striking aspects of Fred's life during this period is the enormous responsibility he had to shoulder as head of a large family. By 1896, he had six children (many of them were then quite young, and all of them seemed to be ill at one time or another), at least five servants,[143] a father and mother to support (though his father passed away in October of 1896), several as-yet unwed sisters, and, of course, beginning in late 1896, when she took up what would turn out to be permanent residency at Berggasse, Minna.[144]

How was Freud able to pay for all this? Based on available evidence, I am not sure how, in fact, he did. He had few outside sources of income. From time to time he might get small "loans" from friends—we know Breuer was one of those who supplied funds periodically, and sometimes Freud's religious teacher at *Gymnasium*, Samuel Hammerschlag, did the same.[145] And from time to time he received similar "loans" from people such as Ernst von Fleischl-Marxow.[146] Though Martha and Minna inherited some money from an aunt—we know Freud asked for and received funds from Minna on at least two occasions in the late 1880s—[147] they were members of a distinguished but impoverished German-Jewish family. Their parents were as poor as Freud's.

The primary source of income during these years came from patient fees, which could be variable at best, so the family lived, in essence, from day to day, literally from patient to patient. Ernest Jones describes how Freud earned income over a several-year period, and how there were both some good and some very bad days, weeks, and months.[148] As we have noted in Chapter 4, how much money Freud earned directly determined how far and long his summer holidays might be. In a good year the family might go as far as Italy. In a bad year it was Bellevue, or other resorts in the Alpine foothills surrounding Vienna.[149]

An indication of just how tight things could get financially is evident in the circumstances surrounding Freud's 1909 trip to America. He had to turn down the first offer from G. Stanley Hall to speak at the Clark University celebrations. Why? The timing was bad. The event was scheduled for the first week of July, and because of that Freud would have to give up three weeks of private practice (and its income). He made that fact clear to Hall in declining the offer. He simply could not afford to miss those fees. When Hall changed the dates for the celebration to the second week in September (and also raised Freud's honorarium from $400 to $750), Freud happily accepted Hall's second invitation.[150]

Freud's financial worries were always deeply on his mind and must have created enormous stress in his life.

Ridicule and Anti-Semitism

Another source of pressure was the constant and often brutal ridicule directed at Freud and his ideas. I see two factors here. One was that many considered Freud's theories outlandish, with their emphasis on sexuality and especially infantile sexuality. The second was blatant and pernicious anti-Semitism. Not the "country club" sort, whispered in corridors and involving restrictions on memberships of one kind or another, but the kind that was shouted openly and could often involve violence or the threat of violence. Sometimes these two factors combined.

Hanns Sachs recalls that there was "the timeworn prejudice that Jewish (or, in another variant, the 'Oriental,' or the 'Mediterranean,' or the 'French') mind was abnormally preoccupied with matters of a sexual nature."[151]

Although Victorian prudery had lessened somewhat in the early years of the twentieth century, when Freud's major works began to appear words like "sex" and "sexuality" were still frowned upon, and newspapers could not use terms such as "homosexuality" and "syphilis." Even a prostitute would euphemistically be called "a woman who works with her hands."[152] As we have seen, it was not merely that establishment medicine objected to Freud's emphasis on sexuality and the libido; some in the medical community actually made fun of him. The psychiatrist Theodor Ziehen, later Professor of Philosophy at Halle University, claimed that "what Freud has written is all nonsense."[153] Ludwig Binswanger reported to Freud in a June 2, 1910, letter that Alfred Erich Hoche—professor of psychiatry at Freiberg—had described Freud's ideas as "a psychic epidemic among doctors ... a reaction ... against extreme physical therapy in order to attract tired patients."[154]

There were signs of trouble right from the beginning. When Freud returned to Vienna in 1886 from studying with Charcot in Paris and presented new ideas on ways to treat hysteria to the conservative members of the Vienna Medical Society, "he was greeted with scorn," Puner notes in her biography.[155] And Jones writes: "We see that Freud was bitterly disappointed at the very outset of his endeavors to convey new ideas to his conservative seniors."[156]

"Instead of encouragement, he received nothing but violent protests and derision from his contemporaries," Hanns Sachs recalls,[157] so much so that when Freud finally reached America in 1909 the New World was a new world in more than one sense. Freud writes in his autobiography: "In Europe I felt as though I were despised; but over there I found myself received by the foremost men as an equal ... psychoanalysis was no longer a product of delusion, it had become a valuable part of reality."[158]

With regard to anti-Semitism, it is hard today to understand how pernicious, in-bred, and vicious it was during Freud's lifetime. It seems to have made his efforts to receive the title of full professor at the University of Vienna more difficult, almost impossible—though according to Hanns Sachs Freud never did achieve the title of professor, at least in the sense that we understand that term today. Through the intervention of a wealthy patient, he was eventually given the title of Professor extraordinarius (our equivalent of associate professor), but the new title did not change his academic status. Sachs remembers: "He had neither the rights nor the duties of a member of the Faculty. Much later, after the war, when Freud was a

world-celebrity, the title of 'Professor ordinarius' was shamefacedly con-
ferred on him, but without giving him a seat on the Faculty."[159] Freud's
situation was that while he was *allowed* to give lectures if he wanted to, and
he did want to, he was not required to. His title in today's academic world
would probably be most equivalent to "adjunct professor."

Martin Freud has written that the driving force behind his father's edict
that his sons not follow in his footsteps in the study of medicine was the
anti-Semitism Freud experienced in the field of academic medicine. He
did not want them to experience the same misery he had been through.[160]

Freud's children had their own anti-Semitic experiences. Martin
Freud has written about one particularly ugly incident. On holiday during the summer of 1901, the Freud family was staying near a little green
lake in Thumsee, not far from Bad Reichenhall. Martin and his brother
Oliver, while fishing in a rowboat on the lake, were surprised one morning to hear a number of men who were standing on an adjoining road
hurling anti-Semitic insults at them. The two boys rightly ignored the
men, but later that same afternoon Freud had to go to Reichenhall, and
the two boys were rowing him across the lake to a nearby highway to
shorten his walk. As Martin Freud recalls: "The men who had abused
Oliver and me that morning were now reinforced by a number of other
people, including women, and stood on the road ... apparently prepared
to block the way to Reichenhall. As we moored the boat, they began
shouting anti-Semitic abuse." Without the slightest hesitation, Freud
"jumped out of the boat and, keeping to the middle of the road, marched
toward the hostile crowd ... swinging his stick." Charging the men, the
crowd "gave way before him and promptly dispersed." The incident made
a deep impression on Martin: "After more than fifty-five years I can still
recall the faces of these crusaders in racial hatred," he remembers.[161]

Martin Freud also experienced anti-Semitism in the army during World
War I[162] and in 1913 while at university, where he was "badly hurt in a
brawl between German-Austrian and Jewish students."[163] Anti-Semitic
violence on university campuses seems to have been common and did not
dissipate with time. Edmund Engelman—who grew up in Vienna and is
justly appreciated as the person who, at great risk to himself because the
Nazis had Freud's apartment under constant surveillance, photographed
Freud's Berggasse home just prior to Freud's escape from Vienna in 1938—
had his own tale of horror:

> During my years as a student, 1926–1931, [the university] was a center
> of intense, often violent, conservative "pan-German" political activities.

Jews and other "aliens" walked carefully on campus, pitifully intent on not "causing trouble"—yet Jewish students were regularly beaten up by gangs from the nationalistic fraternities. The police, meanwhile, stood off-campus, scrupulously avoiding interference with traditional "academic freedom" that allowed the university to pretend to be a state unto itself.[164]

The effect of all this was not only to cause Freud deep concern about his career and his ability to support his ever-growing household because of outside hostility, but, as Helen Puner points out, he also "worried constantly and ceaselessly about his children's futures, and their fates, as individuals and, understandably, as Jews."[165]

THE ABSTINENT FREUD

Added to all these challenges and the emotional toll they must have exacted, Freud's romantic ardor toward Martha began to cool—apparently not many years after their marriage began, though the overall picture is rather muddled. Peter Gay notes: "we know that in August 1893, when he was only thirty-seven, he [Freud] was living in sexual abstinence."[166] Yet he must have had intercourse with Martha after that date, since his last child, Anna, was born in December 1895, so his abstinence must have been interrupted—at least once, perhaps more often. There is also evidence of sexual activity after 1895. Freud writes to Wilhelm Fliess on December 17, 1896, about the latter's ideas concerning human periodicity: "I noticed that on certain dates, which clearly recur every 28 days, I have no sexual desire and am impotent—which otherwise is not yet the case."[167] Although Freud uses the phrase "not yet the case," which seems to imply it might soon be the case, it seems reasonable to assume that during the other days of the four-week cycle he did have sexual desires and was not impotent.

In 1900 Freud becomes more declarative and apparently more definitive about his sexual abstinence with Martha. As we have seen, he writes to Fliess on March 11 of that year: "I am done begetting children."[168] I take this to mean that Freud had stopped having sex with Martha, for, as Peter Gay points out, Freud "deplored the untoward psychological consequences of contraception. Except in the most favorable circumstances, he believed, the use of a condom is likely to produce neurotic malaise. *Coitus interruptus* and other means are no better; depending on the method employed, either the man or the woman is probably doomed to end up a victim of hysteria or of an anxiety neurosis."[169]

Freud's abandonment of sex with Martha seems confirmed by a November 6, 1911, letter that Emma Jung sends to him, in which she reminds him that during his 1911 visit to Küsnacht he had told her that his "marriage had long been 'amortized,' now there was nothing more to do except—die."[170] Freud's rejection of contraception could also have been a convenient excuse not to have sex with Martha. In any case, since he didn't want more children and didn't believe in contraception, sexual activity with Martha was apparently no longer an option.

Yet the issue of Freud's sexual activity with his wife is confused once again by an incident in 1915 reported by Peter Gay. Gay tells us that in July of that year Freud had a series of dreams, one of which was about Martha. In interpreting how the previous day's residue contributed to the content of the dream, a standard tool in dream interpretation, Freud notes that it "has to do with successful coitus Wednesday morning." Freud was then fifty-nine years of age.[171] At Martha's menopausal or post-menopausal age at the time—fifty-four—maybe the issue of contraception was no longer relevant. Or perhaps the "successful coitus" was not with Martha at all, though it seems unlikely that Freud would raise with Fliess the specter of a possible affair, so it appears it was coitus with Martha.

So what does all this mean? The evidence is obviously sketchy and seems at times contradictory, but Freud appears to have been driven into abstinence because of fears that Martha might become pregnant again. There were two concerns here. One is about adding another child that Freud would be forced to support. He was struggling just to keep his present family afloat. A second is about Martha's health and what a new pregnancy might mean. She was already worn out from six pregnancies in just nine years.

An additional factor was Freud's lack of interest, the cooling of his ardor. Freud writes in his 1908 paper on "'Civilized' Sexual Morality and Modern Nervous Illness" about how common it is after several years of marriage to see sexual interest wane. "Satisfying sexual intercourse in marriage takes place only for a few years," he points out. "After these three, four or five years, the marriage becomes a failure in so far as it has promised the satisfaction of sexual needs."[172] It seems that Freud is writing about his own situation here.

THE SEXUAL FREUD—HOMO AND HETERO

This was the so-called abstinent Freud. On the other hand, while Freud could write to friends about his impotence and lack of sexual desire fairly early on in his marriage, a constant and at times burning sexuality never left him. Some of this was directed at Martha, seemingly in fits and starts. Much more of it was directed at others—toward certain men as well as other women, such as Minna.

Concerning the transfer of Freud's affection from Martha to Minna, Paul Roazen writes in *Freud and His Followers*: "The evidence for the premature falling off in Freud's sex life might be interpreted ... instead of merely the cooling of his ardor for Martha, what may have happened is that he transferred his physical and/or emotional needs to another woman, Minna."[173]

The conventional notion that, as Puner puts it, Freud "would never once swerve from the path of marital rectitude that grew from the seed of his general rigid morality,"[174] or as Jones writes, that Freud was "quite peculiarly monogamous ... of few men can it be said that they go through the whole of life without being erotically moved in any serious fashion by any woman beyond the one and only one"[175]—that is, Martha—seems at best superficial. If we accept these characterizations at face value, then Freud becomes a hypocrite. What he preached, sexual freedom, was not how he acted or how he even felt. But Freud was not a hypocrite.

Words

Freud's words and most importantly his feelings (and actions) indicate a strong sexuality. First, his words. One of the keystones of Freud's theories is the recognition of the role of sexuality in human motivation and the need to free repressed sexual feelings. He was the great sexual liberator of his time, an ardent champion of sexual freedom. We have already noted his letter to Putnam and his answers to the 1905 questions concerning the divorce law in the Austro-Hungarian Empire. There is abundant additional evidence of his liberal sexual views.

As early as 1893 in a draft paper he sends to Fliess, Freud argues that "the only alternative [to masturbation] would be free sexual intercourse between young men and unattached young women."[176] And in the same 1908 paper mentioned above, "'Civilized' Sexual Morality and Modern Nervous Illness," Freud maintains that civilization makes impossible demands upon the individual. It asks us to practice abstinence until we are married, and those who do not marry are required to remain abstinent throughout their lives. But deflecting powerful sexual instincts through sublimation is near impossible for the vast majority of people, and even for a minority, can be achieved only intermittently. Attempting to do so only causes neuroses or other harmful consequences. He writes, "Experience shows that the majority of the people who make up our society are constitutionally unfit to face the task of abstinence."[177]

One wonders how well Freud was able to sublimate his strong sexual feelings. We already know that he apparently found it difficult to confine his sexual activity to a single partner.

In a 1912 paper titled "On the Universal Tendency to Debasement in the Sphere of Love," Freud seems to justify his own infidelity with Minna, who, as we have seen, he often called "dear sister." Freud writes, "anyone who is to be really free and happy in love must have surmounted his respect for women and have come to terms with the idea of incest with mother or sister."[178]

Feelings

Beyond the words, of course, were the actual feeling, what I will call Freud's simmering sexuality. I see this taking two forms. One homosexual; the other, and the more powerful, heterosexual.[179]

Freud tended to develop "crushes" on intelligent, handsome men. His first homosexual attachment was to the brilliant Ernst von Fleischl-Marxow, who was Ernst von Brücke's laboratory assistant and who supervised some of Freud's work when Freud was a student there. Freud thought of Fleischl as a "dazzling personality."[180] Jones indicates that Fleischl was one of six people whom Freud idealized as a student at the University of Vienna,[181] and whose "friendship meant much to Freud and whose untimely death he deeply deplored." Fleischl was "young, handsome, enthusiastic, a brilliant speaker, and an attractive teacher," Jones tells us. "He had the charming and amiable manners of old Viennese society." At twenty-five he contracted an infection while conducting research in the pathology laboratory. "An amputation of his right thumb saved his life," Jones informs us, "but continued growth of neuromas required repeated operations."[182]

Freud, Jones continues, had "first admired [Fleischl] from a distance, but after leaving the Brücke Institute had come to know him more personally. In February 1884 ... [Freud] speaks of his 'intimate friendship' with Fleischl." Earlier, Freud had written of him:

Yesterday I was with my friend Ernst v. Fleischl, whom I have hitherto ... envied in all respects. ... He is a most distinguished man, for whom both nature and upbringing have done their best. Rich, trained in all physical exercises, with the stamp of genius in his energetic features, handsome, with fine feelings, gifted with all the talents ... he had always been my ideal and I could not rest till we became friends and I could experience a pure joy in his ability and reputation.[183]

Another time Freud writes to Martha: "I admire and love him [Fleischl] with an intellectual passion, if you will allow such a phrase. His destruction [coming death] will move me as the destruction of a sacred and famous temple would have affected an ancient Greek. I love him not so much as a human being, but as one of Creation's precious achievements."[184]

In April 1885, Freud sat up all night with Fleischl, who spent the entire time in a warm bath by Freud's side, presumably nude. Soaking in warm water was the only way Fleischl could find relief from his terrible pain. "It was the first of many such nights [Freud] passed in the following couple of months," Jones points out.[185]

Freud's interest in cocaine led him to recommend it to Fleischl as a way to shed the latter's addiction to morphine which he was taking for his pain.[186] Unfortunately, Fleischl became as addicted to cocaine as he had been to morphine. Freud felt guilty as a result.[187]

Freud did not understand the homoerotic component in his affection for Fleischl, nor have Freud scholars who have commented upon the relationship. With regard to the deep "crush" Freud developed with the next male target of his affections, Wilhelm Fliess, the matter is different, though it took Freud some time to realize the homosexual element in his feelings.[188] He and Fliess began corresponding in 1887, and by 1893 we have evidence that Freud's admiration and affection for Fliess were set. Freud writes to Minna on April 7 of that year: "He [Fliess] is a most unusual person, good nature personified: and I believe, if it came to it, he would for all his genius, be goodness itself. Therefore his sun-like clarity, his pluck."[189]

In the mid- and late-1890s Fliess continues to be Freud's irreplaceable Other, as Peter Gay phrases it.[190] Freud writes to his friend on January 3, 1899, shortly after one of their "Congresses" (meetings): "Now look at what happens. Here I live in ill humor and in darkness until you come; I get things off my chest; rekindle my flickering flame at your steadfast one and feel well again; and after your departure, I again have been given eyes to see, and what I see is beautiful and good."[191]

Gay points out that at the time no one, not even "his witty, intelligent sister-in-law Minna Bernays," could do for Freud what Fliess was able to do, and much of that was because of Freud's idealized sense of who Fliess was.[192]

At about the turn of the century, Freud's friendship with Fleiss begins to dissolve. It was Fliess who was withdrawing from Freud, the result, at least in part, of Fliess's jealous wife Ida, who did "everything possible to sow discord between the two friends."[193] But even at that time Freud had strong, affectionate feelings for Fliess. Freud writes to him in a May 7, 1900, letter, "But no one can replace for me the relationship with the friend which a special—possibly feminine-side—demands,"[194] and a year later, on August 7, 1901, Freud writes again to Fliess: "I do not share your contempt for friendship between men, probably because I am to a high degree party to it. In my life, as you know, woman has never replaced the comrade, the [male] friend."[195]

By 1908, Freud was able to get in touch with "remnants of unconscious homoerotic feelings [about Fliess] that were bubbling up" in him,[196] and by 1910 Freud could write to Ferenczi that he was well on his way toward overcoming the remnants of his homosexual feelings toward Fliess. Freud notes in an October 10, 1910, letter: "This [homoerotic] need has been extinguished in me since Fliess' case, with the overcoming of which you just saw me occupied. A piece of homosexual investment has been withdrawn and utilized for the enlargement of my own ego. I have succeeded where the paranoiac fails."[197]

Freud believed that disguised homosexuality was the foundation of paranoia. In fact, in a letter to Jung of February 17, 1908, Freud writes about this process with regard to Fliess: "The paranoid form is probably conditioned by restriction to the homosexual component. ... My one-time friend Fliess developed a dreadful case of paranoia after throwing off his [homosexual] affection for me, which was undoubtedly considerable."[198] In the case of Fliess, it seems that homosexual feelings went both ways; hence Ida Fliess's concern. By 1908 Freud is already referring to his "one-time friend Fliess." Obviously, Freud had for some time seen the writing on the wall.

Freud also had homosexual feelings toward Jung as did Jung toward Freud. As we will remember, Jung talked openly about the "undeniable erotic undertone" of his feelings toward Freud in a letter dated October 28, 1907,[199] and we have noted the open affection he expressed toward Freud in his 1953 interview with Eissler.

It seems that Freud's "affectionate" feelings toward Jung reawakened many of his old homoerotic feelings toward Fliess—feelings which he had worked so diligently to extinguish. When other possibly homosexual situations appeared, Freud sought to shut them down immediately. He writes to Jung on September 24, 1910, complaining about Ferenczi's homoerotic emotional needs: "My travelling companion [Ferenczi] is a dear fellow, but dreamy in a disturbing kind of way, and his attitude towards me is infantile. He never stops admiring me, which I don't like. ... He has been too passive and receptive, letting everything be done for him like a woman, and I really haven't got enough homosexuality in me to accept him as one. These trips arouse a great longing for a real woman."[200]

A real woman? In other words, not a "fake" woman like Ferenczi? I suspect the "real" woman Freud has in mind is Minna, the female with whom he felt most comfortable travelling—and simply being with.

Homosexual feelings, as Peter Gay has pointed out, apparently played a role in a fainting spell Freud experienced in Munich in 1912. It was in the same room in the Munich Park Hotel where Freud had fainting spells twice before, in 1906 and 1908. He attributed the latest incident to his concern about Jung's growing belligerence (which probably signaled his eventual departure from the psychoanalytic movement, though Freud does not mention this), but also to the fact that Freud first saw Munich when he visited Fliess during the latter's illness. "This town seems to have acquired a strong connection with my relation to this man," Freud writes to Ernest Jones on December 8, 1912. "There is some piece of unruly homosexual feeling at the root of the matter." Jones writes back on December 23, 1912, saying he "had suspected a homosexual element." He thought that Freud "would find it difficult to give up your feeling for Jung (meaning that perhaps there was some transference to him of older affects in you)." Freud agreed, writing back on December 26: "You are right in supposing that I had transferred to Jung homosex[ual] feelings from another part but I am glad to find that I have no difficulty in removing them for free circulation."[201]

While Freud was attempting to keep his homosexual feelings under control and hopefully eradicate them, in part by trying to understand them better, there is ample evidence he had powerful heterosexual feelings at the same time. Many of these took the form of amorous feelings toward Minna.

With regard to Minna and, I suspect, women in general, it is important to remember Jung's recollection in his 1953 interview with Kurt Eissler about the nature of Freud's sexual musing. Jung tells Eissler: "He [Freud] always told me that in his neurosis: 'Well, now I'm an old man, and, and, … Yeah, if one had a young woman, one could rejuvenate oneself!'"[202]

In *The Psychopathology of Everyday Life*, Freud reveals his ongoing interest in young women—in this case a very attractive one. But here he is not only musing but taking action, almost to the point of touching. Freud recalls:

> In the house of some friends I met a young girl who was staying there as a guest and who aroused a feeling of pleasure in me which I had long thought was extinct. As a result I was in a jovial, talkative and

obliging mood. … As the girl's uncle, a very old gentleman, entered the room, we both jumped to our feet to bring him a chair that was standing in the corner. She was nimbler than I was and, I think, nearer to the object; so she took hold of her chair first and carried it in front of her with its back towards her, gripping the sides of the seat with both hands. As I got there later, but still stuck to my intention of carrying the chair, I suddenly found myself standing directly behind her, and throwing my arms around her from behind; and for a moment my hands met in front of her waist.[203]

In 1909 during Freud and Jung's trip to America for the Clark University celebrations, he often had prostitutes on his mind, so much so that he found he could not sleep. He complains to Jung one morning at breakfast: "I haven't been able to sleep since I came to America. I continue to dream of prostitutes."

"Well," Jung shrugged, "why don't you do something about it?"

"But," Freud replied, appalled at the suggestion, "I'm a married man."[204]

In 1919 the theme of prostitutes comes up again. He seems inextricably drawn to their section of a small Italian town—perhaps, by that time, actually wanting to "do something about it." He writes:

As I was walking, one hot summer afternoon, through the deserted streets of a provincial town in Italy which was unknown to me, I found myself in a quarter of whose character I could not long remain in doubt. Nothing but painted women were to be seen at the windows of the small houses, and I hastened to leave the narrow street at the next turning. But after having wandered about for a time without enquiring my way, I suddenly found myself back in the same street, where my presence was now beginning to excite attention. I hurried away once more, only to arrive by another *détour* at the same place yet a third time.[205]

"Freud visibly enjoyed the admiration of good-looking women," Peter Gay writes about Freud's eye for the opposite sex, "the handsome and formidable Lou Andreas-Salomé was only the most striking of these." I would add that Minna might not have been the most striking of this sort, but she was certainly the first. "Freud … long remained hospitable to the pleasures of the senses," Gay continues:

He expressed some sympathy for Horace's dictum *carpe diem*—"seize the day"—a philosophical defense of grasping the pleasure of the moment that appeals to "the uncertainty of life and the unfruitfulness of virtuous renunciation." After all, he confessed, "each of us has had hours and times in which he admitted that this philosophy of life is right." At such moments, we are apt to criticize the pitiless severity of moral teachings: "They only understand how to make demands without offering compensations." Stern moralist though he was, Freud did not deny pleasure its innings.[206]

In a May 31, 1897, letter to Fliess, Freud reports a dream where he "was going up a staircase with very few clothes on. I was moving, as the dream explicitly emphasized, with great agility. … Suddenly, I noticed, however, that a woman was coming after me, and thereupon set in the sensation, so common in dreams, of being glued to the spot, of being paralyzed. The accompanying feeling was not anxiety but erotic excitement."[207]

"Like some of … [Freud's] dreams," Gay writes, "some of his papers and casual comments whisper of luxuriant erotic fantasies persisting through the years. They may have been fantasies for the most part."[208] Then again, I would add, they might not have been.

Freud went so far as to propose to his Wednesday Psychological Society the founding of "an academy of love where the *ars amandi* would be taught."[209] *Ars amandi* is Latin for "the art of love," usually in the sense of sexual love. It is also the title of a famous book by the Roman poet Ovid. Gay comments: "'How much he practiced what he would have taught in such an academy remains his secret."[210]

Roazen is skeptical of any decrease in sexual interest on Freud's part as he grew older. "Freud's Puritanism could be construed as a reaction formation to his own passions having burnt very brightly," Roazen writes; "It is difficult to reconcile the vibrant man we know from his works and letters with the man who responded to his self-analysis in the 1890s with a relative loss of potency." Yet, he adds, as we have had occasion to note earlier, even with Freud's sexual interests continuing, Roazen would be inclined "to reject the notion that a physical relationship existed between Freud and Minna. She did indeed speak to Jung about Freud's involvement with her; his attentions did worry her." At least Roazen believes Jung did not lie. "But according to Jung's account," Roazen's argument continues, "it was Freud's affection for her that was worrisome, not an actual affair."[211]

Perhaps, but as we have seen, in Billinsky's original notes of his interview with Jung he writes that Minna told him she and Freud had had "sexual relations," which Billinsky softened in the published version to "their relationship was indeed very intimate."[212] This sounds like something more than feelings of "affection."

Roazen concludes that it is less important whether the two had an affair than to understand "the power [Minna] gained over him. ... Freud seemed to have a split in his love life, his sexuality remaining with Martha and his spiritual involvement shifting to Minna."[213] The facts do no not support Roazen's division. The shift appears to have occurred on the sexual level as well. It is not clear how Roazen is using the phrase "spiritual involvement" in this context. If he means shared intellectual interests, then certainly that shift from Martha to Minna occurred as well.

Elsewhere, however, Roazen seems to believe that the shift occurred on a sexual level as well. On the same page where he writes about Freud's "sexuality remaining with Martha," he also points out, as we have just seen, that the "evidence for the premature falling off in Freud's sex life" might be interpreted not only as a cooling of his ardor for Martha but as a transfer of his "physical and/or emotional needs" to Minna.[214]

It is not easy to differentiate Freud's homosexuality and heterosexuality when it comes to his interests in Minna. Two important psychic transformations seem to have taken place with regard to his feelings for her. A transformation of heterosexual affection from Martha to Minna. This much seems clear. But also a transformation of his sexual feelings for Fliess to Minna as well.

Didier Anzieu, the French psychoanalyst, has written on this subject. While, like Roazen, Anzieu feels that a sexual affair between Freud and Minna never developed, he does see the link between Freud's homosexual feelings for Fliess and their transformation into heterosexual feelings for Minna. Anzieu points out:

Freud never once mentions Minna in his [dream] associations despite the fact that she is manifestly involved in several of his dreams and that all other members of his family and close friends feature sooner or later in his analyses of dreams. Minna, then, is censored. That censorship materializes the incest taboo which must have operated between them throughout their lives.

And hence the reason Anzieu believes that Freud and Minna did not have sex together.

Anzieu's analysis continues: Freud's "upright, loyal and somewhat prim nature and the strict morals of the Jewish milieu in which he lived" are apparent, but

[they] did not stop him being aware of the sexual instinctual basis of his friendship and profound empathy with his sister-in-law, while

at the same time remaining determined to keep the consequences of that awareness strictly to himself. ... In 1900, then, Freud's sublimated homosexual friendship for Fliess was in its final phase, giving way, in his psychical economy, to a sublimated incestuous heterosexual friendship for Minna. This oscillation between a homosexual object and a heterosexual object reflects the notion of bi-sexuality ... much cherished by Fliess, and now in the process of being appropriated, at his expense, by Freud.[215]

I would present the formulation a bit more starkly than Anzieu. I think we can view Minna, in terms of Freud's affections for her, as something of a "She-Man"—strong, capable, commanding, intellectually astute, yet also empathetic, caring, companionable, and supportive in Freud's darkest days. In this sense, she could meet *all* of Freud's sexual needs, homo- as well as hetero-. Even Jones admits that Freud was drawn to women of what he calls "a more intellectual and perhaps masculine cast. Such women several times played a part in his life, accessory to his men friends though of a finer caliber." But, Jones emphasizes, "they had no erotic attraction for him."[216] This last contention is hard for me to believe.

Jones does admit that Minna was the most important of these intellectual/masculine women. The others, in chronological order: Emma Eckstein, Loe Kann, Lou Andreas-Salomé, Joan Riviere, and Marie Bonaparte. Peter Gay also talks about Freud savoring "the companionship and admiration of handsome, interesting, accomplished" women. He adds to Jones's list Hilda Doolittle, Helen Deutsch, Jeanne Lampl-de Groot, Ruth Mack Brunswick, and Freud's own daughter Anna.[217]

I think it is significant, at least as far as I am aware, that Freud is never drawn again to anyone of Martha's type: fragile, extremely feminine, passive, dainty, non-engaged. Opposites do attract. The question is for how long do they? In Freud's case, I would suggest, not for very long.

IN FREUD'S MIND

As we have seen, Freud's life was one long struggle. He felt battered and alone. He was desperately stretched financially. He had to see a certain number of patients each day just to keep his family afloat, just to pay bills. He had discovered some rather amazing ideas, concepts he knew were revolutionary, insights which could change our understanding of the nature of man, but no one seemed to want to take his ideas seriously. Worse, the medical establishment appeared more than happy to malign him— marginalize him; make fun of him; drive him into a deep, dark corner.

Some of this opposition can be attributed to the fact that he was Jewish, though he was a secular member of that religion. A lot more of it had to do with the mores of the period, the fact that Victorian prudery seemed to be so pervasive a part of social custom at the time. Talking of sex and its impact on human behavior was strictly taboo.

If all this wasn't bad enough, deep fissures began to appear in the foundations of his marriage. We will go into more detail about Freud's marriage in the next chapter. Suffice it to say here that while he may have loved Martha and appreciated everything she did for him and the family, he was no longer drawn to her romantically; she no longer interested or aroused him. She was too rigid, too interested in making and enforcing a variety of rules. And she thought many of his ideas were obscene. Can you imagine, his own wife thinking his ideas were obscene? He found it hard to talk to her about anything that was important to him outside of family matters.

I suspect he felt guilty about his relationship with Minna. He knew it was dangerous, perhaps diabolical as well. But he needed someone who would listen to him, share his struggles, empathize, offer solace, have the intelligence to realize what he was doing and why it was important. Fliess had been that person for a long time, but he began moving away from Freud, perhaps as a result of Ida Fliess's jealousy. Minna was not like that. She supported Freud from the beginning, and she continued to do so. She was also fun to be with: smart, creative, sardonic. She was strong where Martha was weak, colorful where Martha was bland. As suggested previously, perhaps she also liked to do adventuresome things in bed. We can never know what happens behind closed doors. Also, like Freud, Minna would not suffer fools—or indeed, anyone she did not like—gladly. And her attitude toward religion was as secular as Freud's, which he must have greatly appreciated, in sharp contrast to Martha's views—which, though she was forced to consciously repress them, were as orthodox as her mother's.[218] Given the pressure and stress, Freud could find solace in the arms of someone he trusted implicitly and who brought him great comfort.

Where was this relationship going? He didn't know, and perhaps it didn't matter. He (as well as Minna) felt they were superior people, in both an ethical and an intellectual sense. They were a class apart and could do things that ordinary people might be afraid to do. Their talent and knowledge, their elevated sensitivity and intellectuality, justified their actions.

POOR JUDGMENT

But why would Freud do something so fraught with peril, seemingly so "out of character" as having an affair with his own sister-in-law? In addition to feeling that he was superior and that, as a result, his actions were justified, the simple answer is that Freud often displayed *poor judgment* when it came to relationships, especially with those in which there was an "affective" attachment. For someone so intelligent and insightful, it is amazing how blind he could be when it came to certain friends; how much Freud could be a victim of wishful thinking and self-deception, like ordinary mortals. Hanns Sachs recalls that Freud

> had Adler made his successor in the presidential chair [of the Wednesday Psychological Society], a mistake which he repeated very soon afterwards on a larger scale by insisting on the installation of Jung as president of the newly founded International Association. ... This continuous series of errors in judging those around him seems out of keeping with Freud's reputation as one of the great psychologists for whom the mind should hold no secrets. ... He saw passionate zeal, strength, endurance, and high-minded motives where only a trace of these fine things existed.[219]

Freud had similar experiences with Breuer and later with Fliess. With Fliess, Freud seems to have greatly inflated his friend's abilities, even though he was no match for Freud intellectually, in order to make the relationship with his Berlin colleague seem all the more important. His reasoning seems to have been that if someone as "talented" as Fliess thought highly of his ideas, maybe they actually did have merit. Of course, at the time Freud was desperate for support from any quarter. He had none, except for the constant encouragement Minna provided and, after 1902, the interest shown by members of his Wednesday Psychological Society, most of whom, he eventually concluded, were not particularly talented. "All my Viennese won't amount to anything, except for little [Otto] Rank," Freud writes Karl Abraham in 1911.[220]

I think Freud's emotions could often get in the way of his reasoning, as Barry Silverstein has already pointed out.[221] A rational Freud would have thought twice about having an affair with his own sister-in-law; might never have even considered it. But an emotional Freud? Especially an emotionally needy Freud? That was a different matter. Reason and reality were no barriers. He seems to have followed his emotional needs wherever they might lead him; stayed with "friends" long after they were interested in keeping him close; acted frequently without regard to the possible consequences of his actions.

It is interesting that in Freud's highly-charged "emotional" relationships, and there were more than several, it was always the other person—Breuer, Fleischl (by dying), Fliess, Jung, Adler, Rank—who left Freud. He never left them, desperately holding onto these people even after everyone else could see that the relationships were no longer viable.

FROM MINNA'S PERSPECTIVE

Minna's feelings toward Freud were complex and sometimes contradictory. She appreciated what he did for her. She had no income and was entirely dependent upon him for support.[222] Although the custom of the time was to find a home for unmarried women of the family, Freud could have pushed her onto somebody else's lap, some blood relation such as her brother Eli who, as we know, along with Freud's sister Anna and their children, had emigrated to America. But Freud didn't do that. In fact, he did just the opposite, arguing that she *had* to join him and Martha at Berggasse. They wanted her; they needed her. In an April 28, 1887, letter we have previously referenced, Freud writes Minna, "we actually intend to keep you with us until you establish your own house. ... Martha is lonely, after all, and she misses you ... and no one can replace you."[223] Martha the dispensable one; Minna the indispensable one.

As mentioned, Freud seemed to quickly assume Ignaz's role after the latter died. He would be Minna's intellectual interlocutor, as Ignaz had been. He would take care of her as Ignaz would have, had he lived. Freud would keep the original "circle" together, or at least what remained of it. He recognized Minna's talents—her broad knowledge, her intellect, her remarkable capabilities—and sought to create a role for her commensurate with these. He built her up, made her feel important. He forgave her fractiousness, just as he forgave himself his own. His friends soon became her friends. Remember the greetings Freud's colleagues sent her? In the case of Karl Abraham, even Abraham's wife sent her greetings.[224]

And Minna gave a lot back to Freud in return for his generosity. She made his life more bearable. She was interesting, witty. She helped him relax. While Martha thought her husband's ideas were obscene, Minna was fascinated by them. Moreover, Minna seemed to instinctively understand Freud's needs, his pain, how much he felt life had hurt him. Anzieu writes:

> She [Minna] had not been worn out, like her sister, by household tasks and repeated pregnancies. She was more vivacious, wittier, and more intellectual. ... Sigmund found it easier to discuss his work with her than with his wife, easier to ask her to accompany him on his mountain excursions ... as she was unmarried and unattached, she must have been for Freud an available, desirable and prohibited libidinal object.[225]

I am not sure how "prohibited" Minna was, but available and desirable—those she certainly was.

Any notion that Minna might have been some passive, maiden aunt whose only role was to support Martha in her household duties, including helping supervise the children, does not comport with history, though she did do all those things as well. Yet she was also an accomplished person in her own right—aggressive, demanding, sexual, perhaps even predatory—at least in Esti Freud's eyes. Minna knew what she wanted and the steps needed in order to achieve her goals. She became a force to be reckoned with; in some ways a larger-than-life personality. Remember how Jones describes her in his biography of Freud: "One of the sons remarked to me that 'Tante Minna' deserved a book to herself, so interesting and decided was her personality."[226]

Large and commanding, we know Anna Freud, as she grew up, became jealous of her.[227] Anna felt Minna was too close to her father. She wanted Minna's role for herself. And eventually she got it. But that was years later. Anna was only an infant when Minna joined the Freud family in 1896 (Anna was born in 1895) and was only fifteen years old in 1910, no match at that point for the sharp-tongued, multitalented Minna and her forceful, brusque personality. Probably no match for Minna for some years beyond as well.[228]

Minna ceded command of the household to Martha but, pushing her sister to one side, assumed the more important and more valued role in Freud's eyes: intellectual confidante and muse. But her desires did not appear to stop there. She wanted to capture Freud in all his various manifestations—Freud the intellectual, Freud the revolutionary, most importantly, Freud the lover.

Yet she also must have felt guilty about the impact her rise to prominence within the family must have had on her dear sister. She loved Martha yet, at the same time, callously sought to steal her sister's husband—or at the very least, her husband's affection. That must have weighed heavily on her, and perhaps that is what she meant when she told Jung during his 1907 visit to Berggasse that she "was very much bothered by her relationship with Freud and felt guilty about it."[229] Her dilemma was clear: she was caught between her love for Freud and her love for Martha, with the former becoming stronger than the latter over time. This must have tormented her. No wonder she was willing to risk telling Jung her secret. She was desperate, anxiously seeking someone who would show her forgiveness, provide her with some measure of consolation; someone besides Freud who would tell her that what she was doing was all right. She needed someone to hear her "side" of the story. That love was not rational and could be demonic.

That it had a mind of its own. That she was as much a victim as Martha was. That none of this was her fault.

There may have been other reasons why she wanted to share her secret with Jung, an act which, objectively, was preposterously dangerous. Perhaps she wanted to signal to the new heir and successor that she was important, a key player in Freud's intellectual world, someone whom Jung needed to take seriously—and from what he saw of the relationship between Minna and Freud, he did not need much convincing.

While Minna was grateful and appreciative for all Freud had done for her and she reciprocated in numerous ways, she must also have felt angry, perhaps even bitter. While *de facto* Freud's confidante, lover, and second wife, she must have resented the fact that she was not his wife *de jure*. How frustrated she must have felt. This may be why she sometimes answered the telephone, "Frau Professor Freud." She felt that was her *rightful* title.

She might also have felt Freud owed her something more than she was getting. After all, she had devoted her whole life to him. Maybe their affair was winding down—had ended or was on its last legs. Perhaps Freud had less need for her now that he had Jung and was on the verge of gaining international recognition for psychoanalysis. He was fifty-one in 1907, while Minna was nine years younger. He always thought she was more energetic than he. Maybe he couldn't keep up with her continuing demands—emotional and sexual. It's hard to know precisely what motives were at work, but the very fact that she shared details of the affair with Jung—at a minimum, a frighteningly rash thing to do—suggests there was a good deal of anger and resentment simmering within her.

CHAPTER 6

FREUD AND MARTHA

The most important fact to remember regarding the Freud/Martha relationship was that it began in deep intimacy and was initially filled with scintillating romance, but by the early 1890s it had lost much of both. Even the ardent embraces and kisses had disappeared.[1] And by 1893, Freud indicates he was living in sexual abstinence,[2] with some sexual activity after that time.

DOMINATION AND SUBMISSION

Who was Martha? What was she like? She was small and delicate, patient and feminine, reserved and punctual. Above all, she was accommodating, displaying devotion and strict obedience. From the beginning, we see Freud dominating her to an unusual degree, demanding that she renounce many cherished traditions. He insisted that she turn her back on her Jewish cultural heritage. Her grandfather, you'll recall, had been the chief Rabbi of Hamburg, and her mother, Emmeline, was strictly orthodox. Freud forced the family to celebrate the Christian holidays, with the children painting Easter eggs and decorating a Christmas tree. Their son Martin Freud had no memory of him or his brothers and sisters ever going to a synagogue.[3]

In a family environment where everyone, with the exception of Minna, walked on eggshells, Martha reluctantly acquiesced to her husband's strict demands, which pleased him in one sense, but in another upset him. He wanted her to fight back, show spunk, but she could not. It was not in her nature. Yet the more she avoided standing up to him, the angrier he became. There was little room for Martha to find emotional peace in her relationship with her husband.

Compulsive, Martha sought refuge in household management tasks, where, because of her organizational skills, she shone and where she was able to substitute duty and hard work for the intimacy that was missing in her marriage.[4] She became Freud's gatekeeper extraordinaire, and home life settled into a rigid, invariable routine, if not always a pleasant one. Strict schedules were set up for breakfast, lunch, and dinner, as well as work and rest times, all with one specific goal in mind: to allow Freud time to work, think, and create.[5]

Freud sometimes bristled at his wife's rigidity and her devotion to cleanliness and perfect order, as well as her many rules, but he saw the dividends it paid for him in terms of his work—complete freedom from household duties and responsibilities. The German psychoanalyst Dr. Ernst Simmel commented drily on one occasion when visiting Freud that if he had a wife like Martha he too could have written all those books.[6] Managing the household was not only Martha's job but also Minna's when she joined the family, as well as that of several household servants whom the Freuds employed, though there is no doubt that Martha was in charge.

While Freud clearly appreciated Martha's hard work on behalf of the family, he seemed to keep her role narrowly circumscribed, excluding her from important family decisions. He rented their apartment at Berggasse 19 without ever consulting her. When she saw it, she was appalled—she thought the neighborhood a poor one, did not like the stone stairs, which she felt were dark, steep, and dangerous, and found the apartment too small for their growing family[7]—but she did not say anything. Also, he named their six children himself—after his friends, his relatives, or people he admired. But Martha did not protest; at least we are not aware that she did. It is not even clear if Freud ever consulted her.[8]

By the time Jung visited the Freuds in 1907, the effects of six pregnancies and the impact of years of stress were apparent in Martha's physical appearance. You'll recall Freud referred to her as his "rather elderly housewife," though she was only in her mid-forties at the time. "Completely extinguished," was Jung's judgment when he first encountered her.[9]

CONTROL: SON AS MASTER

How could such an awkward and cold relationship, one apparently devoid of affection, develop between two intelligent and well-meaning people—both of whom at one time loved each other dearly? It has its roots in Freud's boyhood and the special role young Sigmund assumed in his parents' household.

Freud's parents saw their son, Martin Freud tells us, as an extraordinary child, gifted, "destined to become famous," a person for whom "no sacrifice was too great."[10] Freud was the eldest child, and Ernest Jones believes that was significant, "since an eldest child differs, for better or worse, from other children. It may give such a child a special sense of importance and responsibility," which Jones sees being facilitated by "his mother's love and, indeed, adoration."[11] Helen Walker Puner makes a similar point. She sees Freud's overindulgent mother granting the young boy privileges "as naturally and inevitably as if they had been part of his birthright ... his mother's devotion was so complete that she could not bring herself to deny him anything, even when his wishes and needs came into conflict with those of the rest of the family."[12]

It seems only natural "that this immensely promising young man should be declared the family favorite," Peter Gay points out. The family "accepted Freud's boyish imperiousness with equanimity and fostered his sense of being exceptional." Like Puner, Gay also sees Freud always getting his own way: "If Freud's needs clashed with those of ... others, his prevailed without question ... the Freuds' golden boy could do no wrong—and did no wrong."[13]

Years later, Ernest Jones remembers finding it strange as a young Freudian disciple visiting Vienna to hear Freud's mother Amalie "refer to the great Master as 'mein goldener Sigi,'" obvious evidence of the close relationship between mother and son.[14] And Martin Freud relates how anxious Freud's mother would become when her princely son did not appear promptly at her Leopoldstadt apartment on such important occasions as Christmas and New Year's Eve, recalling:

[A]s the evening went on, an atmosphere of growing crisis was felt by all as Amalie became unsettled and anxious. ... My father always came to these gatherings ... but his working day was a long one and he always came much later than any one else. Amalie knew this, but perhaps it was a reality she could never accept. Soon she would be seen running anxiously to the door and out to the landing to stare down the staircase. Was he coming? Where was he? Was it not getting very late? This running in and out might go on for an hour, but it was known that any attempt to stop her would produce an outburst of anger which it was better to avoid.[15]

Gay points out that it wasn't only Freud's mother who showed pride and complete faith in young Sigmund's abilities; it was also Freud's father, Jakob Freud, who saw his son's talents emerge at a tender age. On Sigmund's thity-fifth birthday, Jakob presented his son with his own Bible. In it was an inscription in Hebrew, which in English read, "It was in the seventh year of your age that the spirit of God began to move you to learning."[16]

Freud's young and proud mother felt certain her son was destined for greatness. She even had "evidence" to prove it. Freud tells us that at the time of his birth an old peasant woman had prophesied that "with her first-born child she [his mother] had brought a great man into the world," and several years later, when Freud was eleven or twelve and the family was sitting at a café in the Prater one evening, a poetaster, who was going from table to table devising verses to delight visiting families, assured the impressionable Freuds that one day their son would someday attain the rank of Cabinet Minister, which at that point in Austro-Hungarian history was indeed possible for a Jewish boy to achieve.[17]

Later, Freud recognized the psychological impact that a mother's favored treatment could have on the eventual success of the child: "A man who has been the indisputable favorite of his mother keeps for life the feeling of a conqueror," he writes, "that confidence of success that often induces real success."[18]

PRIVILEGES

With Freud's favored status came certain privileges, which must have made him the envy of the family. No matter how strained his parents' financial circumstances and crowded their quarters, young Sigmund always had a room of his own. In 1875 the Freud family moved into a six-room apartment. Freud's brother Alexander, his five sisters, and his parents crowded into three bedrooms, yet young Sigmund still had a room of his own. Anna Freud Bernays, Sigmund's sister, describes Freud's so-called "cabinet" as "a single room separated from the rest of the apartment. This cabinet, long and narrow, with a window looking on the street" was where Sigmund "lived and worked until he became an interne in the General City Hospital. All through the years of his school and university life, the only thing that changed in this room was the increasing number of crowded bookcases added to the writing desk, bed, chairs and shelf which furnished it." Even as a teenager, Anna Bernays continues, her brother "did not join us at our evening meals, but took them alone in the room where he pored endlessly over his books."[19]

The allure of the "cabinet" for Freud is apparent in how difficult it was for him to separate himself from it even after he was no longer living at home. Martin Freud remembers: "The cabinet in the humble flat in the Leopoldstadt reserved for the favorite son was not abandoned when my father went to live at the hospital in Vienna. He returned to it for week-ends and, according to my Aunt Anna, many of his friends came to see him there."[20]

Perhaps this is the beginning of Freud's sense of extraterritoriality. His "cabinet" was part of the overall Freud apartment yet also decidedly apart from it. In addition to his own room, Freud had an oil lamp for himself, while those in the other bedrooms had to use messy candles.[21]

A third privilege was that young Freud had the right to lecture his younger siblings about life and discipline them at times, so even as a boy he was already playing the authoritarian father, a role he would hone to perfection within his own family some years later. Some of this was playing the big brother role—helping his siblings with their school lessons, inform-ing them about what was happening in the world at large.[22] Yet at the same time young Freud could display a certain strictness—a priggish attitude which had a lasting impact upon at least one sister. Martin Freud recalls:

> According to my Aunt Paula [Freud's sister], he could show severity if he found them erring. He caught Paula herself spending money in a sweet shop, something she was, apparently, not supposed to do. She was admonished with so much severity that fifty years later she had neither forgiven nor forgotten it when she told the story to the small schoolboy son [that is, Martin Freud] of the respected, and feared, big brother.[23]

The feared big brother also censored what his siblings might want to read. "Not only did he read a great deal himself," Anna Freud Bernays recalls,

> but he exercised definite control over my reading. If I had a book that seemed to him improper for a girl of my age, he would say, "Anna, it is too early to read that book now." When I was fifteen, I remember, he felt that I should not read Balzac and Dumas. I read them, of course, notwithstanding, hiding the forbidden volumes among the linens.[24]

He even instructed his siblings with regard to social niceties. Ernest Jones writes: "In a letter of July 1876, to his sister Rosa, four years younger than himself ... he warned her against having her head turned by a slight social success."[25]

"He was an attentive but somewhat authoritarian brother," Peter Gay has noted, "his didactic streak was marked from his school days on."[26] This authoritarian behavior was out of tune with the democratic and liberal environment promoted by his father Jakob. Jakob had established a "Family Council" in which he consulted the children regarding various family decisions. One "Council" verdict came up with the name "Alexander" for the last Freud child, a suggestion proposed by Sigmund. At the time he was captivated by the exploits of Alexander the Great.[27]

TWO CHARACTERISTICS

Two personality characteristics of the young Freud, both fostered by the overindulgent atmosphere created by his parents, seem to have been fixed in these early years: a need to control his environment (and the people within it) and an inflexibility of purpose. These would have both positive and negative consequences for Freud and those around him, and would become even more pronounced when he assumed the role of head of his own family when he married Martha.

One early story features both characteristics. His sister Anna recalls:

When I was eight years old, my mother, who was very musical, wanted me to study the piano, and I began practicing by the hour. Though Sigmund's room was not near the piano, the sound disturbed him. He appealed to my mother to remove the piano if she did not wish him to leave the house altogether.

I would say this was more a threat than an appeal. In any case, Anna continues, "the piano disappeared and with it all opportunities for his sisters to become musicians."[28]

This set the Freuds apart, but not in a good way. Peter Gay notes: "The Freuds must have been among the very few middle-class Central European families without a piano, but that sacrifice faded in face of the glorious career they imagined for the studious, lively schoolboy in his cabinet."[29]

Martin Freud adds an interesting note regarding what he terms his father's "inflexible demand that no piano be played in the flat," no matter the consequences:

He had his way then and, I might mention here, he had his way later when he had a home of his own. ... There was never a piano in the Berggasse and not one of his children learnt to play an instrument.

This was unusual in Vienna then and would probably be thought unusual today: because to be able to play the piano is considered an essential part of middle-class education.[30]

Thus the decision not to have a piano had social consequences. That "essential part of middle-class education" was probably most important to Freud's sisters, who might have feared they would appear less attractive in the eyes of potential suitors compared with young ladies who did play the piano, which was to say, just about all of their contemporaries.

CONTROL: FATHER AS MASTER

The Sigmund-centric world of his youth did not have to miss a beat when Freud married Martha. He was still the center of the universe around which everyone else circled and for whose benefit everyone else worked tirelessly.

Freud's autocratic stamp was obvious to everyone within the Freud household, as he continued to tightly control the environment at Berggasse. He hated "noise," as we have already witnessed with regard to his sister's piano playing. But his dislike extended beyond the sounds emanating from musical instruments. Like most physicians at the turn of the century, the Freuds had a telephone installed when it became available. But Freud could not stand the ringing. "My father hated the telephone and avoided its use whenever possible," Martin Freud recalls. "As everything in our home was arranged to harmonize with his wishes, all precautions were taken to save him from using it."[31] Freud also hated bicycles and motorcycles, when they appeared in the early part of the century.[32] I can understand his dislike of motorcycles because of the noise they produce, but it is puzzling that he would also dislike bicycles.

Martin Freud tells us noisy radios also posed a threat when they became generally available. None appeared in his father's part of the flat or in the family living room.[33] The same was true of record players. Only Minna was allowed to have one of these bothersome things, and it was banished to the far reaches of the flat.[34]

It was as if Freud wanted to keep Berggasse as quiet as a mausoleum and as private. He even insisted on controlling his family's movements in and out when patients were visiting Berggasse. "Family members were not supposed to leave the apartment when patients might be arriving or departing," Paul Roazen writes, "the family was expected to exercise discretion."[35] How they would actually know when patients were arriving or departing is not clear, but there must have been some overall schedule of appointments that was shared with family members. Perhaps this was another household task handled by Martha.

"The whole household revolved around Freud's work," Paul Roazen writes further, "and he was a man with predictable rituals." Anything out of the ordinary roused anxiety and discomfort. "This need for control extended from the most insignificant detail—the use of a particular coffee-cup, for example—to the most important part of his life. ... Each activity, which cup he favored ... would be avidly reported within the family."[36] He also kept guard lest Jewish traditions enter into life at Berggasse, to the deep dismay of Martha.[37]

As head and master of the family, Freud's powers extended far beyond the confines of Berggasse. With regard to travel, Freud insisted that he be the one to choose the destination for the family's summer holiday each year, and he worked diligently at this task. Remember what Martin had said: "The selection of a family summer holiday resort was always father's duty."[38] And when the family was under financial pressure, arrangements were made that he alone travelled in comfort while Martha, Minna, the children, and whatever servants they took along travelled third class. Martin Freud again:

> In Austria in those days a third-class compartment could only offer hard wooden benches; but mother, with the help of rugs, cushions and pillows, soon turned the shabby place into luxurious sleeping-quarters with quite a home atmosphere. ... She always calculated precisely how many children could be fitted comfortably along the seats and, if there were surplus children, a hammock or two might be slung. She and the nurse, if any, huddled themselves in corners.

Martha, always the dutiful protector, made certain that Sigmund travelled "alone and in comfort," Martin informs us. Presumably first class. Freud apparently did not complain about this special arrangement.[39]

He also lectured members of his family about what they should or should not do regarding a variety of subjects, as rigorously as he had lectured his siblings in his parents' apartment years before. There was no doubt as to who was boss in the Freud family.[40] Helen Walker Puner writes: "Just as the sons of his spirit in psychoanalytic circles were expected to accept his dictates without exception, so his own children were expected to accede to his authority. At home, as abroad, his word was the law."[41]

You'll remember that Freud banned medicine as a profession for his sons.[42] When Martin wanted to enter the cavalry as part of his national military service, he also ran up against his father's strict demands. Martin

recalls, "But father objected firmly … and I had, in consequence, to abandon the idea."[43]

Freud's need to control even reached to Martin's wife, Esti. Paul Roazen
writes:

> Freud himself was so patriarchally in charge of those around him that
> he was hard to challenge. He convinced Esti not to choose for his
> grandchildren the pediatrician she had had as a child, for he objected
> to the man's having published some premature scientific findings
> which had not been validated. … Esti told me, drawing a deep breath,
> that she would not have dared to oppose Freud's will, despite her
> appreciation of her own pediatrician.[44]

Freud was even more dictatorial during his four-year engagement to
Martha, if that can be imagined. Here his behavior was characterized by
intense, often irrational jealousy. "He had already informed her [Martha]
that she must expect to belong entirely to his family and no longer to her
own," Ernest Jones writes.[45] "Freud was a tyrannical, jealous lover," Lisa
Appignanesi and John Forrester point out in their book *Freud's Women*.
Freud was intent on "possessing [Martha] exclusively, repeating his childhood desire to eliminate all rivals from the field and recapture the original
and singular adoring relation to his mother."[46]

Freud's "intermittent bouts of jealousy at times bordered on the pathological in their intensity, their sheer irrational anger," Peter Gay has
commented.[47] Freud demanded that Martha forsake all others for him,
including former admirers Max Meyer and Fritz Wahle,[48] as well as her
mother and her brother Eli. Even the docile, accommodating Martha could
not agree to turn her back on her own mother and brother. Her failure to
do so, Gay believes, "generated strains that took years to dissipate."[49]

Freud's dictatorial bullying was not something he was proud of; nor, on
the other hand, was it a characteristic he felt he needed to hide. It was just
part of who he was. As he candidly reveals to Martha in a letter of August
22, 1883: "I am afraid I do have a tendency toward tyranny, as someone
recently told me. … I let myself go in a kind of youthful high spirits of
immaturity, which used to be quite alien to me." Freud again on August
29, 1883, also to Martha: "I must admit to myself that I do have a tyrannical streak in my nature and that I find it terribly difficult to subordinate
myself."[50]

The net result of Freud's godlike persona within the family—Martin
Freud describes his father periodically coming down from his "Olympian
heights" when something might require his attention[51]—meant that Freud

did absolutely nothing around the house and was not required to. Martin Freud believes that there was only one occasion in his father's entire life when he went shopping for groceries for the family, and that was an emergency situation. The family was on holiday in Berchtesgaden when severe flooding cut them off from their supply of food.[52]

MARTHA THE FACILITATOR

For her part Martha worked diligently to protect her husband from anything that might interrupt or divert him from the main task at hand—the focus on his work—and her efforts tended to heighten his role as family master and lord. The relationship between husband and wife became what Martha's biographer Katja Behling calls one of "authority and submission."[53]

"Martha arranged the life of the house so as not to disturb her husband," Paul Roazen writes:

> The apartment was unusually quiet, especially considering the number of people it housed, and the family's life revolved around his work. Martha did far more for Freud than was usual even in those times. Much of Freud's own fastidiousness may have come from Martha's compulsive orderliness.[54]

Martin Freud's wife Esti confirms the unusual nature of just how far Martha went to subordinate herself to her husband and his needs. She told Roazen that it was "definitely not the custom of the time for a wife to extend herself as much as Martha had"; that her own mother "would not have dreamt of doing the things for her [Esti's] father that 'Mama' did for Freud."[55]

And how far did Martha's help go? "Early riser as he was," Katja Behling points out, "Freud is even said to have been given a helping hand [by Martha] in getting washed and dressed in the mornings. Martha had his clothes brushed and laid out ready for him, and rumour had it she would even put the toothpaste on his brush for him."[56] The toothpaste story might not have been apocryphal. "A disciple of Freud's once saw that Martha had put toothpaste on Freud's toothbrush," Paul Roazen reports.[57]

And Martha made certain that her husband was dressed to perfection. Although parsimonious in most everything pertaining to the family, such was not the case when it came to "dressing" Sigmund. Martin Freud recalls:

> My mother, who ordered all my father's clothes, tried to reach absolute perfection, always taking the greatest care in ordinary well-cut clothes made from British cloth. Thus he appeared as respectable

[during our summer holidays] as he did in Vienna in his dark suits and black ties.[58]

And Freud liked to dress well. He saw it as a matter of self-respect and being consistent with the "deeply entrenched medical tradition that a doctor should be well turned out," Martin tell us.[59]

Helen Walker Puner suggests Martha's care for her husband constituted a re-creation of Freud's mother's earlier care for him. "Martha Freud organized the household to revolve around the convenience of *der Papa*, as the children referred to their father," Puner writes:

> the household and all who lived in it were rigidly regimented to move only in their prescribed orbits around the sun who was *der Papa* ... she would provide for him ... the same care and devotion to his physical comfort which his mother had shown him. And with his wife, as with his mother, the first women in his life, he would come first. His needs, his desires, his wishes would remain, as in his mother's house, the pivot around which the rest of the family, including his wife, revolved.[60]

But Martha's personal care for her husband was only part of the regimen she established at Berggasse. Every aspect of domestic life seems to have been similarly organized and regulated. Martin Freud remembers the rigid details concerning the daily family lunch, or *Mittagessen*. Martha "believed in punctuality in all things, something then unknown in leisurely Vienna," he writes:

> There was never any waiting for meals: at the stroke of one everybody in the household was seated at the long dining-room table and at the same moment one door opened to let the maid enter with the soup while another door opened to allow my father to walk in from his study to take his place at the head of the table facing my mother at the other end.[61]

Apparently Freud's entrance was accompanied by the sound of a gong, commensurate with his stately position. "The double door to the dining-room would open," Katja Behling writes,

> and Martha and the six children would enter and take their seat at table. Freud would enter the room on the stroke of a gong, sitting down at the opposite end of the table to Martha. The maid would appear

and start to serve the food. If one of the children was missing, Freud would briefly look at the empty seat before pointing at it silently with his knife or fork and giving his wife a quizzical glance—whereupon Martha would explain the whereabouts of the absent child.[62]

Apparently the gong was often the last loud sound that anyone heard at *Mittagessen*, for Freud was a rather taciturn, silent man when he ate. "He often seemed lost in thought or would be closely studying some new acquisition from his collection of antiques," Behling tells us.[63]

If life at Berggasse was a form of theatre, it needed a large supporting cast, and Martha had one in the form of more than several servants, as I briefly mentioned earlier. Martin Freud recalls:

> We had as long as I can remember a *Herrschaftsköchin*, a cook who did no work outside her kitchen; there was a housemaid who waited at table and also received father's patients. There was a governess for the elder children and a nanny for the younger, while a charwoman came each day to do the rough work.[64]

In later years, Martha's emphasis on order, cleanliness, and regulation became extreme, and her behavior seemed a frightening exaggeration of her earlier compulsive self. Peter Gay tells the story about Martha regularly objecting when Dr. Max Schur, Freud's last attending physician, mussed up the bed while examining her husband.[65] Also, Martha developed the habit of bringing to the dinner table a pitcher of hot water and a special napkin in case anyone might soil the table cloth so she could quickly get rid of the offending stain; and her annoyance with the ashes from Freud's constant cigar-smoking was so noticeable that it was commented upon among Freud's followers at the time.[66]

When the family moved to London, Martha once gave some motherly advice to Melanie Klein's daughter Melitta Schmideberg, who was a young analyst at the time. Martha pointed out how important it was to water flowers every day at the same time.[67] Paul Roazen points out that in the later years, "Freud's students tended to make fun of Martha as a pedantic housewife."[68]

Both Ernest Jones and Peter Gay have a special take on Martha and her peculiar behavior as head of the domestic side of the Freud household. They feel she transcended the typical *Hausfrau* role. "There can have been few more successful marriages," Jones writes:

> Martha certainly made an excellent wife and mother. She was an admirable manager—the rare kind of woman who could keep

servants indefinitely[69]—but she was never the kind of *Hausfrau* who put things before people. Her husband's comfort and convenience always ranked first. In the early years he used to discuss his cases with her in the evening, but later on it was not to be expected that she should follow the roaming flights of his imagination any more than most of the world could.[70]

Martha Freud was not "simply a model *Hausfrau*," Peter Gay writes, though he admits she "makes a rather shadowy figure ... her surviving or accessible traces are sparse." Yet he feels comfortable enough to say that "her contribution to family life was far more than dutiful, unpaid, essential drudgery." She was at once

> kind and firm, effective and thoughtful about the all-important domestic details and no less important travel arrangements, capable of reassuring self-control, never rattled. Her insistence on punctuality (a quality which, her son Martin observed, was rare in casual Vienna), gave the Freud household its air of dependability.

Gay goes on to describe Martha as "the complete bourgeoise. Loving and efficient with her family, she was weighed down by an unremitting sense of her calling to domestic duty, and severe with lapses from middle-class morality." She was not "a companion for her husband on his long and lonely progress toward psychoanalysis. She assisted Freud in ways natural to her by presiding over a domestic setting in which he could be at ease, partly by letting him take most of it for granted."[71]

I am puzzled why Jones and Gay insist that Martha need be something more than a *Hausfrau*, as if being a *Hausfrau*, and a competent one, might not have been a sufficient role for her. Does having a traditional *Hausfrau* as wife somehow taint the reputation of the husband, one of the greatest thinkers of the twentieth century? I don't think it does, but perhaps for some it might. And for Jones to say that Martha was "never the kind of *Hausfrau* who put things before people," is simply not true, as long as we're willing to accept the stories about the messed-up bed sheets (in the case of Dr. Schur) and removing stains on the dining room tablecloth (in the case of possibly numerous dinner guests).

And if Martha was not the dutiful and often rigid *Hausfrau* as they maintain, why did Freud often feel irritated (and even embarrassed) by her behavior? Certainly castigating Dr. Schur for messing the bed must have been embarrassing to Freud, and he must have found at least annoying her constant complaints about his dropping cigar ashes all over the apartment.

Bringing hot water to the dining table for spot removal must also have appeared eccentric, both to Freud and to many others.

It is obvious that there were occasions when she took her duties too seriously. Appignanesi and Forrester tell us that soon after their marriage Martha was already scolding Freud for "his messy disruption of the domestic order she imposed,"[72] so much so that he could describe himself in a January 24, 1887, letter to Minna as henpecked: "My wife scolds only when I spill something or leave something lying about in disorder, or when I lead her across a filthy spot on the street. It is generally said that I am henpecked. What should one do against that?"[73] Obviously, avoid filthy spots in the street. This was a year after they were married.

We know that Anna Freud, who never got along with Martha, complained of her mother's obsessive regularity. She found her mother "too controlling." Anna is said to have sarcastically remarked, "My mother observed no rules, she made her own rules."[74]

While Freud was irritated, there is evidence that he was also trying to be understanding. Paul Roazen notes in his *Freud and His Followers*: "As one [Freud] pupil put it, 'there was an air of understanding forgiveness for her [Martha's] increasingly pedantic attitudes.'"[75]

Remember how embarrassed Freud was about Martha when the Jungs first visited Berggasse in 1907 and what he said about her: "I am sorry that I can give you no real hospitality; I have nothing at home but an elderly wife."[76] While at the time Martha was only in her mid-forties, perhaps she looked "elderly" by then—six pregnancies and the constant tension of having to meet a demanding husband's requirements for quiet and absolute order. Apparently she also failed to keep up her appearance, according to Peter Gay: "Once married, she took little time to attend to whatever beauty she possessed."[77] Given the breadth of her responsibilities, and the constant demands that they be met, perhaps her looks became the least of her priorities.

WALLS

In this mélange of master and obedient wife, several metaphorical walls were erected. One was massive and surrounded the entire Freud household. Anyone not part of the family was excluded from entering its gates. This included not only eager historians and snoopy biographers, but even close disciples of Freud, people such as Hanns Sachs. This wall I term Fortress Freud, a foreboding edifice which will be discussed in more detail in our concluding chapter.

A second wall Freud constructed around himself. In it he lived his own regimented, sheltered life, able to focus exclusively on research, writing, and, most importantly, the movement to which he gave birth, psychoanalysis. To enter this world required Freud's permission. Minna got it regularly. Martha and the children received it infrequently, if ever.

A third wall surrounded Martha and her life. It provided her sanctuary. It defined a small but important universe where she was queen and where she could gain a measure of self-respect she could not find elsewhere. Martha controlled this world with as much ruthless determination as Freud did his.

Within Freud's demarcated area, quiet, hard work, and the discovery and discussion of ideas prevailed. It was a severe, isolated place, where activities were planned down to the minute and nothing was allowed to distract—not even pleasure. Hanns Sachs recalls: "He [Freud] had eliminated almost everything that did not fit in with his planned life. Visits, social calls, and parties did not exist for him."[78] And there was a fierceness in this world which took the form of what Sachs calls a "magnificent pride." To Sachs that helped explain "what seemed otherwise a glaring contradiction: he [Freud] was kind without softness, benevolent yet not compassionate. Having hardened himself like a lancet of finest steel he had little sympathy for those who were weak and cringing. … He was disdainful of people who lived by half measures."[79] Does Sachs mean people like Martha? We shall shortly see.

Behind Freud's wall emotions were severely constrained. Martin Freud tells us that his "father's perfect self-control seldom, or never, permitted him to show emotion."[80] The Freud family did not show feelings openly; they were not warm; they did not hug and kiss.[81] Freud apparently felt awkward expressing feelings to his children or, really, anyone close to him.[82] His nephew Harry remembers his uncle as "always on very friendly terms with his children" but not "expansive … always a bit *formal* and *reserved*" (Emphasis Harry's). Indeed, "it rarely happened that he kissed any of them; I might almost say, really never. And even his mother, whom he loved very much, he only kissed perforce at parting."[83] It is difficult to know how different the Freuds were from the average Austrian bourgeois family at the time, but Harry Freud's recollections seem to suggest his uncle exercised unusually tight control over his feelings.

Aggressive and driven, Freud found it hard to relax—at home, anyway. On holiday with the children he could, at least at times, "abandon his usual reserve and even … become a little playful," according to Martin Freud's reminiscences.[84] He could even become a bit less formal. "He drank from the actual bottle instead of using the small flat aluminium beaker he

carried in his waistcoat pocket," Martin remembers. "He removed his tie
and unbuttoned his collar. He did not, however, go so far as to take off
his coat."[85] Given Freud's reticence, that would have certainly been going
too far.

Holidays were also when the children got a chance to see him, because
at home they rarely did. Martin Freud again: "we children saw little of our
father when, for much of the year, he worked for anything from sixteen to
eighteen hours a day."[86] Katja Behling describes Freud as "a ghostly half-
presence at home, busy at work in the remotest rooms of their spacious
flat."[87] And Peter Roazen notes: "the consensus among Freud's followers
seemed to be that he had spent an inadequate amount of time with his
children."[88]

In reading Martin Freud's memoir of his father, *Sigmund Freud: Man
and Father*, it struck me that most of the book was about Martin rather
than his father. I soon realized why: Martin didn't really see much of his
father. He saw him primarily during the holidays, much less frequently at
home. And he saw him only for those initial weeks at the beginning of the
holidays when Freud was with the family. Yet, even when Martin did see
him, he seemed standoffish and cool.

In his book Martin reproduces several letters his father sent him while
Martin was in the Austrian army during World War I. They seem rather
formal and distant and are signed "Most cordial greetings," or "I greet you
cordially and look forward to your reply," as if they were impersonal business letters. Martin senses this coolness himself and seeks to explain his
father's attitude to the reader:

> I am aware that these samples of my father's letters to me can have
> little interest to those who merely know him as a name; they are not
> adorned with any expressions of affection and certainly not of sen-
> timent. His letters were nearly always very much to the point and
> severely practical.

Nevertheless, Martin concludes, he knew "full well" that his father "was
deeply concerned about the dangers he believed I was facing and the priva-
tions he was certain I was exposed to."[89]

Although I do not doubt that Freud loved Martin and was concerned for
his safety, I wonder how Martin *knew* his father felt that way. The letters are
devoid of warmth and feeling. So, too, were Freud's actions when Martin
was about to return to the Russian front following a period of leave during the First World War. Hanns Sachs was a witness: "Freud was quite …
undemonstrative in emotional situations," Sachs tells us; "I saw him taking

leave of his oldest son [Martin] who, after a short furlough, returned to the front in Russia, by no means a safe place for an artillery officer. After a 'good-bye' and a hearty handshake Freud turned to me and continued our conversation."

Later, Sachs continues, he had occasion to observe just how much Freud's children meant to him, though Sachs does not provide details.[90] It is obvious Freud loved his children and Martha as well, in his own sort of way, but simply could not express that love openly. But if you don't tell someone you love him, how does that person really know?

The result of this lack of affection is summed up well by Peter Gay: "In the midst of a lively, crowded household, Freud was alone."[91] Just how alone he felt is revealed in a December 8, 1895, letter he writes to Fliess: "When I see your handwriting again, those are moments of great joy, which allow me to forget much of my loneliness and privation."[92] This was sent shortly after the birth of his daughter Anna, which should have been an occasion for joy. But apparently not. According to Gay, while Freud could cherish his family, his family did not "assuage his dismaying sense of isolation." That, Gay believes, was Fliess's task.[93] I would add that it was Minna's task as well, all the more so after the turn of the century when Freud and Fliess went their separate ways.

During his engagement to Martha, with her far away in Wandsbek, Freud lamented that he could not kiss her, which he obviously wanted to do at the time. In a letter dated January 22, 1884, he suggests, apparently half-jokingly, cigar smoking as a substitute: "Smoking is indispensable if one has nothing to kiss."[94] We know from Hanns Sachs that Freud smoked at least twenty cigars a day; he was a "chain-smoker in the fullest sense of the word." Sachs tells us that Freud was so fond of smoking that he was irritated when men around him did not smoke. Given the power of Freud's personality, "nearly all who formed the inner circle became more or less passionate cigar-smokers."[95] All alone in his study, a ready supply of cigars might have provided Freud all the romantic affection he could get without having to deal with real people and express intimate, personal feelings, both of which he obviously did not feel comfortable doing.

Behind Martha's wall there was less loneliness, because there were more people. The children, the servants, Aunt Minna—she served both Martha and Freud. This was because managing people was one of the key features of Martha's world, and Martha was more sociable than Freud and could adapt better on an interpersonal level.

Ostensibly Martha did everything she could to spare her husband the worries of everyday life and allow him the time he needed to do his work. This is what, from the outside, she seemed to be doing, and that is how she justified the rigid schedule she set up for daily household activities at Berggasse. She certainly received great kudos for doing that—at least from those outside the Freud family. To those within, especially Freud and certainly Anna Freud, she seemed, as previously pointed out, to go too far at times.

The question is, why? She appears to have acted so on purpose, though perhaps not consciously. Her behavior was saying, "If you want rules and regulations, boy will I give you rules and regulations." It was her way of expressing her anger while at the same time appearing to be helpful. Freud was an overpowering figure. She was no match for him. But he had hurt her deeply by stripping away her cherished beliefs as well as cherished friends. She must have been furious. But how does someone as docile as Martha confront such a formidable husband? Not by frontally attacking him, certainly. So she was forced to use deception—causing him pain while ostensibly trying to protect him. Making regimentation at Berggasse a caricature of what reasonable regimentation might have been. It was the only way for her to get even, preserve whatever self-esteem remained following her often bitter battles with him to define what family life would be like in their marriage.

In the end, Martha's efforts were only partially successful. She certainly gained Freud's respect by efficiently organizing his life and the life of the household, but it did not gain what she really wanted from him, and that, or course, was his love and affection. A love and affection she desperately needed and which he, for whatever reason, was unable or unwilling to provide.

CONSEQUENCES

The problem with walls, even metaphorical ones, is that they bring consequences. They have emotional costs. They stifle communication, wreak havoc with feelings, make people keep grievances to themselves, where they fester. Separation may have helped Freud and Martha in one sense. It allowed them space for their feelings; it helped keep conflict on the surface to a minimum. But it provided a false safety. In one way or the other, those pent-up emotions would find expression. They often seemed to do so in the form of psychosomatic illnesses.

Martha suffered from severe migraines and vomiting fits,[96] as well as intestinal colic and severe menstrual pain.[97] Some three months after the birth of her daughter Anna in late 1895, Martha developed a writing block. Freud mentions this in a March 7, 1896, letter to Fliess. He calls it a *Schreiblähmung*.[98] Katja Behling comments: "It was as though she had been robbed of the power of the (written) word, and was no longer in full possession of a means of communication and a creative possibility for self-expression and self-disclosure."

Behling asks: Was this a form of resistance, a way for Martha to withdraw into herself? I assume Behling means a form of resistance with regard to her domineering husband. Behling, who is a trained psychotherapist, points out that "A 'writing paralysis' characterized by manifest motor failure would bring Martha's short-term symptom complex close to a conversion neurosis, the sort of disorder from the tradition of classical hysteria where a mental experience produces a somatic manifestation."[99]

Remember, this was about the same time Freud was writing to Fliess, telling him of his "loneliness and privation." To describe the emotional lives of both Freud and Martha as mentally distraught at that time would not be an exaggeration, even though Martha had just given birth to a healthy baby girl. Something else is obviously amiss in the Freud marriage, something of an emotionally debilitating sort. Perhaps post-partum depression on Martha's part, though it is not clear what the cause is. But walls do not help.

Freud also suffered from psychosomatic illnesses: like Martha, digestive troubles and migraines, but also rheumatic pains, fear of travelling, fatigue, various heart conditions (perhaps psychosomatic), incontinence (as we have seen in his trip to America)—but especially depression. Dismayed over the tepid reception his beloved *The Interpretation of Dreams* was receiving and the lack of success he was having at the time with several patients, he writes openly of his depression in a letter to Fliess dated March 11, 1900:

> For two months I have not written a single line of what I have learned or surmised. ... You know how limited my pleasures are. I am not allowed to smoke anything decent; alcohol does nothing for me; I am done begetting children; and I am cut off from contact with people. So I vegetate harmlessly.[100]

Even the children were not immune from somatic disturbances apparently related to emotional dysfunction. Katja Behling tells us that with the exception of Freud's eldest child, Mathilde, all the Freud children had serious lisps, which, according to Anna Freud, severely impaired their performance at school. The impediments were so acute that the children's teachers complained to the Freuds that something needed to be done about the problem. A speech therapist was brought in to help.[101]

There were long-term impacts as well. While Anna Freud would go on to a successful career, "not all the Freud children," Behling writes, "were

equally successful in emerging from the overpowering shadow cast by the.
father."[102] The Freud genius, however, would reappear a generation later.
Martin's son Lucian would become the preeminent British painter of his
time, and his other son, Clement (later Sir Clement), a famous journalist
and chef who served as aide to Field Marshall Montgomery during the Second World War. Still later, Martin's grandson David would become Baron
Freud, a British journalist, businessman, politician and Parliamentary
Undersecretary of State.

FROM FREUD'S POINT OF VIEW

While Freud wanted to mold Martha in ways he thought would make
her and their marriage better, he was only able to achieve mixed results. He
appears to have found her lacking in several respects, certainly as a wife
and perhaps as a person as well. One wonders, in retrospect, just how good
a fit they were for each other.

Love, for Freud, meant conflict and struggle, to be followed by the joy of
making up. In a January 16, 1884, letter to Martha, he lays out a prescrip-
tion for what he feels the best sort of relationship would be for them: "I
would love to have a good squabble with you. It wasn't so bad ... to read
something every month that came from the depths of passion. When you
are mine we must have a little quarrel at least once a week, so that your love
can always start fresh again."[103] Or, to put it another way, Freud "wanted to
goad her [Martha] into opposition, to provoke her, in order then to lavish
her with affection."[104]

On their honeymoon on the Baltic coast in Lübeck and Travemünde,
Freud and Martha write a joint letter to Mama Bernays in alternating sentences in which he expresses a similar hope for a vital, decidedly combative
relationship. He writes: "Given at our present residence at Lübeck on the
first day of what we hope will prove a Thirty Years' War between Sigmund
and Martha."[105]

But the war never came, not even many skirmishes. Where Freud
sought conflict, Martha took refuge in compromise. Where Freud refused
to accept half-measures,[106] Martha delighted in them. "Sparing each other
can only lead to estrangement," he warned her; "It doesn't help at all: if
there are difficulties they have to be overcome."[107]

She was still reluctant. "If it could possibly be avoided," Katja Behling
writes, "[Martha] would not cast the first stone. For Freud, attacking Martha was often like banging his head against a brick wall, which only served
to make him even angrier. What he liked least was Martha's initial tendency to inhibit her aggressions or express them passively, her propensity

to fight shy of conflict and disputes, to hem and haw and fudge the issue instead of making it unequivocally clear where she stood. Her stonewalling was capable of driving Freud to distraction. He preferred having things out, even when this proved painful."[108]

That powerful temperamental differences between Freud and Martha existed is not disputed, even by so adamant a Freudian as Ernest Jones. Actually, Jones thinks it "remarkable," given these differences between Freud and Martha, that a "successful *modus vivendi*" between the two was ultimately achieved. "She recognized the necessity for mutual adjustment and that up to a point it was the man's place to direct it," Jones writes. However:

> Much more disturbing ... were the occasions where his criticisms seemed to her to be unjustified and his demands either unreasonable or at least of a nature she could not fulfill. This led to many bewildering and perplexing situations which taxed her diplomacy to the utmost. In the issue she emerged successfully, but only after passing through several crises where she felt tried to the limit. Her first instinctive response to those demands was on the lines of what Freud called her mother's typical weakness, a quality he heartily despised: namely, by appeasement. Her mother always took the easy way, at whatever cost of evasion or even lack of candor. This could not be said to be at all true of Martha, but nevertheless she had enough of her mother in her to prefer harmony whenever possible.[109]

Freud was determined to probe the truth to the bitter end. It was as if he always needed to find something wrong in the other person in order to set it right. To act otherwise seemed to him cowardly as well as boring. The path Martha followed, of avoiding unpleasantness, was counterproductive. To these entreaties, Martha's reaction was often silence, which Freud always found difficult to cope with. His letters at the time accuse her of being weak, spineless, "of choosing easy paths instead of bravely facing painful situations."[110]

Freud was, admittedly, oppositional by nature. A born contrarian, he liked taking extreme positions, seemingly just for the sake of doing so. He admits to Martha in a February 2, 1886, letter from Paris: "I wanted to explain the reason for my inaccessibility to and gruffness with strangers, which you mentioned. ... One would hardly guess it from looking at me, and yet even at school I was always the bold oppositionist, always on hand when an extreme had to be defended."[111]

As their relationship settled into a structure where each could feel master in their respective domains—perhaps the only way they could get along with each other successfully—Freud must have been frustrated by Martha's lack of interest in and actual disdain for the work he found so precious, psychoanalysis. René Laforgue, the French psychoanalyst, remembers visiting Freud in Vienna and being asked by Martha about a tic which was afflicting a little boy whom she knew. Laforgue was astonished that Martha, whom he liked, would be asking him and not her husband about the boy, and he told her so. Laforgue recalls: "She replied with her customary frankness, 'Do you really think one can employ psychoanalysis with children? I must admit that if I did not realize how seriously my husband takes his treatments, I should think that psychoanalysis is a form of pornography!'"[112]

"To her [Martha's] mind there was something vulgar about psychoanalysis," Katja Behling writes:

something from which she dissociated herself. Marie Bonaparte described how Martha had once told her how much her husband's work had surprised and even upset her in its permissive treatment of sexuality, claiming that she had almost intentionally refused to become acquainted with it. Freud had replied that his wife was simply "very bourgeoise."[113]

And Theodor Reik, one of Freud's first students and an early lay analyst (someone who used psychoanalysis in the treatment of patients but did not have an MD degree), recalls a similar lack of appreciation by Martha with regard to the value of psychoanalysis:

She really never understood why her husband became famous. Nor did she understand his work. She was not particularly interested in his research. She had little awareness of the important role of the unconscious. Once she said to me about a hysterical woman, "She'll get over it if she'll use her will."[114]

No wonder Jung told Eissler he sensed Freud was embarrassed by Martha during his 1907 visit to Berggasse. Freud had reason to be. What might Martha say if Jung happened to ask her a question about psychoanalysis? More frightening, what if he actually did? And apparently, from Jung's account of his visit, some sort of discussion did take place, or else how could he have drawn the conclusions he did concerning how little Martha knew—and how well versed ("*au courant*") Minna was?

On September 13, 1936, the Freuds celebrated their golden wedding anniversary. On September 27, 1936, Freud writes a matter-of-fact letter to Marie Bonaparte summing up his feelings on the occasion: "It was really not a bad solution of the marriage problem, and she is still today tender, healthy and active."[115] Marriage *problem*? Yes, definitely a problem for Freud. Notice the lack of affection, as if Freud the business manager is closing out an account. Again, we see how he struggles to express feelings. "How intimate they were we will never know," Appignanesi and Forrester conclude.[116] The least we can surmise is that intimacy was not one of the strong features of their marriage.

FILLING THE GAP

Where does Minna fit into this picture? She obviously fills a large gap. Minna had everything Freud wanted which Martha could not give him: acuity of intellect, willingness to engage, toughness, boldness, a fascination with psychoanalysis, and a willingness to support Freud's ideas when no one else would. As Freud grew closer to Minna and became acquainted with other women of substance and accomplishment like her—for a start, Jung's wife Emma and mistress Toni Wolff, both of whom eventually opened analytic practices of their own, later such women as Emma Eckstein, Helen Deutsch, Lou Andreas-Salomé, Joan Rivière, and Marie Bonaparte—Martha must have appeared even more wanting in Freud's eyes.

Even in appearance, Minna looked much more like Freud's mother than Martha did. As Paul Roazen notes: "Physically Minna Bernays was large and heavy, much more like Freud's imperious mother than his wife; like Amalie Freud [Freud's mother], Minna wore a little old-fashioned cap on the top of her head."[117]

FROM MARTHA'S PERSPECTIVE

Responding to Ludwig Binswanger's October 2, 1939, letter of condolence following Freud's death, Martha writes back on November 7, 1939: "It is small consolation for me to know that in the fifty-three years of our marriage we had not one angry word, and that I did my best at all times to spare him everyday worries."[118] When Martha says they never really argued—actually Ernest Jones tells us that they did have one argument, over the weighty question of whether mushrooms should be cooked with or without their stalks[119]—I conclude that someone (either Freud or Martha) was working very diligently to make certain there were no arguments, and my strong suspicion is that it wasn't Freud, who seemed to thrive on conflict.

Apparently Martha didn't like emotional messes any more than she liked physical ones, and she sought to clean up both posthaste. Or if she couldn't clean them up, she could at least make an effort to sweep the dirt under the proverbial rug. How different her husband, who wanted to do just the opposite—pull up all the rugs in order to shine a bright light on whatever dirt (or unacceptable emotions and memories) might lie beneath.

She must have been terrified at times, as her imperious husband sought to shape her into what he felt his wife should be. "She was not really his unless he could perceive his 'stamp' on her," Ernest Jones writes.[120] And Helen Walker Puner comments: "Given the forbidding environment her husband created, and the limitations of her own natural inclinations, she could no more meet him on an equal footing than she could have pulled her weight in 'a marriage of true minds.'"[121] Martha simply could not become someone she was not.

Her refuge? Mindless absorption in household details, strict obedience to her husband and, in the worst case, angry silence. Bad things were to be covered up. That's how she hoped they might go away.

Martha deeply angered her daughter Anna, with whom, as I have mentioned, she did not get along anyway, by her efforts to conceal the less savory facts of life from her. These were facts which Anna felt she had a right to know. Martha once told Anna she was going in to see the doctor for a physical examination when in truth the girl was to undergo an appendectomy. That must have been quite a shock. And Martha concealed from Anna the school test schedule, which was sent to parents, on the theory that Anna would worry less if she did not know when the exams were coming. Did Martha ever consider that maybe Anna didn't mind worrying from time to time? Again, Anna was furious.[122]

The idea was to smooth everything out, whether it was a bedsheet, a tablecloth or a child's concern about a test. That was the way Martha sought to get through life's many vicissitudes. Martha's ability to moderate and soothe served her well when it came to settling disputes involving her often cantankerous husband: "On many an occasion it was Martha who placated friends and acquaintances after her hot-blooded husband had raised their hackles," Katja Behling writes, "not a task to be underestimated considering the impulsiveness he had displayed in his youth and his tendency to break off relationships."[123]

Martha seemed able to hold her fire even when it came to her sister Minna's growing closeness to her husband and his work. "Martha seems not to have minded that her sister clearly had easier access to her husband and his sensitive profession," Behling writes; "She left Minna to play the part of Freud's intellectual companion in this field, even at the risk that this might 'estrange' her from her husband."[124] Martha "seems not to have minded," but did she really not mind? That seems unrealistic to me, though she was expert at keeping angry feelings within herself, even over long periods of time. Witness the fact that on the first Friday after her husband's death she lit the Sabbath candles for the first time in half a century. She finally got her way. I suspect she had been angry every Friday evening for the previous fifty years, when she couldn't light the candles, but didn't say anything. Freud thought that battle had been won long ago. But his victory was not final; it was only temporary, and he had to die for Martha to reveal how temporary it was.

To her credit, Martha was able to make the best out of a difficult marriage with a demanding, dominating husband. She showed tact, forbearance, staying power.[125] And she was willing to absorb the emotional costs associated with keeping her feelings to herself. Perhaps she had no choice. Maybe making the best of things, as opposed to really being happy, was what she felt her lot in life to be. In any case, under the circumstances she at least had her relatives and children to fall back on, just as Freud had his work.[126]

Concluding Thoughts

KEY FINDINGS

I have tried to look at the possibility that Sigmund Freud and his sister-in-law Minna Bernays had an affair from every conceivable perspective, and I have reached the conclusion that the available evidence suggests that they did. I base this on the following findings.

The Confession

Minna confessed to Carl Gustav Jung that she had an affair with Freud when Jung, his wife Emma, and Ludwig Binswanger, then Jung's student at the Burghölzli, visited Freud in Vienna in 1907. This happened in a private meeting at Berggasse that Minna had requested. Jung told John M. Billinsky about Minna's confession in a 1957 interview conducted at Jung's home in Küsnacht, Switzerland. A record of the interview was published by Billinsky in 1969. Others appear to have been told the same story by Jung.

Determining Proof

There are only so many possible ways that an affair between two people can be "proven." Affairs by their very nature are secretive, so it's not always easy to find evidence that they occurred. This is the bane of every private detective hired by some distraught and suspicious spouse. Surely one of the strongest ways is for the people involved to confess that they had an affair, and in the case of Minna Bernays this is exactly what happened.

Freud could also have confessed, but that seems unlikely. He knew how frail human beings could be and how people liked to gossip, their assurances to the contrary notwithstanding. Also, given his analytic skills and self-knowledge, however much he might have felt guilty about his infidelity, he would have been able to deal with these feelings without seeking outside help—unlike Minna, who seemed to have a need to share, a desire for sympathy and understanding. Remember, according to Freud's daughter-in-law Lucie, Minna's emotions were her "Achilles' heel."

Documents, such as love letters and diaries, can be an equally importance source of evidence that an affair took place. But we don't have such evidence in this case. The Freud/Minna letters that have survived do not reveal an affair. However, we know that most of the letters written between the years 1893 to 1910 (the period when we can assume, along with Gay, that an affair might have been most likely) are mysteriously missing. Overall, some *thirty-seven years of correspondence* is missing, so there is obviously a very large gap. Minna seems to have directed that all of Freud's letters to her (and perhaps hers to him as well) be destroyed, so the chance of those letters ever showing up is rather slight. Albrecht Hirschmüller, the editor of the collected letters of Freud and Minna, tells us he excluded all the letters from Martha and Sigmund to Emmeline and Minna, primarily for reasons of space. Adding them would have made his volume one-third again as large, he says.[1] So even some extant letters have not yet been published or otherwise made available.

But even if we had the full correspondence, we might not find evidence of an affair in them. As I have pointed out, Freud was too smart to put anything in writing, and I am certain he would have advised Minna to be careful as well. But the lack of any mention or indication of an affair in the letters that have survived does not guarantee that there is no mention or indication of an affair in the vast number of letters that have gone missing. Fortunately, the relatively small number of letters which have survived do tell us something important: that there is a comfort, at times a joy, when Freud and Minna are together. All this adds to the *plausibility* that there was a Freud/Minna affair, even if it does not prove that there was one.

Independent Confirmation

The story of the affair is only part of what Jung told Billinsky. He also inextricably linked Minna's confession to the incontinence incident in America and Freud's refusal to provide intimate associations to one of the "triangle" dreams he and Jung were analyzing at the time. For this part of the story there is independent confirmation in the form of Sándor Ferenczi, as per the research of Peter Rudnytsky. We should not expect similar confirmation for Minna's confession to Jung because there were apparently no witnesses. It is fair to assume the two were alone when they discussed the issue at Berggasse in 1907.

This independent confirmation for one part of the story is important because, as I have already asked, why would Jung tell the truth in one part of his story but lie in the other? There doesn't seem to be any sensible answer to that question.

Remarkably Consistent

There is remarkable consistency in what Jung told a number of people about the Minna/Freud liaison, so if he did lie, he did so with great skill, and I suspect his memory is better than most people realize. In sorting through the historical record, I count at least six times over a thirty-year period when Jung either told people in private or, with regard to material he published, revealed to the public what Minna confessed to him or the story of what happened in America regarding the incontinence incident or the "triangle" dream episode, or all three.

These instances are:

- Jung's 1925 Zürich lecture;
- the 1951 interview with Saul Rosenzweig;
- the 1953 tape-recorded interview with Kurt Eissler;
- conversations with C. A. Meier and Toni Wolff, both presumably before 1953 (and possibly conversations with others as well, according to John Kerr);
- the 1957 interview with Billinsky;
- and finally Jung's autobiography published in 1961.

A Continuum

From a review of the occasions in which Jung told the story or some part of it, he revealed the most information in settings in which he felt most comfortable: invariably private conversations with Jungians; less when in public or in published form, or with avowed Freudians such as Eissler. Whether the person with whom he was conversing was a Freudian or Jungian *did* matter to him. But even where Jung held back, as with Eissler, the story is basically the same—only, fewer details are provided.

We can construct a continuum of how candid Jung was with regard to the story. On one end are his *published* references, where he reveals very little, just small hints about a dream in America where Freud exerted his authority—though it would be inappropriate, he cautions the reader, to provide details regarding the exact subject of the dream. I find two instances of this: his 1925 Zürich lecture and his 1961 autobiography.

Somewhere in the middle is when he discusses the matter with an orthodox Freudian *in private*, in which case he reveals that he witnessed a strong transference by Minna to Freud and the fact that Freud was "not insensible." In other words, Freud seemed to reciprocate those feelings. This is Jung's 1953 interview with Eissler.

And then at the other end of the continuum are his discussions, again *in private*, with committed Jungians, where he appears to tell all: the 1957 Billinsky interview, some time earlier than that in which he revealed the same information to C. A. Meier, who says he heard exactly what Billinsky said Jung told him and also, at least according to Meier (via Kerr), Jung's mistress, Toni Wolff.

I'm not sure where Saul Rosenzweig's 1951 interview with Jung stands in this continuum, since he did not publish his entire interview but only provided excerpts from it, and those excerpts focused only on the Freud/Jung American visit. Since Rosenzweig studied under Henry Murray at the Harvard Psychological Clinic, and we know that Murray was strongly influenced by Jung, we can probably classify Rosenzweig as a Jungian. How strong a Jungian, I do not know.[2]

But the important point to be remembered is that Jung told a lot to some people and rather little to others (especially the public), but he didn't tell one person one thing and another something else. He was not inconsistent.

Not a Rumor

Those who doubt that an affair took place often describe Jung spreading a "rumor" or being the "source" of a rumor about Freud and Minna. Peter Gay is guilty of this.[3] I think they do this in order to undermine the credibility of the story, implying that Jung was dealing in idle gossip. But Jung did not spread a rumor. He was relating a confession. When other people talked about what Jung had told them then at that point they were spreading a rumor, because, unlike Jung, they had no firsthand knowledge of what Minna had said.

DOUBTING THAT AN AFFAIR TOOK PLACE

Jung's report of a Freud/Minna affair has raised important questions in the minds of those who doubt that an affair took place. One is whether Billinsky got it wrong, misunderstood Jung or simply fabricated the whole story. Another is whether Jung misunderstood what Minna said or was simply lying about what she said. I think there is still another question, which has not been raised before by scholars, and I don't know why it hasn't. This question concerns Minna's credibility. Maybe it was not Billinsky or Jung who lied, but rather Minna herself. In that case, Jung was merely communicating what Minna had told him, and Billinsky, in turn, was communicating what Jung told him. Jung and Billinsky got it "wrong" because Minna gave them bad information. Let us look at each of these questions in turn.

John Billinsky Got It Wrong or Lied

There is no evidence that Billinsky may have distorted what Jung said or simply made things up. In fact, just the opposite seems to have been the case: evidence indicates that the published version of the Jung/Billinsky interview is less explicit than Billinsky's own interview notes. Billinsky tamped down the "racier" language Jung apparently used. Also, we know Jung told the same story of Minna's confession to Dr. C. A. Meier, according to both Peter Gay and Kurt Eissler. Eissler called it "exactly the same account," and although a devout Freudian, vouches for C. A. Meier's integrity, "whose reliability is above doubt," he avers. Also, Meier is quoted in John Kerr's book saying that Jung told the same story to Jung's mistress, Toni Wolff. In fact, Meier thought he and Wolff were the only ones Jung had told about the affair.

Jung Got It Wrong or Lied

Aspects of Jung's story have been questioned by those who do not believe that Freud had an affair with Minna or have serious doubts about such a story. I'll mention here some of the most frequently repeated charges.

Jung wanted revenge

Jung spread the story of Freud's infidelity to get back at Freud, with whom he broke and toward whom he felt great bitterness. Yet there is no evidence that Jung ever fabricated any story about Freud, or anyone else, for that matter. Jung had plenty of opportunities to criticize his one-time colleague, and he took ample advantage of many of those over the years, as did Freud when he had a chance to criticize Jung. I have always felt that Jung's memory of what Minna told him was so specific that it is improbable he simply made the story up. Where could such ideas have come from? Also, there is no evidence to suggest that Jung had attempted himself, or urged others, to publish the story of Freud's extramarital transgressions. If Jung really wanted to hurt Freud, he could easily have done just that. I suspect Jung would have been as shocked as C. A. Meier was when Billinsky published his interview.

Minna was too unattractive for an affair with Freud

Beauty obviously is in the eye of the beholder, but there is no evidence that Freud felt that Minna was unattractive; in fact, there is evidence that he thought just the opposite, that she was attractive both physically and in terms of her energy, strong personality, and powerful intellect. At one point, in a May 7, 1886, letter to her, as we have seen, he calls her beautiful. He also seems to have admired the way Minna dressed. Photos of Minna as a young woman do not depict her as unattractive. Freud seems to have thought that Martha and Minna looked alike, and no one has criticized Martha's looks. Also, a neighbor of the Freuds at Berggasse thought that Minna was prettier than her sister. For a person whom some claim was unattractive, Minna's feminine charms seem to have drawn several intelligent and talented men to her: Schönberg, who became her fiancé; Freud, who made her a center of his intellectual life for years, arranged for her to accompany him alone on many holiday excursions, and was sexually attracted to her; and Jung, who thought she "was very good-looking and she not only knew enough about psychoanalysis but also about everything that Freud was doing," as he told Billinsky.

An affair would have been out of character for Freud

The popular perception of Freud is that he was monogamous and even puritanical; thus an affair would have been out of character for him. It would have been out of character for Minna as well, the argument goes. She is often described as spinsterish. But the more we learn about Freud and Minna, their attitudes and how they behaved, the more "in character" they appear to have acted. Both were emotionally needy. Both wanted someone to lean on, especially Minna after the death of her fiancé. Freud felt especially isolated, alone, and embittered, given the medical community's scornful reaction to his ideas. Both also felt they were intellectually and ethically superior to most of their contemporaries; both wanted to live by their own rules, irrespective of society's mores. This is the idea of extraterritoriality that I have described. Freud believed in successive polygamy, that sex outside of marriage was moral and should be legalized, that marriage was not an indissoluble institution, and that sustained sexual abstinence was almost impossible.

Once he became sexually abstinent with Martha, how could he satisfy his strong sexual needs? Certainly he could sublimate some of them, but a more practical answer is that he could have turned to Minna for sexual gratification, a woman whom he liked immensely and with whom he felt particularly comfortable. Given her strong androgynous personality—at once sharp-elbowed, brazen, and confrontational, and also caring, empathetic, and capable of great sympathy—she could meet all of Freud's sexual desires, homo- and heterosexual. Love, for Freud, involved conflict; Martha wanted to compromise and avoid conflict at all costs. Freud loving a weak, demurring Martha—that would have been out of character. Freud loving the combative and often confrontational Minna—that would have been in character. Throughout his life, Freud sought out strong, "masculine" women, as both Ernest Jones and Peter Gay acknowledge. And he was never attracted again to a passive, extremely feminine woman such as Martha.

But even if the case could be made that Freud and Minna acted out of character—and I think that's far-fetched—don't people sometimes act "out of character," especially behind closed doors? Who can really say for certain what happens behind closed doors?

Why would Minna confide in the callow young stranger, Jung?

Since Minna was at the center of Freud's intellectual life, she must have known about Jung and the fact that by 1907 Freud had been corresponding with him for the past year. She must also have known that Freud was preparing to crown the young, bright psychiatrist heir and successor, hoping that he would take psychoanalysis boldly into the twentieth century. Jung might have been young, but he was extremely capable and had Freud's full confidence. Minna must have heard great things about him from Freud. Why wouldn't she feel comfortable consulting this rising new star?

Also, unlike Freud, Jung had a winning personality; people immediately liked him, especially women. I suspect he had the ability to make Minna feel comfortable—at least comfortable enough to reveal to him her secret relationship with Freud. She may also have wanted to let Jung know her important role in Freud's life and work, lest she be overlooked as psychoanalysis emerged onto the world scene.

Freud never had a "laboratory" at Berggasse

Because Jung mentions his encounter with Minna as occurring in Freud's "laboratory," yet Freud had no room that might be called a laboratory in the flat at Berggasse, the assertion goes, thus Jung must have made the entire story up. It is obvious what Jung meant by the term—the place where Freud did his work—and since Freud himself used the same term to describe his work area in an April 28, 1887, letter to Minna, this charge is without substance.

Jung misconstrued Minna's meaning

Is it possible that Jung might have misunderstood Minna and read more into what she was saying than was really there? Yes, there is that possibility, but I don't think that happened. You'll recall, this issue was raised by Elms, who thought Jung's recollection leaves unclear what Minna might have actually told him as opposed to what he inferred.[4] I don't think it's unclear at all. But beyond that, Jung's story does not seem something he could have simply surmised from the way he saw Freud interacting with Minna or from what Minna might have *hinted at* in her conversations with him. Rather, Jung's recollection seems based on something Minna *told* him. He didn't have to surmise anything, for *she asked* to talk to him. *She* took the initiative. *She* revealed the affair. What he did was to record (mentally) her confession, and that's about all.

So it is not a matter of Jung's perceptions or interpretations, though, in addition to what Minna told him, what Jung perceived cannot be discounted—the strong "transference" between Minna and Freud he described to Eissler in their 1953 interview. But detecting a strong transference between Freud and Minna is substantively (and qualitatively) different *than being told by Minna that she was having sexual relations with Freud!* A transference might involve sex or might not. There can be no doubt what Minna's description means.

Jung's memory was failing

This attempt at discrediting the idea of an affair between Minna and Freud hinges on Jung's age when he revealed Minna's confession in the interview with Billinsky. At that time (1957), Jung was eighty-two, and the event he described had occurred fifty years previously. He was too old, and the event too long ago, the argument runs, for him to recall it accurately.

However, there is no indication that Jung's advanced age must have impacted the accuracy of his story. As evidence, there is a 1957 filmed interview of Jung by a professor at the University of Houston, which shows Jung to be alert, insightful, charming, and funny. He is even complimentary of Freud, calling *The Interpretation of Dreams* a "masterpiece." The interview is currently available on YouTube; you can be the judge of how much in control of his mental faculties Jung was at age eighty-two. As noted, there is also a published version of the interview.

Did Jung at times have trouble remembering things? Yes, he did. I have already mentioned several of these instances.[5] I suspect there are others as well. But I notice that when he does make those kinds of mistakes, they are errors of detail, not substance—such as remembering visiting Freud in 1906 when it was actually 1907, or recalling that he stayed at Berggasse for fourteen days during his first visit there when it was actually more like a week.

Jung did not have time or opportunity to meet with Minna

Contrary to the assumptions that underlie this assertion, Jung had ample opportunity to meet with Minna during his 1907 visit to Berggasse—even more than once, if he had wanted—since for a large part of the week, especially during the day, Freud was busy with patients and could not meet with Jung himself. Freud had warned Jung that Easter weekend would have been a better time for a visit, but Jung could not fit that into his schedule.

Minna's bedroom was only accessible through the master bedroom

If Minna's bedroom at Berggasse was accessible only through Freud and Martha's master bedroom, this argument goes, how could Freud and Minna have been intimate there? In 1990 Peter Gay clears this up by informing us that Minna only occupied that bedroom after 1920—when, one would presume, an affair between her and Freud would have been over or at least on the wane. Before 1920, her bedroom was elsewhere in the large flat, and Anna Freud occupied the bedroom accessible only through Freud and Martha's. If we assume that Minna had simply switched bedrooms with Anna in 1920, which seems most likely, then prior to that her bedroom would have been at the far end of the flat, facing the street—as far as one could get from the bedroom occupied by Freud and Martha, which overlooked the inner courtyard of the building.

The "shocking" confession versus the continued friendship

If Minna indeed told Jung about her affair with Freud, which apparently deeply shocked Jung ("It was a shocking discovery to me, and even now I can recall the agony I felt at the time," he told Billinsky), this argument asks, why did he continue to write Freud letters lavishing him with praise and admiration? Quite simply: because Jung was smart and ambitious. Freud seems to have been the first great man he had ever met. It was obvious that Jung felt it was important to cultivate Freud's friendship as a way of promoting his own career, irrespective of what was happening in Freud's private life.

And then, we must ask ourselves, what would Jung have said? Common courtesy dictated that he remain silent. It would have been absurd to confront Freud on the issue. Lavishing Freud with praise, or not bringing the matter to his attention, does not mean that Jung admired the fact that Freud was having an affair with Minna. Jung could marvel at the man and his work without at the same time admiring every aspect of Freud's private life, including the shocking affair Freud was having with his own sister-in-law.

Freud was more interested in men than women

Although it is true that Freud developed "crushes" on certain handsome, intelligent men, I see no evidence that his homosexual feelings resulted in an actual physical relationship with a man. Freud's homosexual feelings need to be put into context: they did not dominate his sexual life. They were latent. Evidence suggests that his heterosexual desires were much stronger and did not subside over time.

Did Jung ever lie? Yes, he did. When Jung and Freud were in America in 1909, Freud asked Jung to provide associations to a dream of Jung's in which there appear two human skulls. Freud asked Jung to think of a wish connected with those skulls. It was obvious to Jung that Freud was trying to uncover secret death wishes toward him concealed in the dream. But whose death, Jung wondered, would he have wished? To satisfy Freud's desire, Jung named his wife and his sister-in-law, feeling that their deaths were at least worth wishing for, even though these were not actually his associations. Jung later explained: "I wanted to know what he [Freud] would make of my answer, and what his reaction would be if I deceived him by saying something that suited his theories. And so I told him a lie."[6] But while Jung lied to Freud he later admitted that he did.

This sort of fabrication, created under pressure and later acknowledged, is miniscule compared with making up a scandalous story of what Minna might have said about an affair with Freud. When has Jung ever done anything even remotely like that? I don't know of any such instance.

Minna Lied

There is another possible interpretation of Freud's relationship with Minna in which they did not have an affair, and this is based on the assumption not that Jung lied, *but that Minna did*. After all, everything Jung said was based on Minna's confession, and if she did not tell him the truth, Jung could not have told the truth, either. As far as I know, no other scholar working on this subject has raised this question before, and I find that surprising.

But why would Minna lie? Possibly she told Jung was what she *hoped* might be the case (an affair between her and Freud) rather than what was *actually* the case. Perhaps she was in love with Freud, and he with her, and if she could not have him in reality she could at least have him in fantasy.

But what about the "triangle" dream episode in America? How does that fit in? I think one way to interpret this is that Freud did not want to reveal to Jung his strong affection for Minna, which he certainly had, and perhaps his disdain for Martha—both, obviously, very intimate feelings— even though he might not have been having an affair with Minna. So when he halted the dream interpretation with an appeal to "authority," he was not hiding an affair with Minna, but rather some very intimate, personal feelings which he wanted to keep secret. Embarrassing feelings, no doubt. Admittedly this view might be a stretch, but it is at least a possibility.

Using the premise that it was Minna and not Jung who lied as a point of departure, we can see Freud registering with Minna as man and wife at the Schweizerhaus Inn as a (pardon the expression) Freudian slip. It shows that unconsciously Freud would have liked to have had Minna as his wife. The same with Minna answering the phone at Berggasse "Frau Professor Freud,"[7] which she is reported to have done. She did so because she would have *liked* to be Freud's wife.

And the missing letters between the two? This is a more difficult issue, but I think we can interpret that circumstance in a way that is consistent with the new premise as well. Instead of Minna wanting to have all Freud's letters to her, and perhaps hers to him, destroyed because they might reveal an intimacy between the two, under this new assumption she would have wanted all those letters destroyed *because they did not reveal that intimacy*. In other words, from her point of view, it would have been too painful and embarrassing for the world to know that *they were not as intimate as she would have liked*, that they did not have an affair. Admittedly, this is another stretch—perhaps the longest.

In terms of my version of Occam's Razor, in which the fewer the assumptions the stronger the argument, the theory that Minna might have lied to Jung, while possible, is less likely than the theory that she simply told him the truth. To believe that Minna lied doubles the numbers of major assumptions needed. Not only must we assume that Jung told the truth, we must also assume that Minna lied. Possible, but quickly becoming less probable.

There is no doubt that Minna would have liked to be Freud's wife, and perhaps he would have liked her to be as well, so, in retrospect, in choosing Martha Bernays Freud might have chosen the wrong sister. Of course at the time Freud could not have chosen Minna. She was already engaged to Ignaz Schönberg.

ADDITIONAL EVIDENCE

There is additional evidence pointing to an affair between Freud and Minna. This evidence does not "prove" they were lovers—it is certainly not as strong as Minna's confession, especially when her confession is coupled with the events which took place between Jung and Freud in America—yet it does make an affair *more likely* or *more plausible*. It adds *believability* to the notion that Freud and Minna were lovers.

The Schweizerhaus Log

Franz Maciejewski's discovery of a registration log at the Schweizerhaus resort in Switzerland where Freud signed himself and Minna in as husband and wife (*Herr Dr. Sigm. Freud u[nd] Frau/Wien*) is one of these pieces of evidence and adds credence to the idea that there was an affair. That's because *the most likely* explanation of why Freud signed the registration book as man and wife was to cover up the fact that he was sleeping with his sister-in-law. There might be other explanations, and we have seen Zvi Lothane and Albrecht Hirschmüller offer several: the hotel was busy and there was only one room available, Freud was afraid of breaking Swiss law by sharing a room with a woman who was not his wife, and so on. But these explanations seem much less likely reasons why Freud signed the logbook the way he did.

Is Maciejewski's important discovery the "smoking gun" that proves that Freud and Minna had an affair, as he claims? No, because we already have the "smoking gun": Minna's confession to Jung.

Opportunity

To have an affair one needs not only willing participants, but also opportunity for those involved to be alone. Freud and Minna had plenty of opportunity to be by themselves. I see this as another argument in support of there having been an affair.

Freud and Minna took many trips alone together, and some of these trips lasted as long as a month, as we have seen. We have documented all the trips they took together based on available materials. And they seemed to have been very happy when on holiday together.[8]

Minna was as hardy a traveler as Freud, able to keep up with his maddening pace, in which, as we have seen, he would hardly spend more than one night in each place he visited.[9] We know that Freud thought she had great energy, even more than he possessed.[10] The two seem to have been perfectly suited to the rigorous holiday travelling style with which Freud felt comfortable.

Also, we can now say, based on new information provided by Peter Gay concerning living arrangements at Berggasse prior to 1920, that Freud had almost unlimited access to Minna there as well, especially, I would think, during the late evening hours, between the time Martha retired and when Freud went to bed—and we know that he habitually did not get to bed until two or three in the morning.[11] This was presumably an interval when everyone else in the household was asleep. And he need not wake anyone to get to Minna's bedroom. If, as we assume to be likely, in 1920 Minna and Anna simply switched rooms, Freud had direct access to Minna's bedroom, which was situated off one of the two foyers in the large flat.

Family Gossip

All the chatter within the Freud family about Freud and Minna also adds plausibility to the idea of an affair. We have already seen that Freud and Minna's holiday trips together raised eyebrows within the family,[12] as they would even today in a more liberated world. And we have seen that Freud himself knew about the rumor of an affair, because he questioned one of his patients about it—Eva Rosenfeld, who, by the mid-1920s, had become intimate with Anna Freud, her first cherished friend.[13] Then there is Esti Freud's comment that while she was not certain Freud and Minna had an affair, she would not rule it out—but whatever might have happened there was no doubt in her mind that Minna had made a play for Freud.[14]

Esti Freud, who hated Minna because she was always so critical of her, especially of her clothes, gives us hints of a different sort of Minna. No longer the spinsterish, accommodating eternal Aunt of lore but the powerful, perhaps predatory woman who might try to bend Freud to her will.

Closeness

Freud and Minna were always close. She was one of the few people he openly cared about. They played cards together, talked about his work, were both interested in literature and society, shared the same sardonic outlook on life, and were secular rather than religious. He seemed relieved when they were able to be alone together. He wrote letters in secret to her and had her do personal favors for him. She was one of the few people he allowed to pass into his sacred world.

Fear of Discovery

Freud was afraid to reveal to others that he was travelling alone on holiday with his sister-in-law. There is the incident where Freud consciously stays away from a group of university professors whom he knew from

Vienna, lest he have to introduce Minna to them. Freud was afraid to be caught with the "wrong woman."

Solace

For most of his adult life Freud was under immense pressure financially. He lived from day to day depending on the number of patients he was treating. He had pressure from other directions as well: people made fun of his ideas, he was often the victim of anti-Semitism, and the foundations of his marriage began to show fissures beginning in the mid-1890s. For all the activity and people around him, Freud was a terribly lonely person. Minna was there to help, providing solace and steadfast support. She was someone he could always depend on. It would be natural for him to turn to her in time of emotional as well as sexual need.

A Tense Marriage

There is little evidence, after the first several years of their marriage, that Freud and Martha enjoyed each other's company. On the contrary, he seems to have excluded her and others, including his children, from his own little world. This does not mean he did not love them; he just felt more comfortable being by himself or alone with Minna. He seems to have both demanded and at the same time detested the various rules and regulations that Martha established to protect him from distractions. Eventually, she became an embarrassment to him: "I have nothing at home but an elderly wife," he told Jung.

In addition to her excessive demands about how the household should operate—demands which became more onerous with time—she let her personal appearance go and showed no understanding of, or interest in, Freud's work. Worse, she displayed open hostility to it, describing it as "pornographic." The fact that she talked disdainfully about psychoanalysis to Freud's friends and colleagues—and I suspect he became aware of what she said—must have added to the tension that already dominated their relationship.

OTHER FINDINGS

There are several other findings regarding the Freud/Minna affair that deserve attention.

The Tip of the Iceberg

What Jung told Billinsky about Minna's confession is probably only the tip of the iceberg, even though Billinsky was a Jungian and hence someone with whom Jung could feel reasonably comfortable sharing information. I think that if Jung had provided Billinsky with a fuller picture of his conversation with Minna, and Billinsky had published that description, there might have been fewer doubts about the veracity of Jung's story of the affair. Perhaps more details would have made the story more three-dimensional and hence more believable.

Let's recall the essence of what Jung said about Minna as per Billinsky:

> Soon I met Freud's wife's younger sister. She was very good-looking and she not only knew enough about psychoanalysis but also about everything that Freud was dong. When, a few days later, I was visiting Freud's laboratory [that is, his study], Freud's sister-in-law asked me if she could talk with me. She was very much bothered by her relationship with Freud and felt guilty about it. From her I learned that Freud was in love with her and that their relationship was indeed very intimate.

As we have learned from Peter Rudnytsky (and I was able to confirm directly, with Billinsky's son), Billinsky's notes of the interview, which have not been published, are much stronger in tone than the published version. Remember, the "very intimate" description of the Freud/Minna relationship in the published version is actually described by Jung as "sexual relations" in Billinsky's notes.

I count a total of thirty-four words in the interview excerpt quoted above. If that is all Minna told Jung, she could have said as much in thirty seconds while passing him in a hallway. But that in all probability is not what happened. Since she had asked to talk to him and Jung agreed—whether they talked then or arranged to talk later is not clear—I suspect she went into some detail with Jung about what "bothered" her about the affair and the guilt she said she felt, and probably even asked for Jung's advice about what she should do next. After all, Jung was a psychiatrist and a brilliant one at that—the sort of person someone in distress might logically seek out, especially if she knew that Freud thought so highly of his talents that he was about to appoint him heir and successor.

I've already suggested that Jung and Minna probably talked a minimum of ten minutes. But perhaps they talked longer: a half hour or even an hour. Given the free time Jung had that week, it is conceivable that they even talked more than once, a detail Jung need not have shared with Billinsky. Minna had something important to get off her chest, and I suspect Jung was very empathetic toward her and consoled her as much as he could. Charm was one of his great skills. He already liked her, thought she was intelligent, knowledgeable, and "very good-looking," so a brief doctor-patient relationship might have quickly taken root.

I think it is reasonable to assume that the sort of confession Minna made was not done on the run, but required time, privacy, a lot of thought. Jung might have taken the opportunity to probe Minna as to her feelings as she revealed more details: anger at Freud; her possibly feeling trapped between her love for her sister and her love for Freud. Any number of sensitive issues might have come up. This, after all, was an extraordinary circumstance, an agonizing situation for Minna.

So I suspect there is a deep backstory here—a backstory Jung apparently did not discuss with Billinsky.

Billinsky's Mistake

Eager to publish, Billinsky did not check whether the *Time* magazine article was accurate. If he had, today we would not have any solid evidence of an affair between Freud and Minna. No other person with whom Jung apparently shared his knowledge of Minna's confession went public with it.

Jung's Love for Freud

For all the bitterness between the two men, Jung loved Freud and deeply regretted their not having been able to continue their relationship. Freud was the greatest man he had ever met.

Commonalities

Freud had just about everything in common with Minna and very little in common with Martha. One might think this reason enough to cause Freud's alienation of affection vis-à-vis Martha.

Minna's Desire for Recognition

Why did Minna reveal her affair with Freud to Jung? Perhaps 1907 was a pivotal year in her life. Prior to 1900 Minna had shared with Fliess the role of personal confidante to Freud. After the turn of the century, Fliess breaks with Freud, and Minna becomes her brother-in-law's *only* confidante. In 1902, the Wednesday Psychological Society is established and begins to serve as a sounding board for Freud's ideas and psychoanalysis in general. Eventually, Freud does not think those involved in the Wednesday group are very talented, with the possible exception of Otto Rank, but the group does provide support to Freud, which, at the beginning, supplements Minna's. But she might not have seen this group as threatening. However, she must have been more concerned about competition from the Swiss. In 1904 Bleuler begins corresponding with Freud and more significantly, in 1906, Jung does the same, becoming a powerful advocate for psychoanalysis, proselytizing on its behalf.

By 1907, Minna must have seen Jung as a key competitor for her role as confidante. After all, Freud appeared on the verge of naming Jung his heir and successor. This had to make Minna anxious at the very least and wonder what part she would be playing in the new world of psychoanalysis.

As previously mentioned, I suspect Minna's desire to share her secret with Jung was in part a declaration to Jung that she was a central person in Freud's intellectual life and had a special, personal relationship with him. It is obvious she did not want her role diminished as psychoanalysis evolved onto a broader stage, and it appears she wanted to make certain Jung knew that.

Freud: Control and Command

Freud was autocratic, authoritarian, unbending but most significantly, he was controlling, first as son and then as husband and father. He felt he knew what was best for everyone and was determined to get his way. He could also be quite cold, unable to express feelings openly. He dominated not only his parents and siblings, but Martha and the children and eventually even his children's wives (witness Esti Freud). He kept his emotions to himself and carefully limited his interactions with others. Finding it hard to relax, his only pleasure became unrelenting work. He could not tolerate cultural activities because they took too much time away from his research. His rigidly compartmentalized life was filled with tension and often resulted in periods of deep depression with migraines and other psychosomatic illnesses. Psychosomatic illnesses also afflicted Martha and the children. Life at Berggasse was difficult and often filled with stress and anxiety, quite different from the Pollyanna existence portrayed by both Ernest Jones and Kurt Eissler. Freud does not seem to have gained any long-term emotional satisfaction from his marriage to Martha, nor did she seem to have benefited much herself.

Martha's Revenge

Martha set up rules and regulations for the household to protect her husband, and in that she was quite successful. But these same "safeguards" often irritated Freud and others (Anna), because they sometimes went too far, Martha becoming over time a caricature of her former self, a veritable object of humor and ridicule. I suspect that unconsciously she went too far on purpose, as her only way of getting back at her domineering husband.

FINAL POINTS

In closing let me briefly touch upon several final topics.

Evidence That Jung Lied

What would constitute evidence that Jung lied? I can think of several sorts. One would be a confession on his part that he fabricated the story of a Freud/Minna affair. He could have told someone that he had, or have written as much in letters to friends. I have not found any evidence that Jung did make such a confession, though it is possible that he did and friends have been reluctant to go public with what he told them. That would be the strongest evidence.

Another indication that Jung might have lied would be if he had told other stories about Freud which turned out to be false. In other words, was Jung in the habit of making up stories about Freud? We know of at least one instance where he lied *to* Freud, because he publicly admitted it—this was about his associations with regard to a dream of his that Freud was trying to interpret—but there is no indication that he ever lied *about* Freud.

Still another indication that Jung might have lied would be if he ever made up stories about other people. In other words, was Jung in the habit of simply making up stories? I have not found any evidence that he did, but perhaps further research into this question is needed.

Another source of possible "evidence" that Jung lied would be if either Freud or Minna or both ever denied that they were having an affair. It would be unlikely that either would say so publicly, because it might given credence to the rumor, but certainly they could have denied it privately, to friends or associates. Did that happen? Not that I am aware of, but perhaps further research into this question is needed as well.

The Philandering Jung

Another important question concerns Jung's own sexual philandering. Did it color his view of Freud's relationship with Minna? Did it make him more likely to see an affair, when perhaps there was only a close relationship with "affective" components?

We know certain things about Jung's sexual behavior. Women liked him, and he returned their regard. He was tall, dynamic, aggressive, and charming. And he was an inveterate flirt, a compulsive womanizer.[15] He might have had an affair with his patient/student Sabina Spielrein at the time he was just starting to communicate with Freud. There are conflicting opinions as to whether the relationship was ever consummated.[16] We do know that Spielrein wrote Freud on June 10, 1909, asking him to intercede ("mediate") to try to sort things out between her and Jung.[17] Earlier, in a letter to Freud of March 7, 1909, Jung had denied that the relationship was sexual, but suspicions remain. Although Jung and Sabina might not have been lovers, there was undoubtedly a strong transference/counter-transference between them, and Emma Jung had reason to be concerned.

Jung's flirtatious personality may well have made him more sensitive to the interactions between Minna and Freud, the sort of interactions he talks about in his interview with Eissler.[18] Given these sensitivities, Jung might have assumed that Freud and Minna were lovers when in fact they were not. But this does not explain why Minna would talk about having "sexual relations" with Freud and discuss her feelings of guilt about what she and Freud were doing. Based on these sorts of descriptions, Jung did not need to assume anything.

I think a more likely explanation is that Jung saw what Freud was up to, and even though he might have disapproved of the affair because Minna was Freud's sister-in-law, he used the model of Freud's "two wives" arrangement as a template for his own behavior. We know that several years later (about 1915) Jung began to openly keep a mistress, Toni Wolff, with his wife's reluctant consent.[19] The three even had Sunday dinner together.[20] This arrangement lasted for the remainder of Jung's life, and he treated Wolff basically as a second wife. But there was one important difference between Jung's arrangement and Freud's: Jung never fell out of love with Emma the way Freud did with Martha, because Jung felt that his love for each, Emma and Toni, enhanced his love for the other. A true *ménage à trois*.[21]

Fortress Freud

There was a powerful Fortress Freud mentality that dominated life at Berggasse and continued for many years after Freud's death. After his passing, the leadership baton was taken up by his daughter Anna, who exercised her new role with relish, creating more than a little discomfort among Freud scholars. Katja Behling writes:

> Even today ... there are persistent rumours that Anna manipulated the image of her parents by destroying a lot of the letters, especially Martha's. She was considered a tough censor. On the one hand, she was justifiably eager to prevent excessively intimate matters from being made public. On the other hand, she was keen to influence the idea people formed both of psychoanalysis and her parents.[22]

Appignanesi and Forrester make a similar point:

> Once married, it is remarkable how silent Freud was, even to his
> closest friends such as Wilhelm Fliess, about his relations with
> Martha.... [W]e know more about the inner turmoil of their engage-
> ment ... than we do about their marriage. Very few of the many
> letters and papers Sigmund and Martha left have emerged from
> the closed vaults to which daughter Anna and the like-mindedly
> secretive collaborators at the Freud Archive have confined them—
> as if source material on the Freud family were incriminating loot
> to be stashed in an anonymous Swiss bank account.[23]

Hanns Sachs, although a close ally of Freud, sensed the inviolate nature of
the Freud family inner sanctum and chose not to probe it. He reflects on
the subject in his usual understated manner: "The atmosphere of the house
was that of peaceful and temperate friendliness. The innermost and strictly
intimate relations between those who lived in it were never revealed to
me. They were not that sort of family and I had no wish to pry into their
secrets."[24]

When in 1936 the writer Arnold Zweig asked Freud if he could write
his biography, Freud's response was both firm and revelatory as to how
strongly he valued his privacy and what he thought of those who might
wish to violate it. "Whoever undertakes to write a biography binds himself
to lying, to concealment, to hypocrisy, to flummery and even to hiding his
own lack of understanding," Freud writes to Zweig on May 31, 1936, "since
biographical material is not to be had and if it were it could not be used.
Truth is not accessible; mankind does not deserve it."[25]

Secrecy became the dominant theme and mode of operation at Berggasse, but I suspect that "Fortress Freud" existed even before fame came
to Freud and one could argue there was a need for some sort of protective
bastion—to keep out the curious and the ambitious as well as the antago-
nistic. Secrecy was part of Freud's mental makeup. It was part and parcel
of the wall he built around himself to keep others out and to ensure that he
kept things under control.

Kurt Eissler, as the first director of the Freud Archives at the Library of
Congress, carried on the tradition of control and secrecy for Anna Freud
while she was alive and continued to do so after her passing. He combed
the world for materials, conducted interviews of key individuals, Jung
included, and set rules for when material could be released and to whom.
Janet Malcolm, in her *In the Freud Archives*,[26] relates a meeting she had
with Eissler where she repeated a complaint Peter Swales had made to her,

to wit: "locking up material in the Archives for a hundred years favored the unborn and discriminated against scholars working today." Eissler retorted that there were far greater injustices, such as Peter Swales publishing "whatever he wants about Freud, and that Freud cannot defend himself and prove he is being maligned."[27]

But the matter is not so simple. It is one thing to set up rules; it is another to administer them unfairly and without regard to equity and need. Kurt Eissler interviewed the crusty and outspoken Esti Freud, yet he embargoed access to the interview until the year 2053. I can only imagine what she said! I suspect it was not what Eissler wanted to hear. And we have already seen how the Freud family treated Helen Walker Puner—rather shabbily, denying her access to all of Freud's private papers dealing with his life and the life of his family.[28] Also, Paul Roazen tells how he had to finagle a reluctant Anna Freud into several interviews for one of his books. He was lucky in that he was able to enlist the help of her staff.[29]

On the other hand, there are certain favorites who seem to have had unlimited access to what they need. One is Albrecht Hirschmüller, who admits he was given access to "all interviews that concern the Freud and Bernays families" in 1996, though they were embargoed until 2010 for others.[30] Similarly, Deidre Bair had access to Eissler's 1953 interview with Jung while the material remained out of reach to other scholars. She openly thanks Eissler in her book—the material was "generously made available ... by Dr. Eissler and released to me by the LC [Library of Congress] at his request."[31]

In recent years there appears to have been some loosening of the requirements, at least according to Hirschmüller.[32] I had no trouble obtaining promptly from the Archives (for a fee) a digital version of the sixty-one page Eissler/Jung 1953 interview, yet I received no special treatment, since the material was released for general distribution in 2013, the year I requested it. But lack of transparency, the coveting of certain materials and limiting access to them so closely associated with the reign of Eissler et al., seems to have infected the larger world of Freud scholarship.[33]

Appignanesi and Forrester's analogy of the anonymous Swiss bank account and its loot is appropriate. Freud source material is viewed by some as gold, and as such, why share it? The most egregious instance of secrecy involving sources which I have come across in doing research for this book is contained in Deidre Bair's study of Jung. On page 119 of her book she writes of the Jungs' first visit to Freud in 1907 and the strange things they witnessed there. "Both Jungs were keenly observant, and both were struck by what they called 'certain oddities' in the Freud family's dynamic." The source for this statement is Note 47, which reads, "Private source, private archive." Need I say more?[34]

Was there a "coverup" of an affair between Freud and Minna as a way of protecting Freud and psychoanalysis? I'd be surprised if there wasn't, given the track record of concealment and obfuscation which must be laid at the feet of the Freud family and their allies. If they did know, and I think it is a safe bet that they did, it was certainly in their interest to make certain no one else knew. Such revelations, because of Freud's emphasis on sexuality in his theories, would have been embarrassing at best, devastating at worst. Whether the "coverup" was systematic or not, or just part of their general tendency not to share information, I have no idea.

Minna's Contribution

Like many of the issues pertaining to Freud and Minna, that of Minna's possible contribution to the corpus of Freud's ideas is a complex one. Since a large quantity of the Freud/Minna correspondence is missing, one has to be careful about generalizing too quickly. We know Freud and Minna communicated about dreams, cocaine, aphasia, and other subjects. But I don't see any direct impact Minna might have had on Freud with regard to these or other areas of research. Psychoanalysis and issues related to it are not a prominent theme in their (limited) extant correspondence.

I've also checked Freud's correspondence with Fliess, and although Minna is mentioned at least several times in their letters—her visits to Fliess and his wife in Berlin, her serious illness of 1900–1901, and Freud's deep concern and affection for her—she is not mentioned as a participant in any of the substantive discussions. In the Freud/Jung letters, she is referred to even less frequently. One would have thought that if she was an intimate partner in the development of Freud's ideas he would have mentioned to Fliess or Jung things like, "I ran this idea by Minna, and she said the following," or, "Minna came up with this interesting notion which could greatly strengthen my ideas concerning repression," or something to that effect. But none of that is there.

As co-confidante to Freud for a number of years as well as a resident at Berggasse, Minna had a different relationship to Freud than Fliess did. Freud did not need to write her letters to discuss his research. He could have simply asked her to come into his study or gone to her room to run some ideas past her. And I suspect he did this quite often. That's what a confidante is for. So we might not expect to find many letters to or from Minna in which discussions of psychoanalysis take place.

Yet I remain suspicious of just how deeply Minna became involved. If she was a key intellectual interlocutor of some sort, why didn't Freud take her to some of his meetings (or "Congresses") with Fliess, or at the very least why wasn't she invited to attend the international psychoanalytic associations meetings when they were established? Because she was a woman? Perhaps, but Jung's wife Emma did attend, and so did Toni Wolff.

Paul Roazen also has his doubts about the extent of Minna's contribution. For him "she was more a listener, a projective screen for his ideas, than anything like a collaborator."[35]

Minna was certainly fascinated by Freud's ideas and was intelligent enough, and perhaps eager as well, to converse with him on various psychoanalytic subjects, in sharp contrast to Martha, who, as we have seen, had no interest in psychoanalysis and even felt disdain for it. Yet I see the emotional support Minna gave Freud, during his period of isolation and deep anxiety, as her main contribution. I think that for many years her daily encouragement was as important as any intellectual contribution she could have made, and Minna, serving as Freud's confidante and muse, seems to have provided unqualified support when Freud most needed it.

Implications for Psychoanalysis

I don't believe that Freud having an affair with his sister-in-law in any way impacts the validity of psychoanalysis, or its value, whether it pertains to its theories of the mind or those regarding therapeutic technique. Freud's ideas have to stand on their own and need to be evaluated by objective criteria which have nothing to do with the fact that he may have gone outside his marriage to seek sexual gratification with his sister-in-law.

However, looking carefully at Freud's affair with Minna does tell us a lot about Freud the man and how his personality may have contributed to the development of psychoanalysis in the first place, as well as some of the problems he encountered later in finding long-term adherents for his ideas.

We see an immensely talented, creative person, with a vast capacity for work, but also a lonely, unbending figure, someone who above all needed to dominate and control. These latter traits helped him gain initial recognition for his ideas against powerful and often unreasonable opposition, but they also caused irreparable harm when he demanded of his adherents undeviating obedience.

Freud was correct. He did not possess the sort of personality that made people like him. As he himself realized, he needed a Jung, with the latter's enthusiasm and charm, to represent psychoanalysis to the outside world, just as Darwin, for other reasons, needed Huxley. The control and domination that Freud was able to exercise in the narrow confines of the home, either as son or later as husband and father, could not be replicated successfully in the broader world, with so many different personalities and such a diversity of issues and opinions, and with many people who often thought they were as talented and determined as he. That I see as Freud's tragic flaw: his inability to reshape his personality to meet the demands of a complex and ever-changing world, which he found impossible to control.

Notes

PREFACE

1. See John M. Billinsky, "Jung and Freud: The End of a Romance," *Andover Newton Quarterly*, Volume 10, Number 2, 1969, pages 39–43.

2. Franz Maciejewski, Jeremy Gaines, "Freud, His Wife, and His 'Wife,'" *American Imago*, Volume 63, Number 4, 2006, pages 497–506; Franz Maciejewski, "Did Freud Sleep with His Wife's Sister? An Expert Interview with Franz Maciejewski, PhD," Interviewed by Alma Bond, *Medscape Psychiatry Mental Health*, 2007, http://www.medscape.com/viewarticle/555692; Franz Maciejewski, Jeremy Gaines, "Minna Bernays as 'Mrs. Freud': What Sort of Relationship Did Sigmund Freud Have with His Sister-in-Law?" *American Imago*, Volume 65, Number 1, 2008, pages 5–21.

3. Peter Gay, *Freud: A Life for Our Time*, New York: W. W. Norton, 1988, page 76; Ernest Jones, *The Life and Work of Sigmund Freud*, 3 volumes, New York: Basic Books, 1953–1957, I, page 153.

4. See Ralph Blumenthal, "A Century-Old Swiss Hotel Log Hints at an Illicit Desire That Dr. Freud Didn't Repress."

5. Katja Behling, *Martha Freud: A Biography*, translated by R. D. V. Glasgow, Cambridge, England: Polity Press, 2005, pages 26, 73–78.

6. Compare, for example, Gay, 1988, pages 76, 502–503; Maciejewski, Gaines, 2006, page 499.

7. Jeffery M. Masson, Ed., Trans., *The Complete Letters of Sigmund Freud to Wilhelm Fliess, 1887–1904*, Cambridge, MA: Belknap/Harvard University Press, 1985, page 73.

CHAPTER 1: THE ANTAGONISTS: FREUD AND JUNG

1. Gay, 1988, pages 4–5; Jones, I, page 2.

2. Gay, 1988, page 8; Jones, I, pages 12–13.

3. Jones, I, page 20.

4. Gay, 1988, pages 34–35; Jones, I, pages 40–41.

5. Sigmund Freud, *An Autobiographical Study (1927), The Standard Edition of the Complete Psychological Works of Sigmund Freud, Translated from the German under the General Editorship of James Strachey, In Collaboration with Anna Freud, Assisted by Alix Strachey and Alan Tyson,* 24 volumes, London: The Hogarth Press, 1951–1974, Volume XX, page 8.

6. Gay, 1988, page 37. Anti-Semitism seems to have also been a factor. See Ibid., pages 138–139.

7. Gay, 1988, page 41; Freud, *An Autobiographical Study (1927), The Standard Edition,* Volume XX, page 12.

8. Gay, 1988, pages 48–49.

9. Freud, *An Autobiographical Study (1927), The Standard Edition,* Volume XX, page 21.

10. Ibid., pages 33–45, 76–78.

11. Gay, 1988, pages 141–142.

12. Ibid., pages 173–179, 221–224.

13. Ibid., page 200. Gay writes: "Once initiated, their [Freud and Jung's] friendship flourished mightily."

14. Deirdre Bair, *Jung: A Biography,* Boston: Back Bay Books/Little Brown, 2003, page 7; Frank McLynn, *Carl Gustav Jung,* New York: St Martin's Press, 1996, pages 7–11.

15. McLynn, *Jung,* page 6.

16. Bair, *Jung,* pages 20–21. Jung's mother seemed to have had two very different personalities.

17. C. G. Jung, *Memories, Dreams, Reflections,* A. Jaffé (editor), Revised Edition, New York: Vintage Books/Random House, 1961, page 91; McLynn, *Jung,* page 7.

18. McLynn, *Jung,* page 8.

19. Jung, *Memories, Dreams, Reflections,* pages 41–42.

20. McLynn, *Jung,* page 9.

21. Jung, *Memories, Dreams, Reflections,* pages 33–35.

22. Jung, *Memories, Dreams, Reflections,* page 24; Bair, *Jung,* page 29.

23. Jung, *Memories, Dreams, Reflections,* page 44.

24. Ibid., pages 27–30.

25. Ibid., page 31.

26. Ibid., pages 68–72.

27. Ibid., pages 72–75, 95.

28. Ibid., page 86.

29. Ibid., pages 97, 100.

30. Ibid., pages 113–115.

31. Jung said this in a filmed interview conducted by University of Houston psychology professor Dr. Richard I. Evans, August 5–8, 1957. This filmed interview is available on YouTube at http://www.youtube.com/watch?v=-kdF-qV6PpE. There is also a printed version of the interview in William McGuire and R. F. C. Hull, *C. G. Jung Speaking, Interviews and Encounters,* Princeton, New Jersey: Princeton University Press, 1977, pages 276–352.

32. Jung, *Memories, Dreams, Reflections,* pages 114–115.

33. Bair, *Jung,* pages 72–81.

34. Jung, *Memories, Dreams, Reflections,* page 148.

35. Ibid., pages 146–151.

CHAPTER 2: THE RUMOR AND ITS ORIGINS

1. For an intriguing portrait of Jones, his role in the development of psychoanalysis, and his relationship with Freud, see Brenda Maddox, *Freud's Wizard: Ernest Jones and the Transformation of Psychoanalysis,* Cambridge, MA: Da Capo Press, 2007.

2. I have always felt that Peter Gay's 1988 biography of Freud did not supersede Jones's work but actually complimented it. Jones's biography is full of wonderful details; Gay's tome adds insight, a needed dose of objectivity, and a rich cultural perspective.

3. Jones, I, page 139.

4. Ibid., page 271.

5. Ibid., page 153.

6. Ibid.

7. Jones, II, page 386. See Helen Walker Puner, *Sigmund Freud, His Life and Mind,* foreword by Erich Fromm, with a new introduction by Paul Roazen and afterword by S. P. Puner, New Brunswick, NJ: Transaction Publishers, 1992 (originally published 1947).

8. Jones, II, page 387. Jones indicates in II, page 482, Note 8, that he got this information about "Tante Minna" from Lucie Freud. Lucie Freud was the wife of Freud's son Ernst and the mother of the celebrated British painter Lucian Freud.

9. Jones, II, page 387.

10. Puner, *Freud,* page 134.

11. Ibid., page 135.

12. Ibid., page 137.

13. Ibid., page 57.

14. Ibid., pages 214–216.

15. *Psychoanalysis and History,* Volume 10, Number 1, page 117.

16. Jones, I, pages 3, 7, 22, 28; II, pages 17, 19, 382, 386.

17. Puner, *Freud,* page ix. According to Samuel P. Puner, who wrote an afterward to the 1992 edition of Helen Puner's 1947 study, Puner was treated rather shabbily by the Freud family, denied access to Freud's private papers dealing with his life and the life of his family. More on the inequities which seem to be prevalent

in the world of Freud scholarship when we take up the topic again in our concluding chapter.

18. Jones, I, page 153.

19. Jones, II, page 386.

20. Maciejewski and Gaines, 2006, page 499; Albrecht Hirschmüller (Ed.), *Sigmund Freud /Minna Bernays: Briefwechsel 1882–1938,* Tübingen, Germany: Edition Diskord, 2005, pages 18–19.

21. Jones first met Freud in 1908, and he almost immediately became "Jung's
understudy as Freud's Gentile." Maddox, *Freud's Wizard,* page 63.

22. "C. G. Jung, a Witness or, the Unreliability of Memories," Madison, CT:
International Universities Press, page 108.

23. New York: Knopf, 1976, pages 62, 556.

24. How intimate was Anna Freud's relationship with Eva Rosenfeld? It is difficult to know exactly, but certainly their relationship was close. Anna often ended
her letters to Eva with "Love and Kisses" or "With a kiss." See Peter Heller, *Anna
Freud's Letters to Eva Rosenfeld,* translated by Mary Weigand, Madison, CT: International Universities Press, 1992, pages 102, 109, 113. Heller's volume contains
only the letters from Anna Freud to Eva Rosenfeld and only those from the 1920s
and early 1930s. Extant correspondence from later years (1946–1977) is restricted
to business or brief communications. See Heller, page ix. Eva Rosenfeld did not
complete her analysis with Freud but with Melanie Klein, who had a theory of
child psychotherapy that did not sit well with Anna, so that fact must have grated
on her. See Paul Roazen, *The Historiography of Psychoanalysis,* New Brunswick,
NJ: Transaction Publishers, 2001, pages 133–134.

25. Gay, 1988, page 752.

26. Eissler, *Three Instances of Injustice,* page 111.

27. Peter Gay, *Reading Freud: Explorations and Entertainments,* New Haven,
CT: Yale University Press, 1990, page 164.

28. Gay, 1988, page 753.

29. Kurt Eissler, *Interview with C. G. Jung,* unpublished manuscript, Library of
Congress; in German, 61 pages, Tape No. 74, August 29, 1953.

30. See Eissler, *Three Instances of Injustice,* page 109. The information about
Billinsky is from an obituary notice that appeared in the *Boston Globe* on March
15, 1984, and is quoted by Eissler.

31. Billinsky, page 39; *Time* magazine, "People" section, page 32. Eissler says
that the article appeared in *The New York Times* on that date, but I cannot find it
there, so there must have been some confusion on Eissler's part between *Time* and
The New York Times. Eissler, *Three Instances of Injustice,* page 110.

32. According to the American psychologist Saul Rosenzweig, when Clark
University president Howard B. Jefferson was about to retire in 1967, Jefferson did
a search of old files that were located in "the lower recesses of the administration
building" and discovered these letters and with them other material pertaining
to the 1909 Clark University celebrations. See Rosenzweig, *Freud, Jung, and Hall
the King-Maker: The Historic Expedition to America (1909), Including the Compete*

Correspondence of Sigmund Freud and G. Stanley Hall, Seattle: Hogrefe & Huber Publishers, 1992, page 7.

33. Billinsky is quoting the *Time* magazine article almost verbatim here.

34. To date, I have not been able to find the Hall letter to Freud which Billinsky mentions, if it ever existed, which I rather doubt. While Rosenzweig, in his *Freud, Jung, and Hall,* claims his book contains the full extant correspondence between Freud and Hall—*Including the Complete Correspondence of Sigmund Freud and G. Stanley, Hall,* as Rosenzweig's subtitle proclaims—it does not include Hall's letter to Freud. Rosenzweig's study came out in 1992, many years after Billinsky's interview was published, so if there was a letter it seems Rosenzweig would have tracked it down and included it in his collection, or at the very least referenced it, but it is nowhere to be found in his book.

35. Saul Rosenzweig, in his *Freud, Jung, and Hall,* translates this passage slightly differently, but the message is the same. It's not really the father trying to control sons who want their freedom. On the contrary, it's the sons' desire to murder the father. Rosenzweig's translation of the same passage is: "Had the actual events been better known to you, you would probably not have concluded that here again is a case of a father who will not permit his sons to come into their own. Instead you would have seen that the sons wanted to depose their father—exactly as in primal times." The whole letter can be found in Rosenzweig, *Freud, Jung and Hall,* pages 381–382. There is also a third attempt at translation, which appears in an article by John C. Burnham, "Sigmund Freud and G. Stanley Hall: Exchange of Letters," *Psychoanalytic Quarterly,* Volume 29, 1960, pages 307–316. Here's Burnham's version (page 312): "If you were more familiar with what really happened, you would probably not have judged that here was another case in which a father would not let his sons come into their own; rather, you would have seen that the sons wanted to get rid of their father, just as at the dawn of time." These three passages—from *Time,* Rosenzweig, and Burnham—are essentially the same, and all quote the same paragraph in the August 28, 1923, letter from Freud to Hall. Burnham also provides a copy of the German original, so readers can decide for themselves which is the best translation. (See Burnham, 1960, pages 310–311.) The original brief *Time* article of September 5, 1969, that Billinsky quotes from, is as follows (*Time,* page 32): "Sixty years ago last week, Sigmund Freud paid his only visit to the U.S. to deliver a series of five lectures at Clark University in Worcester, Mass. The $750 fee was a great help to the hard-pressed doctor, and the warm reception, he later noted, 'encouraged my self-respect in every way.' Now a collection of 13 letters discovered in the basement of Clark's library indicates that Freud kept up a correspondence with the university's president, Psychologist G. Stanley Hall. The letters abound with expressions of gratitude and courtesy. But one with a sharper tone replied to Hall's suggestion that Prize Disciple, Carl Jung's bitter split with Freud was a classic case of adolescent rebellion. 'If the real facts were more familiar to you,' Freud wrote, 'you would very likely not have thought that there was again a case where a father did not let his sons develop, but you would have seen that the sons wished to eliminate their father, as in ancient times.'"

36. Alliance for Audited Media, "The Top 25 U.S. Consumer Magazines for June 2013," http://www.auditedmedia.com/news/blog/2013/august/the-top-25-us-consumer-magazines-for-june-2013.aspx.

37. This picture looked familiar to me, and then I remembered it was the one that Freud took with G. Stanley Hall and Jung at the Clark University celebrations, which appears on the front dust jacket of Rosenzweig's *Freud, Jung, and Hall*. The *Time* photograph cuts out Hall and Jung.

38. Kurt Eissler first pointed out Billinsky's error in 1993 in *Three Instances of Injustice*, page 110.

39. Rosenzweig, *Freud, Jung, and Hall*, page 377.

40. Billinsky, 1969, page 39.

41. Ibid., page 42.

42. Interview with Karl Schmid. May 1970. *Jung Biographical Archive.* Quoted in Linda Donn, *Freud and Jung: Years of Friendship, Years of Loss,* New York: Scribners, 1988, pages 98, 206.

43. Jung is mistaken. It was not that evening but the next day.

44. Billinsky, 1969, page 42.

45. Peter L. Rudnytsky, "Rescuing Psychoanalysis from Freud: The Common Project of Stekel, Jung, and Ferenczi," *Psychoanalysis and History,* Volume 8, Number 1, 2006, page 134. Also, Rudnytsky pointed this out to me in a December 24, 2013, personal communication.

46. Personal communication, January 27, 2014.

47. See Bair, *Jung,* page 101, for background information regarding the emergence of psychoanalysis at the Burghölzli.

48. Jung, *Memories, Dreams, Reflections,* page 114.

49. Ibid., page 149.

50. Quoted in Donn, *Freud and Jung,* page 98, based on her interview with Franz Jung.

51. There appears to be disagreement among scholars on exactly how many days, but it was at least five and probably not more than seven. Binswanger did stay on for an extra week.

52. Donn, *Freud and Jung,* pages 71–72.

53. Ibid., page 74.

54. Jones, II, page 33.

55. Bair, *Jung,* page 119.

56. William McGuire, editor, *The Freud/Jung Letters: The Correspondence between Sigmund Freud and C. G. Jung,* translated by R. Manheim & R. F. C. Hull, Princeton, NJ: Princeton University Press, 1974, page 23.

57. Jones, II, page 33.

58. Martin Freud, *Sigmund Freud: Man and Father,* Lanham, MD: Jason Aronson, 1977 (originally published 1958), page 109.

59. McGuire, *The Freud/Jung Letters,* page 26; also see Donn, *Freud and Jung,* page 75.

60. A. A. Brill, *Lectures on Psychoanalytic Psychiatry,* New York: Alfred A. Knopf, 1949, Lecture I, page 11; Donn, *Freud and Jung,* page 76.

61. Donn, *Freud and Jung*, page 77.

62. McGuire, *The Freud/Jung Letters*, page 82.

63. Donn, *Freud and Jung*, pages 78–79.

64. Jung's letter to Freud, October 28, 1907, McGuire, *The Freud/Jung Letters*, pages 94–95.

65. Freud's letter to Jung, November 15, 1907, McGuire, *The Freud/Jung Letters*, page 98.

66. Donn, *Freud and Jung*, pages 84–86.

67. Ibid., pages 87–88.

68. Ibid., pages 88–90.

69. McGuire, *The Freud/Jung Letters*, page 207. For detailed analyses of the Jung/Spielrein relationship and Freud's connection to it, see John Kerr, *A Most Dangerous Method, The Story of Jung, Freud, and Sabina Spielrein*, New York: Knopf, 1993; and Aldo Carotenuto, *A Secret Symmetry: Sabina Spielrein between Jung and Freud*, translated by Arno Pomerans, John Shepley, Krishna Winston, New York: Pantheon Books, 1982.

70. McGuire, *The Freud/Jung Letters*, page 210.

71. Jones, I, pages 223–225. The woman in this case was the famous Anna O., real name Bertha Pappenheim. Breuer's counter-transference to Pappenheim was so strong that his wife became jealous and he had to break off the treatment.

72. Carotenuto, *A Secret Symmetry*, page 94.

73. Rosenzweig, *Freud, Jung and Hall*, page 44.

74. Ibid., pages 19–49. Saul Rosenzweig, whose study is a comprehensive account of the Clark celebrations and the events leading up to it, including Freud and Jung's travels, is surprised that Jung was invited. He was only thirty-four at the time, Rosenzweig argues, and not that well known; his record of publications neither lengthy nor that impressive; and although Hall was already using Jung's association experiments in his own work, he referred to those as the "Jung–Freud tests," yet Freud had nothing to do with them. Rosenzweig concludes from this that "Hall did not consider Jung an important scientific innovator in his own right" (ibid., page 34). I think Rosenzweig is correct. Just looking at the list of honorary doctorates awarded at the ceremony, Jung is not even included under the category of psychology, but instead receives his degree under the designation "Education and School Hygiene." See the Clark University website for the list of honorees by category: https://www.clarku.edu/micro/freudcentennial/history/1909psych.cfm.

Rosenzweig thinks Jung may have been a replacement for the more eminent Dr. Ernst Meumann, professor at the University of Münster and a specialist in the field of experimental pedagogy. Meumann apparently first accepted Hall's invitation and then had to decline. Rosenzweig, *Freud, Jung, and Hall*, pages 35–36, 45–46. Jung offers his own explanation, which is different than Rosenzweig's. Jung writes in *Memories, Dreams, Reflections*: "During the years 1904–5 I set up a laboratory for experimental psychopathology at the Psychiatric Clinic. ... There were ... a number of Americans among our associates, including Carl Petersen and Charles Ricksher. Their papers were published in American journals. It was these association studies which later, in 1909, procured me my invitation to Clark University." Ibid., page 120.

75. Rosenzweig says he learned of Freud's view of the fainting episode in Bremen from a travel diary Freud kept and is now deposited in the restricted portion of the Freud Collection at the Library of Congress. He indicates that Anna Freud gave him permission to access the documents. Rosenzweig, *Freud, Jung, and Hall*, pages 52–53, 287. I might add here, another example of the selective distribution of information in the field of Freud studies. See the concluding chapter of this book for more on this subject.

76. Ibid., pages 51–53.

77. Ibid., pages 56, 58, 61.

78. Ibid., page 64.

79. Ibid., page 291.

80. Ibid., pages 64–67.

81. Ibid., page 64.

82. Maciejewski, Gaines, 2006, pages 497–506.

83. Ibid., pages 499–500.

84. Ibid., page 502. In a September 5, 1900, letter to Martha from Riva, Freud indicates that he is sensitive about people he might know seeing him with Minna (the "other woman"). See Christfried Tögel, *Unser Herz Zeigt Nach Dem Süden, Reisebriefe 1895–1923*, Berlin: Aufbau Tashchenbuch Verlag, 2002, page 131.

85. Maciejewski, Gaines, 2006, page 500; Tögel, 2002, page 109.

86. Maciejewski, Gaines, 2006, pages 500–501.

87. Albrecht Hirschmüller, 2005, page 242. Minna's statement could have a second meaning: not his own bed but maybe Minna's.

88. Eva Brabant, Ernst Falzeder, Patrizia Giampieri-Deutsch, eds., *The Correspondence of Sigmund Freud and Sàndor Ferenczi, Volume I, 1908–1914*, translated by Peter T. Hoffer, introduction by André Haynal, Cambridge, MA: Belknap Press of Harvard University Press, 1992, page 453.

89. Maciejewski, Gaines, 2006, page 501.

90. Masson, *The Freud/Fliess Letters*, page 322.

91. Maciejewski, Gaines, 2006, page 504.

92. Maciejewski, Gaines, 2008, pages 5–21.

93. Ibid., page 5.

94. Ibid., pages 5, 15–18.

95. Rudnytsky, 2006, pages 125–129.

96. Ibid., page 135. Sándor Ferenczi, *Ohne Sympathie keine Heilung: Das klinische Tagebuch con 1932*. Edited by J. Dupont. Frankfurt am Main: Fischer, 1988, pages 246–247.

97. Rudnytsky, 2006, page 137. Brabant, *The Correspondence of Freud and Ferenczi*, pages 304–305.

98. Brabant, *The Correspondence of Freud and Ferenczi*, pages 304–305.

99. Rudnytsky, 2006, page 137.

100. Ibid. For the letter, see McGuire, *The Freud/Jung Letters*, page 526.

101. *The New American Review*, Spring/Summer 1982, pages 1–23.

102. Jones, I, pages 336–337.

103. Pages 422–425.

104. Jones's description of this trip is in some respects different from the one that Freud describes to Fliess, but all major elements are the same.

105. Swales, 1982, page 2.

106. Masson, *The Freud/Fliess Letters*, page 423.

107. Examples, all in ibid., May 21, 1894, letter (page 73); September 15, 1895, letter (page 139); November 29, 1895, letter (page 152); April 4, 1900, letter (page 408).

108. Ibid., pages 423–424.

109. Swales, 1982, pages 11, 14.

110. Freud, *The Psychopathology of Everyday Life (1901)*, *The Standard Edition*, Volume VI, Chapter II, "The Forgetting of Foreign Words," pages 8–14.

111. Jones, I, page 336.

112. See Swales, 1982, pages 14–15.

113. *The American Journal of Psychoanalysis*, Volume 51, Number 2, 1991, pages 173–184.

114. O'Brien, 1991, pages 174, 182; the letter can be found in Masson, *The Freud/Fliess Letters,* pages 191–192.

115. O'Brien, 1991, pages 173–174.

116. Full reference details for Kerr's book are provided in note 69 for this chapter.

117. As I mentioned earlier, I have communicated with Dr. John M. Billinsky, Jr., Billinsky's son, from whom Kerr indicates in his book he got a copy of the notes (Kerr, *A Most Dangerous Method,* page 529), and Billinsky Junior says that he remembers reading the notes as his father was preparing a sanitized version for publication, and he confirms that the handwritten notes contain a more explicit account of the relationship between Freud and Minna than does the published version.

118. Kerr, *A Most Dangerous Method*, page 138.

119. Bair, *Jung*, pages 195, 248–249.

120. Kerr, *A Most Dangerous Method*, pages 137, 529–530. See Vincent Brome, *Jung: Man and Myth,* New York: Atheneum, 1978, page 264.

121. Brome, *Jung*, page 264.

122. Ibid., page 305.

123. See page 13 of this chapter.

124. Kerr, *A Most Dangerous Method*, page 137.

125. *American Imago*, Volume 64, Number 2, Summer 2007, pages 283–289.

126. Their first trip together was in 1897. For a comprehensive description of the trips Freud took alone with Minna, see Chapter 5 of this book.

127. Silverstein, 2007, page 285.

128. Ibid., pages 286–287.

129. Paul Roazen, *Meeting Freud's Family,* Amherst, MA: University of Massachusetts Press, 1993, page 139; Silverstein, 2007, page 287.

130. Silverstein, 2007, page 287.

131. Ibid., page 288.

132. *Psychoanalysis and History*, Volume 10, Number 1, pages 115–130.

133. Burston, 2008, page 116.

134. McGuire, *The Freud/Jung Letters*.

135. Burston, 2008, page 118.

136. Ibid. See Richard Schoenwald, "Review of The Freud/Jung Letters," *Journal of Modern History*, Volume 47, Number 2, 1975, pages 360–363.

137. Schoenwald, 1975, page 361.

138. Burston, 2008, pages 121, 125.

139. Ibid., page 122.

CHAPTER 3: THE FREUDIAN RESPONSE

1. See Chapter 2 of this book.

2. *Freud, The Man and the Cause*, New York: Random House.

3. Ibid., page 52.

4. Ibid.

5. "Freud and Minna," Volume XVI, December 1982, pages 41–46.

6. Elms, 1982, page 43.

7. See McGuire, *The Freud/Jung Letters*, page 26.

8. Elms, 1982, page 43.

9. Ibid.

10. Ibid.

11. Ibid., page 45.

12. Ibid., pages 45–46.

13. Gay, 1988, page 76.

14. Hirschmüller later disputes this and says Freud only called *Martha* "My Treasure." See Hirschmüller, 2005, page 25. Based on Hirschmüller's and Tögel's collection of letters, I agree with Hirschmüller, although Gay may have had access to other letters of which I am not aware, and perhaps Hirschmüller and Tögel also were not aware.

15. Gay, 1988, page 76.

16. This is according to what Freud told Princess Marie Bonaparte, a strong supporter who helped extricate him from Nazi Austria in 1938. Gay's reference is to a December 16, 1953, letter from Bonaparte to Ernest Jones (*Jones Papers, Archives of the British Psycho-Analytic Society*, London). We have already seen in a May 21, 1894, letter to Fliess, Freud also refers to Minna as "my closest confidante" (see Masson, *The Freud/Fliess Letters*, page 73). Gay also references this letter (see Gay, 1988, page 665).

17. Gay, 1988, page 76.

18. Ibid., pages 752–753.

19. Ibid., page 752.

20. Ibid. I am referring to the December 3, 1912, letter from Jung to Freud discussed in Chapter 2 of this book.

21. Gay, 1988, pages 642, 752.

22. Ibid., page 752.

23. Ibid., pages 752–753.

24. Ibid., page 753.

25. January 29, 1989.

26. Gay, 1989.

27. Ibid.

28. Both letters have now been published in Hirschmüller, 2005; see pages 235–238 for the April 27, 1893, letter; and pages 185–187 for the April 28, 1887, letter.

29. Gay, 1989. See Nathan G. Hale, Jr., editor, *James Jackson Putnam and Psychoanalysis; Letters between Putnam and Sigmund Freud, Ernest Jones, William James, Sàndor Ferenczi, and Morton Prince, 1877–1917*, Cambridge, MA: Harvard University Press, 1971, page 189.

30. New Haven, CT: Yale University Press, this time with references. The title of the new essay is "The Dog That Did Not Bark in the Night," Gay, 1990, pages 164–179.

31. Ibid., page 164.

32. Edmund Engelman, Peter Gay, and Rita Ransohoff, Chicago: University of Chicago Press, 1976, page 73.

33. Gay, 1990, page 165.

34. Martin Freud, *Sigmund Freud,* pages 26–27: "My father began work at eight every morning and it was not uncommon for him to work through until perhaps three o'clock the following morning"; and page 164: "Since he never went to bed before the small hours of the morning …."

35. Personal communication with Ralph Blumenthal, December 16, 2013.

36. Pages 107–184.

37. Eissler, *Three Instances of Injustice*, page 110.

38. Ibid., pages 110–111.

39. Ibid., page 111.

40. McGuire, *The Freud/Jung Letters,* pages xxi–xxvi.

41. Billinsky, 1969, page 42.

42. Eissler, *Three Instances of Injustice*, page 117.

43. Ibid., page 118, Note 5.

44. McGuire, *The Jung/Freud Letters,* page 23.

45. Eissler, *Three Instances of Injustice*, page 118.

46. Ibid., page 121.

47. Ibid.

48. Ibid.

49. Ibid., page 122.

50. Ibid.

51. See Chapter 3, page 38.

52. We have referenced this letter before. Ibid.

53. Eissler, *Three Instances of Injustice,* page 123; McGuire, *The Freud/Jung Letters*, page 26.

54. Eissler, *Three Instances of Injustice,* page 123; McGuire, *The Freud/Jung Letters,* page 30.

55. Eissler, *Three Instances of Injustice,* page 124; McGuire, *The Freud/Jung Letters,* page 95.

56. Eissler, *Three Instances of Injustice,* page 124.

57. Ibid., page 125.

58. Billinsky, 1969, page 42; Eissler, *Three Instances of Injustice,* page 125.

59. Eissler, *Three Instances of Injustice,* pages 125–126.

60. Eissler, *Three Instances of Injustice,* page 127; Billinsky, 1969, page 42.

61. Eissler, *Three Instances of Injustice,* page 129; McGuire, *The Freud/Jung Letters,* page 526.

62. *Introduction to Jungian Psychology: Notes of the Seminar on Analytical Psychology Given in 1925 by C. G. Jung,* edited by Sonu Shamdasani, Princeton, NJ: Princeton University Press, 1989, page 22; Eissler, *Three Instances of Injustice,* page 130.

63. Jung, *Memories, Dreams, Reflections,* 1961, page 158; Eissler, *Three Instances of Injustice,* page 129.

64. Eissler, *Three Instances of Injustice,* page 164.

65. Ibid., page 171.

66. Ibid., page 177.

67. Ibid., page 178.

68. Ibid., pages 178–179.

69. Ibid.

70. *American Imago,* Volume 64, Number 1, Spring 2007, pages 129–133; hereinafter referred to as Lothane, 2007a.

71. Lothane, 2007a, page 129.

72. Billinsky, 1969, page 43.

73. See Gay, 1988, pages 277–283.

74. Lothane, 2007a, page 131.

75. Ibid.

76. See Murray's obituary in *The New York Times,* June 24, 1988.

77. See Chapter 3, page 44. As mentioned previously, Gay also indicates Meier told him. Gay, 1990, page 164.

78. Lothane, 2007a, pages 131–132.

79. Gay, 1988, page 752.

80. Bair, *Jung,* page 702, Note 27; Lothane, 2007a, page 132; Anthony Storr was an Englishman who wrote extensively about Jung and his psychological theories and was a devoted Jungian. See Bair, *Jung,* pages 573, 589.

81. *Psychoanalytic Psychology,* Volume 24, No. 3, 2007, 487–495; hereinafter referred to as Lothane, 2007b.

82. Lothane, 2007b, page 489.

83. Kanton Graubünden, 1851, provision 146.7; Lothane, 2007b, page 489.

84. Lothane, 2007b, page 489.

85. Ibid.

86. Ibid., page 490.
87. See Gay, 1990, page 165; also see Chapter 3, page 42.
88. Lothane, 2007b, page 491.
89. Ibid., page 493.
90. *American Imago*, Volume 64, Number 1, Spring 2007, pages 125–129.
91. Tübingen: Edition Diskord, 2005. See Chapter 2, Note 21.
92. Hirschmüller, 2007, page 126.
93. See Eissler, *Three Instances of Injustice*, pages 107–184; Hirschmüller, 2007, pages 126, 128 (Note 1).
94. Hirschmüller, 2007, page 126.
95. Hirschmüller, 2005, pages 243–245; Hirschmüller, 2007, pages 126, 128 (Note 2).
96. Tögel, 2002, pages 129–131. This last letter was actually written from Riva on Lake Garda. Lake Maggiore is located some 250 kilometers from Riva.
97. Hirschmüller, 2007, page 126.
98. Hirschmüller, 2007, 126–127. Maciejewski had also talked to Wintsch.
99. See Maciejewski, Gaines, 2006, page 501.
100. Hirschmüller, 2007, page 127.
101. Hirschmüller, 2007, page 128; Maciejewski, Gaines, 2006, page 501.
102. Dunn, *Freud and Jung*, page 98.
103. New York: Other Press, 1992, 2000.
104. Appignanesi and Forrester, *Freud's Women*, page 52.
105. McLynn, *Jung*, page 100.
106. New York: John Wiley & Sons, 2000.
107. Breger, *Freud*, page 397.
108. Roazen, *The Historiography of Psychoanalysis*, page 85; see also ibid., page 110 for similar thoughts.
109. Roazen, *Meeting Freud's Family*, page 153.
110. Roazen, *Freud and His Followers*, page 62.

CHAPTER 4: SORTING OUT THE ARGUMENTS

1. See page 41 of Chapter 3.
2. For Jung's views on the subject, see *Memories, Dreams, Reflections*, page 148.
3. For the sake of completeness, I will include in this list, in slightly enlarged versions, the several instances already mentioned by Kurt Eissler. See Eissler, *Three Instances of Injustice*, pages 129–130.
4. McGuire, *The Freud/Jung Letters*, page 526; also Eissler, *Three Instances of Injustice*, page 129.
5. See Chapter 3, page 42.
6. Jung, *Notes of the Seminar*, page 22.
7. Jung, *Memories, Dreams, Reflections*, 1961, page 158; Eissler, *Three Instances of Injustice*, page 129.
8. Rosenzweig, *Freud, Jung, and Hall*, pages 64, 291.

9. Ibid., page 64.

10. Jung, *Notes of the Seminar*, page 22.

11. I assume this was the "triangle" dream.

12. Jung is mistaken here. He might have been away from Switzerland for fourteen days, but he was in Vienna only about a week. It was Ludwig Binswanger, accompanying Jung and his wife Emma to Vienna, who stayed on with Freud for an additional week. Jung and his wife went on to Budapest, where they visited a friend, Philip Stein, and then to Fiume in Italy and finally by boat to Abbazia for a holiday before returning to Zürich. See McGuire, *The Freud/Jung Letters*, page 24.

13. Some examples of the adoration: "And I was of course, God, a naïve young man then, and, and enthusiastic, and loved Freud a great deal, admired and loved him so much. ..." "So he was utterly brilliant, and when he was in a good mood, he was exceptionally entertaining." "He *felt* things, *noticed* them, in a very keen way. He could make extraordinarily keen and accurate observations"—Emphasis Jung's. "He could grasp all emotional states in others wonderfully. So, in that he was admirable!" "He had a vivid feel for beauty and very good taste." "He has a very keen, a very keen taste for beautiful things. Particularly beautiful jade, beautiful stones." "... he had a very lively feel, an intense appreciation, for art." "So, everything that was good in literature, he knew it and appreciated it." "He was very gracious, very gentle and gracious." "Yes, it was, yes, it was! Yeah, it goes to show, doesn't it, what bigness, what depth he had, you know?!"

Some examples of the regrets: "We had a very good friendship, until we just came up against the things that were incompatible. That's how it was—it was a terrible disappointment to him that I turned away from him. And for me it was the same!" "So, for me, it [Jung's break with Freud] was a terrible loss. I didn't come off it for a long time. [This seems to be the so-called psychotic episode that Eissler describes in *Three Instances of Injustice*] But it just didn't work anymore. It was impossible!" "God, if he only could have gotten away from himself, you know! But that was this neurotic element, you know? ... If he could have gotten away ... it would have been crazy, you know, to ever have wanted anything other than to work together with him!"

14. Maciejewski, Gaines, 2006, page 502.

15. Gay, 1988, page 753: "[If] a statement that Freud makes concerning someone else may well apply to himself," Gay had argued, "Swales accepts it as evidence [that the person in question is a disguised Freud]; when a statement fails to fit, he accuses Freud of disguising the material, or of brazen deception."

16. Kerr, *A Most Dangerous Method*, pages 529–530.

17. Brome, *Jung*, page 264.

18. Kerr, *A Most Dangerous Method*, page 137.

19. Silverstein, 2007, pages 284–285.

20. Remember what Freud wrote: "I stand for a much freer sexual life. However, I have made little use of such freedom, *except in so far as I was convinced of what was permissible for me in this area*"—emphasis mine. The letter is contained in Hale, *James Jackson Putnam and Psychoanalysis*, pages 188–190.

21. Gay, 1988, page 45.

22. Burston, 2008, page 116.

23. McGuire, *The Freud/Jung Letters*, 1975.

24. Burston, 2008, page 118.

25. Ibid., page 122.

26. Eissler, *Three Instances of Justice*, page 179.

27. Jones, I, page 153; II, page 387.

28. Jones, II, page 386.

29. Clark, *Freud,* page 52.

30. See Silverstein, 2007, page 283.

31. See Chapter 2, pages 19–20.

32. See Rudnytsky, 2006, page 134.

33. McGuire, *The Freud/Jung Letters*, page 3.

34. See A. A. Brill, *Lectures on Psychoanalytic Psychiatry*, Lecture I, pages 10–11.

35. McGuire, *The Freud/Jung Letters*, page xvi.

36. See, for example, Martin Freud, *Sigmund Freud*, page 109.

37. Bair, *Jung*, page 114.

38. Martin Freud, *Sigmund Freud*, pages 108–109.

39. Eissler, *Interview with C. G. Jung*, 1953.

40. McGuire, *The Freud/Jung Letters*, page 23.

41. Martin Freud, *Sigmund Freud*, page 109.

42. This is the letter dated March 31, 1907; McGuire, *The Freud/Jung Letters*, page 26.

43. See Eissler, *Three Instances of Injustice*, pages 123–124.

44. In an October 23, 1906, letter to Freud, Jung writes about Spielrein: "I am currently treating an hysteric with your method. Difficult case, a 20-year-old Russian girl student, ill for 6 years." Jung wants to know what Freud thinks. On October 27, 1906, Freud responds with a detailed analysis. See McGuire, *The Freud/ Jung Letters*, pages 7–9.

45. For those who think there was an affair, however imperfect, see Aldo Carotenuto, *A Secret Symmetry*, page xliii; and John Kerr, *A Most Dangerous Method*, page 197. For someone who doubts Jung and Spielrein ever became intimate, see Zvi Lothane, "Tender Love and Transference: Unpublished Letters of C. G. Jung and Sabina Spielrein," *International Journal of Psycho-Analysis*, Volume 80, 1999, pages 1189–1204.

46. See Kerr, *A Most Dangerous Method*, pages 3–15, for the state of Spielrein documents.

47. Since Wolff only became Jung's mistress in 1913, though he knew her earlier. See Bair, *Jung*, page 248.

48. Some of their sharpest criticisms came in their respective autobiographies. In Jung's, Freud is criticized for an all-consuming bitterness, which Jung ties to Freud's emphasis on sexuality (Jung, *Memories, Dreams, Reflections*, pages 152–153); and in Freud's, he laments ever having appointed Jung president of the

International Psychoanalytic Society, "a most unfortunate step," and he criticizes Jung for not recognizing the importance of infantile sexuality and the Oedipus Complex (Freud, *An Autobiographical Study (1927), The Standard Edition*, Volume XX, pages 50 and 53).

49. Martin Freud, *Sigmund Freud*, page 48.

50. Masson, *The Freud/Fliess Letters*, page 423.

51. Gay, 1988, page 76.

52. For the bibliographical essay, see Gay, 1988, pages 752–753; for the brief notes, see Gay, 1988, pages 76 and 225.

53. Jung, *Notes of the Seminar*, page 20.

54. Gay, 1988, page 203.

55. Billinsky, 1969, page 42.

56. Gay, 1988, page 225.

57. Jung, *Memories, Dreams, Reflections*, page 120: "During the years 1904–5 I set up a laboratory for experimental psychopathology at the Psychiatric Clinic. I had a number of students there with whom I investigated psychic reactions (i.e., associations)." Also see Aniela Jaffé, editor, *C. G. Jung: Word and Image*, Princeton, NJ: Princeton University Press, 1979, pages 40–41, for some additional information, including a graphic, about the experiments.

58. Hirschmüller, 2005, page 186.

59. Gay, 1988, page 76.

60. Ibid., page 752.

61. Hirschmüller, 2005, page 67.

62. Ibid., page 63.

63. Ibid., facing page 7.

64. Ibid., page 258.

65. Page 62.

66. See Chapter 6 of this book.

67. Billinsky, 1969, page 42.

68. Bair, *Jung*, page 118. Bair's quotes about Viennese culture are from Carl E. Schorske, *Fin-de-Siècle Vienna: Politics and Culture*, New York: Random House, 1981, pages xxv–xxvi. Schorske writes that Vienna was "rich in cultural creativity," not "culture and creativity," as Bair quotes him; see Schorske, *Fin-de-Siècle Vienna*, page xxv.

69. *The New York Times* book review, January 29, 1989.

70. Hirschmüller, 2005, pages 235–238.

71. Ibid., pages 260–61.

72. Ibid., pages 23–24.

73. Eissler, *Three Instances of Injustice*, page 178.

74. Ibid., pages 178–179.

75. Hirschmüller, 2005, pages 23–24.

76. Ibid., pages 241–247.

77. Ibid., page 241.

78. Ibid., page 248.

79. Martin Freud, *Sigmund Freud*, pages 38–39: "My father hated the telephone and avoided its use whenever possible. As everything in our home was arranged to harmonize with his wishes, all precautions were taken to save him from using it."

80. Hirschmüller, 2005, pages 248–249.

81. Tögel, 2002, pages 151–154.

82. Ibid., pages 156–162.

83. Ibid., pages 197–205.

84. Hirschmüller, 2005, pages 255–256.

85. Ibid., pages 298–300.

86. Hirschmüller, 2005, pages 248–249; Tögel, 2002, pages 113–115.

87. Tögel, 2002, pages 151–154.

88. Hirschmüller, 2005, page 24.

89. Gay, 1990, page 164.

90. See Martin Freud, *Sigmund Freud*, pages 26–27, 164.

91. Billinsky, 1969, page 42.

92. Eissler, *Three Instances of Injustice*, page 117.

93. Bair, *Jung*, page 318.

94. Rosenzweig, *Freud, Jung and Hall*, page 291.

95. Eissler, *Three Instances of Injustice*, page 121.

96. Ibid.

97. Jones, I, page 328.

98. Engelman, *Berggasse 19*, page 73.

99. Eissler, *Three Instances of Injustice*, page 122.

100. Gay, 1988, page 199.

101. Eissler, *Three Instances of Injustice*, page 122.

102. Remember, Eissler points to two letters Jung wrote to Freud immediately after his visit as evidence. One, a March 31, 1907, letter in which Jung points out the "tremendous impression" Freud had on him, and his hope, even "his dream," that Freud might come to Zürich. "A visit from you would be seventh heaven for me personally," he adds poignantly (Eissler, *Three Instances of Injustice*, page 123; McGuire, *The Freud/Jung Letters*, page 26). A second letter, sent April 11, 1907, expresses similar sentiments (Eissler, *Three Instances of Injustice*, page 123; McGuire, *The Freud/Jung Letters*, page 30). Even six months later, Jung's praise is unrestrained. He writes in an October 28, 1907, letter: "I have a boundless admiration for you both as a man and a researcher. … my veneration for you has something of the character of a 'religious' crush" (Eissler, *Three Instances of Injustice*, page 124; McGuire, *The Freud/Jung Letters*, page 95). These passages, Eissler argues, are "irreconcilable with an agonizing experience involving discovery of Freud's alleged intimate relationship with Minna Bernays" (Eissler, *Three Instances of Injustice*, page 124).

103. Gay, 1988, page 216.

104. Eissler, *Three Instances of Injustice*, page 125.

105. Ibid., page 126.

106. Ibid.

107. Rosenzweig, *Freud, Jung, and Hall*, pages 52–53.

108. Jung, *Memories, Dreams, Reflections*, page 158.

109. Eissler, *Three Instances of Injustice*, page 164.

110. Ibid., pages 171, 177.

111. Bair, *Jung*, pages 241–247; Jung, *Memories, Dreams, Reflections*, pages 170–199.

112. See John Kerr's list in *A Most Dangerous Method*, page 137.

113. Eissler, *Three Instances of Injustice*, page 178.

114. Ibid., pages 178–179.

115. Lothane, 2007a, "The Sigmund Freud/Minna Bernays Romance: Fact or Fiction?" *American Imago*, Volume 64, Number 1, Spring 2007, pages 129–133; and Lothane, 2007b, "Sigmund Freud and Minna Bernays: Primal Curiosity, Primal Scenes, Primal Fantasies—and Prevarication," *Psychoanalytic Psychology*, Volume 24, No. 3, 2007, pages 487–495.

116. Lothane, 2007b, page 489.

117. Ibid., page 493.

118. Maciejewski, Gaines, 2006, pages 500–501.

119. Tögel, 2002, page 109.

120. Martin Freud, *Sigmund Freud*, page 47. According to Martin Freud, when Freud's financial situation gradually improved over the years, the family went on vacations further afield, travelled more comfortably, and stayed at more expensive hotels.

121. See ibid., page 51.

122. Maciejewski, Gaines, 2006, page 501.

123. Hirschmüller, 2005, pages 243–244.

124. Lothane, 2007a, page 131.

125. Hirschmüller, 2007, pagers 125–129.

126. *Sigmund Freud/Minna Bernays: Briefwechsel, 1882–1938*, Tübingen: Edition Diskord, 2005.

127. Hirschmüller, 2007, page 126.

128. Hirschmüller, 2005, pages 243–245.

129. Hirschmüller, 2007, page 126.

130. Ibid.

131. Ibid.

132. Ibid., page 127.

133. Maciejewski and Gaines, 2006, page 501.

134. Letter of August 6, 1898 (Hirschmüller, 2005, page 242).

135. Ibid., pages 243–245.

136. Ibid., page 128.

137. Tögel, 2002, pages 129–130.

138. Hirschmüller, 2007, page 128; Maciejewski and Gaines, 2006, page 501.

139. Donn, 1988, page 98.

140. Appignanesi and Forrester, 1992, page 52.

141. McLynn, 1996, page 100.

142. Breger, 2000, page 397.

143. Roazen, 2001, pages 85 and 110.
144. Roazen, 1993, page 153.
145. Roazen, 1976, page 62.
146. Breger, *Freud,* page 397.

CHAPTER 5: FREUD AND MINNA

1. Maciejewski and Gaines, 2008, pages 7–8; Gay, 1990, page 165.
2. 1976, page 63. Roazen quotes a letter from Ernest Jones to Max Eitingon, October 21, 1939.
3. Quoted in Hirschmüller, 2005, pages 20–21.
4. Jones, I, page 153.
5. You'll recall his letter to Martha of August 10, 1898, written while he and Minna were alone on holiday: "Yesterday's tour was tiring, at least for me; Minna cannot be worn out by any exertion" (Hirschmüller, 2005, pages 243–245).
6. Recall Peter Gay's comments regarding Minna's unattractive looks (Gay, 1988, page 76): after the death of her fiancé Schönberg, Gay writes, Minna "apparently resigned herself to spinsterhood. She grew heavier, more jowly, becoming exceedingly plain; she looked older than her sister Martha, though she was in fact four years younger."
7. Hirschmüller, 2005, pages 150–151.
8. Ibid., page 142.
9. Ibid., page 151.
10. Ibid., pages 243–245.
11. Roazen, *Freud and His Followers,* page 62.
12. Tögel, 2002, page 100.
13. Jones, I, page 164.
14. Ibid., pages 116–117.
15. Letter to Fliess of November 12, 1899 (Masson, *The Freud/Fliess Letters,* page 385).
16. Hirschmüller, 2005, page 35, letter of August 22, 1882; and page 87, letter of October 12, 1884.
17. Ibid., page 187, May 8, 1887, letter.
18. Ibid., page 235, letter of April 27, 1893.
19. Ibid., page 97, letter of November 15, 1884; and page 255, letter of July, 18, 1910.
20. Gay, 1990, page 171.
21. Hirschmüller, 2005, page 97, letter of October 29, 1884.
22. Ernst Freud, editor, *Letters of Sigmund Freud,* trans. Tania and James Stern, New York: Basic Books, 1960, page 125, letter of August 28, 1884.
23. Behling, *Martha Freud,* page 77.
24. To see how Freud sought to compartmentalize his life at Berggasse in order to keep out unwanted distractions, even from members of his own family, see Chapter 6 of this work.
25. Behling, *Martha Freud,* page 75.

26. Young-Bruehl, *Anna Freud, A Biography*, Second Edition, New Haven, CT: Yale University Press, 2008, page 449.

27. Billinsky, 1969, page 42.

28. Bair, *Jung*, pages 119–120.

29. Gay, 1988, page 76. Gay indicates that his source is a December 16, 1953, letter from Marie Bonaparte to Ernest Jones, *Jones Papers, Archives of the British Psycho-Analytical Society*, London.

30. Masson, *The Freud/Fliess Letters*, page 73.

31. For a brief history of the Wednesday Psychological Society, see *Minutes of the Vienna Psychoanalytic Society, Volume I: 1906–1908*, edited by Herman Nunberg and Ernst Federn, New York: International Universities Press, 1962, pages xviii–xix.

32. Gay, 1990, page 170.

33. See the concluding chapter of this book for an assessment of Minna's possible contributions to the development of psychoanalysis.

34. Jones, I, page 103; Gay, 1988, page 37.

35. Jones puts Minna's age at sixteen; see Jones, I, 164.

36. Maciejewski, Gaines, 2008, page 7.

37. Sachs, *Freud*, page 153.

38. Hirschmüller, 2005, pages 86–88.

39. Ibid., pages 138–139.

40. Jones, I, page 164.

41. Ibid., pages 164–165.

42. Ibid., page 165.

43. May 7, 1886, letter to Minna (Hirschmüller, 2005, pages 150–151).

44. Jones, I, page 153; Gay, 1988, page 76.

45. Hirschmüller, 2005, pages 138–139, 150–151.

46. Jones, I, page 104.

47. Roazen, *Meeting Freud's Family*, page 139.

48. Hirschmüller, 2005, page 96.

49. Ibid., page 96, Note 5.

50. Ibid., page 96.

51. Jones, I, page 79.

52. Gay, 1990, page 170.

53. Hirschmüller, 2005, page 237.

54. Gay, 1989.

55. Lothane, 2007b, page 491.

56. Gay, 1990, pages 169–170.

57. Ernst Freud, *Letters of Sigmund Freud*, page 229.

58. Hirschmüller, 2005, pages 37–38.

59. Jones, I, page 114.

60. Hirschmüller, 2005, pages 86–87.

61. Gay, 1990, pages 172–173; the letter can be found in Hirschmüller, 2005, pages 185–187.

62. Hanns Sachs, *Freud*, page 84. Sachs does not mention Minna, but, as you will see, she often accompanied Freud as well.

63. Jones, I, page 335. In 1898, while traveling with Minna, she came down with "some gastric disturbance," and Freud continued on to Cattaro with a stranger.

64. Ibid., page 334.

65. Ibid., pages 334–335.

66. Ibid., page 335.

67. Hirschmüller, 2005, pages 243–245.

68. See Chapter 2, pages 29–31.

69. Masson, *The Freud/Fliess Letters,* pages 423–424; see also Jones, I, pages 336–337.

70. See Chapter 4 of this book.

71. Tögel, 2002, pages 129–131.

72. Ibid., pages 151–154.

73. Jones, II, page 23.

74. This according to Jones, II, page 25. I don't see in Tögel or Hirschmüller a Freud postcard sent from Isola dei Pescatori in which Minna is described as handling the journey pretty well. There is a September 9, 1905, postcard from Isola dei Pescatori, where Freud mentions their eating in a small Italian restaurant. Freud does mention that Minna is comfortable and fresh in a postcard sent the next day, September 10, from Pallanza, but perhaps Jones had access to correspondence that Tögel and Hirschmüller did not. See Tögel, 2002, pages 201–202, for both the aforementioned postcards.

75. Jones, II, page 25.

76. Tögel, 2002, pages 195–208.

77. Hirschmüller, 2005, pages 249–254.

78. Sachs, *Freud,* page 95.

79. I cannot find any information about the 1906 Lavarone holiday.

80. Jones, II, page 35.

81. Ibid.

82. See Tögel, 2002, pages 209–236.

83. Ibid., page 236. Last postcard from Rome is dated September 25, 1907.

84. Jones, II, page 36. Jones reproduces (II, 36–37) one of Freud's letters home (written from Rome on September 22, 1907) to illustrate how detailed Freud's descriptions of his excursions are. It is indeed amazing just how much detail Freud provides, even in some of the brief postcards he writes.

85. Ibid., page 52–53.

86. See Tögel, 2002, pages 266–271 for all five letters/postcards sent from Salò. An English translation of the September 25, 1908, letter to Martha from Salò, one of the five I mention, can be found in Ernst Freud, *The Letters of Sigmund Freud,* pages 276–277.

87. Jones, II, page 98.

88. Ibid., page 103.

89. Brabant, *Correspondence of Freud and Ferenczi,* Volume I, pages 508–509.

90. Ernst Freud, *Letters of Sigmund Freud,* pages 302–303.

91. Jones, III, page 10.

92. Ibid., page 79.

93. Ibid., pages 97–98.

94. Gay, 1988, page 158.

95. It is curious, as you'll recall, Gay does mention Minna going off with Freud on some summer trips elsewhere (earlier) in his biography: "the two occasionally visited Swiss resorts or Italian cities alone." I am not sure why Gay drops Minna's name when he summarizes how Freud travelled for the last part of his summer holidays. See Gay, 1988, page 76, for the earlier reference. Also, see Chapter 3 of this work.

96. Jones, I, page 331.

97. Masson, *The Freud/Fliess Letters*, page 73.

98. Jones, I, pages 164–165.

99. Puner, *Freud*, page 134.

100. Sachs, *Freud*, page 76; Puner, *Freud*, page 58.

101. Jones, I, page 180.

102. Gay, 1990, page 168.

103. Roazen, *Freud and His Followers*, page 60.

104. Hirschmüller, 2005, page 260.

105. Sachs, *Freud*, page 20.

106. Ibid., pages 56–57.

107. Ibid., page 82.

108. See Gay, 1988, page 76, for a reference to Freud's statement that at the beginning only Fliess and Minna believed in his work.

109. Hirschmüller, 2005, pages 18–19.

110. Sachs, *Freud*, page 75.

111. See "Heroine Addict, What Theodor Fontane's Women Want," by Daniel Mendelsohn, *The New Yorker*, March 7, 2011, available on the Internet at http://www.newyorker.com/magazine/2011/03/07/heroine-addict

112. Gay, 1988, pages 166–169; Sachs, *Freud*, pages 104–108.

113. Sachs, *Freud*, pages 101–102.

114. Gay, 1988, page 168.

115. Sachs, *Freud*, pages 104–105.

116. We have seen in Chapter 1 that both Freud and Jung were eager for international recognition "After World War I," Roazen writes in his *Meeting Freud's Family* (page 144), "patients often came from abroad. By the 1920s the best-paying clients were Americans, and Freud's practice was largely confined to them."

117. Gay, 1988, page 157. In describing Freud's daily schedule, Gay writes: "Then came supper, sometimes a short game of cards with his sister-in-law Minna, or a walk with his wife or one of his daughters, often ending up at a cafe."

118. Martin Freud, *Freud*, page 48.

119. Hirschmüller, 2005, page 244; letter of August 10, 1898.

120. Tögel, 2007, page 131. Letter of September 5, 1900. As mentioned earlier, Tögel provides short biographies of those referenced in his notes to the letter.

121. Martin Freud, *Sigmund Freud*, page 145.

122. Hirschmüller, 2005, page 256.

123. Behling, *Martha Freud*, page 6.

124. Sachs, *Freud*, page 21.

125. Ibid., page 37.

126. Ibid., page 21.

127. Hirschmüller, 2005, page 18.

128. See page 105 in this chapter. See also Gay, 1988, page 630.

129. Sachs, *Freud*, page 128.

130. McGuire, *The Freud/Jung Letters*, page 7.

131. Ibid., page 107.

132. Silverstein, 2007, pages 286–287.

133. *Meeting Freud's Family*, page 111.

134. Sachs, *Freud*, page 30.

135. Gay, 1988, page 143.

136. Hale, *James Jackson Putnam and Psychoanalysis*, page 189; letter from Freud to Putnam dated July 8, 1915.

137. Gay, 1988, page 143.

138. John W. Boyer, "Freud, Marriage, and Later Victorian Liberalism: A Commentary from 1905," *Journal of Modern History*, I (1978), pages 91–93. The original German version of these questions and answers is contained in an appendix to this article, pages 99–102.

139. Masson, *The Freud/Fliess Letters*, page 398.

140. Gay, 1988, page 45.

141. Roazen, *Meeting Freud's Family*, page 111.

142. See Gay, 1990, page 179.

143. In Chapter 6 of this book, Martin Freud provides details as to the roles of these several servants.

144. Jones, I, page 153.

145. Ibid., page 160.

146. Ibid, pages 160–161.

147. Ibid., pages 50–51.

148. Ibid., pages 337–339.

149. Ibid., pages 332–333. See also Martin Freud's recollections in Chapter 4, Note 120 of this book.

150. Rosenzweig, *Freud, Jung, and Hall*, page 24.

151. Sachs, *Freud,* page 19.

152. Ibid., pages 23–24.

153. Gerhard Fichtner, editor, The *Sigmund Freud–Ludwig Binswanger Correspondence, 1908–1938,* translated by Arnold J. Pomerans, New York: Other Press, 2003, page 26.

154. Ibid., page 37; see also Bair, *Jung*, page 100.

155. Puner, *Freud,* page 59.

156. Jones, I, page 232.

157. Sachs, *Freud*, pages 91–92.

158. Freud, *An Autobiographical Study (1927), The Standard Edition,* Volume XX, page 52.

159. Sachs, *Freud*, Pages 78–79.

160. Martin Freud, *Sigmund Freud*, page 23.

161. Ibid., pages 70–71.

162. Ibid., page 169.

163. Ibid., page 156.

164. Engelman, *Berggasse 19*, page 132.

165. Puner, *Freud*, page 141.

166. Gay, 1988, page 162.

167. Masson, *The Freud/Fliess Letters*, page 217.

168. Ibid., page 404.

169. Gay, 1988, page 163.

170. McGuire, *The Freud/Jung Letters*, page 456.

171. Gay, 1988, page 163.

172. Freud, "'Civilized' Sexual Morality and Modern Nervous Illness (1908)," *The Standard Edition*, Volume IX, page 194. See Silverstein, 2007, page 284.

173. Page 62.

174. *Freud*, page 214.

175. II, page 421.

176. Masson, *The Freud/Fliess Letters*, page 44; see also Gay, 1988, page 63.

177. Freud, "'Civilized' Sexual Morality and Modern Nervous Illness (1908)," *The Standard Edition*, Volume IX, page 193.

178. Freud, *The Standard Edition*, Volume XI, page 186. See also Puner, *Freud*, page 213.

179. Even Jones admits that Freud had a "pronounced mental bisexuality"; see Jones, II, page 422.

180. Gay, 1988, page 32.

181. Jones, II, page 3.

182. Jones, I, page 44.

183. Ibid., page 89.

184. Ibid., page 90.

185. Ibid., page 91.

186. Gay, 1988, page 43.

187. Ibid., pages 44–45.

188. Ibid., page 86.

189. Masson, *The Freud/Fliess Letters*, page 2. Masson notes that this letter was given him by Anna Freud. I do not find it in Hirschmüller's or Tögel's collection of Freud/Minna letters.

190. Gay, 1988, page 86.

191. Masson, *The Freud/Fliess Letters*, page 339.

192. Gay, 1988, page 86.

193. Masson, *The Freud/Fliess Letters*, page 3. Quoted material is from Marie Bonaparte's unpublished notebook, which Masson excerpts.

194. Ibid., page 412. See also Gay, 1988, page 86.

195. Masson, *The Freud/Fliess Letters*, page 447; see also Gay, 1988, page 86.

196. Gay, 1988, page 275.

197. Braband, *The Correspondence of Freud and Ferenczi*, page 221.

198. McGuire, *The Freud/Jung Letters*, page 121; Gay, 1988, 274.

199. Jung's letter to Freud dated October 28, 1907 (McGuire, *The Freud/Jung Letters*, pages 94–95).

200. Ibid., page 353; also, Gay, 1988, page 275.

201. Letters quoted in Gay, 1988, pages 275–276.

202. Kurt Eissler, *Interview with C. G. Jung*, 1953, Library of Congress.

203. Freud, *The Psychopathology of Everyday Life (1901)*, *The Standard Edition*, Volume VI, pages 175–176. See also Puner, *Freud*, pages 214–215.

204. Puner, *Freud*, page 120.

205. Freud, *The "Uncanny" (1919)*, *The Standard Edition*, Volume XVII, page 237. See also Roazen, *Freud and His Followers*, page 62.

206. Gay, 1988, page 164. The quotes are from Freud's *Jokes and Their Relation to the Unconscious* (1905), though not from the James Strachey *Standard Edition*, where they can be found in Volume VIII, page 109. Gay's translation is a bit different.

207. Masson, *The Freud/Fliess Letters*, page 249; Gay, 1988, page 162.

208. Gay, 1988, page 163.

209. Nunberg, *Minutes of the Vienna Psychoanalytic Society*, Volume I, page 311.

210. Gay, 1988, page 163.

211. Roazen, *Freud and His Followers*, page 62. He cites for his information on this subject an interview with Henry Murray on November 10, 1965.

212. Ibid.

213. Ibid.

214. Ibid.

215. Didier Anzieu, *Freud's Self-Analysis*, translated from the French by Peter Graham, with a preface by M. Masud R. Khan, London: Hogarth Press, 1986, pages 542–543.

216. Jones, II, page 421.

217. Gay, 1988, page 503.

218. Behling, *Martha Freud*, page 75. See Young-Bruehl, *Anna Freud*, page 32: "With Minna as his ally, Freud … did not have to stand alone in his criticism of Frau Bernays or in his later efforts to raise his own children non-religiously."

219. Sachs, *Freud*, pages 58–59.

220. Letter of March 14, 1911; Gay, 1988, pages 178–179. Earlier, Freud had had a higher opinion of some members of the group; ibid., 173–178.

221. See Chapter 2 for a discussion of Silverstein's ideas.

222. Anzieu, *Freud's Self-Analysis*, page 542.

223. Hirschmüller, 2005, pages 185–186.

224. Freud's letter to Karl Abraham, September 21, 1913, in Ernst Freud, *Letters of Sigmund Freud*, pages 302–303.

225. Anzieu, *Freud's Self-Analysis*, page 542.

226. Jones, II, 387.

227. Young-Bruehl, *Anna Freud*, page 449.

228. I think that by 1920 Anna had replaced Minna as her father's muse and confidante. That was the year, you'll remember, when Anna and Minna apparently

switched rooms in order to allow Anna to have adjoining rooms in the Berggasse apartment. Anna was then twenty-five years of age.

229. Billinsky, 1969, page 42.

CHAPTER 6: FREUD AND MARTHA

1. Breger, *Freud*, page 91.

2. Masson, *The Freud/Fliess Letters*, page 54; August 20, 1893, Freud letter to Fliess.

3. Martin Freud, "Who Was Freud?" in *the Jews of Austria, Essays on their Life, History, and Destruction*, Second Edition, edited by Josef Fraenkel, London: Vallentine/Mitchell, 1970, page 203.

4. Breger, *Freud*, page 93.

5. Martin Freud, *Sigmund Freud*, pages 32–33; Gay, 1988, pages 59–60, 157–158; Behling, *Martha Freud*, pages 67–68.

6. Behling, *Martha Freud*, page 67.

7. Appignanesi and Forrester, *Freud's Women*, page 46.

8. Gay, 1988, page 59.

9. Eissler, *Interview with C. G. Jung*, 1953, Library of Congress.

10. Martin Freud, *Sigmund Freud*, page 19.

11. Jones, I, page 14.

12. Puner, *Freud*, page 26.

13. Gay, 1988, pages 13, 14, 23.

14. Jones, I, page 3.

15. Martin Freud, *Sigmund Freud*, pages 11–12.

16. Gay, 1988, page 12. For the inscription, see Ernst Freud et al., eds., *Sigmund Freud: His Life in Pictures and Words*, New York and London: Harcourt Brace Jovanovich, 1976, page 134.

17. Sigmund Freud, *The Interpretation of Dreams(1900), The Standard Edition*, Volume IV, pages 192–193. Peter Gay writes: "In the liberal mood dominating Austria in the 1860s, the prophecy seemed no more than sensible"; see Gay, 1988, pages 12–13.

18. Quoted in Jones, I, page 5.

19. Anna Freud Bernays, "My Brother, Sigmund Freud," *American Mercury*, Volume LI, 1940, page 336.

20. Martin Freud, *Sigmund Freud*, page 20.

21. Anna Freud Bernays, "My Brother, Sigmund Freud," page 339; Jones, I, page 17.

22. Martin Freud, *Sigmund Freud*, page 20.

23. Ibid.

24. Anna Freud Bernays, "My Brother, Sigmund Freud," page 337; Gay, 1988, page 14.

25. Jones, I, pages 20–21.

26. Gay, 1988, page 14.

27. Jones, I, page 18.

28. Anna Freud Bernays, "My Brother, Sigmund Freud," page 337.

29. Gay, 1988, page 14.

30. Martin Freud, *Sigmund Freud,* pages 19–20.

31. Ibid., pages 38–39.

32. Ibid., page 106.

33. Ibid., page 121.

34. Behling, *Martha Freud*, page 71.

35. Paul Roazen, *Meeting Freud's Family*, page 158.

36. Ibid., page 152.

37. Clark, *Freud,* page 89.

38. Martin Freud, *Sigmund Freud,* page 51.

39. Ibid., page 44.

40. See Gay, 1988, page 38.

41. Puner, *Freud,* page 139.

42. Martin Freud, *Sigmund Freud*, page 160.

43. Ibid., page 168.

44. Roazen, *Meeting Freud's Family*, pages 153–154.

45. Jones, I, page 139.

46. Appignanesi and Forrester, *Freud's Women*, page 30.

47. Gay, 1988, page 40.

48. Appignanesi and Forrester, *Freud's Women*, page 31.

49. Gay, 1988, page 40.

50. Ernst Freud, *Letters of Sigmund Freud,* pages 43 (the August 22, 1883, letter) and 52 (the August 29, 1883, letter).

51. Martin Freud, *Sigmund Freud,* page 39.

52. Ibid., page 63.

53. Behling, *Martha Freud*, page 80.

54. Roazen, *Freud and His Followers,* page 56.

55. Roazen, *Meeting Freud's Family*, page 149.

56. Behling, *Martha Freud*, page 67.

57. Roazen, *Meeting Freud's Family*, page 149.

58. Martin Freud, *Sigmund Freud*, page 125.

59. Ibid., page 25.

60. Puner, *Freud*, pages 57–58.

61. Martin Freud, *Sigmund Freud*, pages 32–33.

62. Behling, *Martha Freud*, page 68.

63. Ibid.

64. Martin Freud, *Sigmund Freud*, page 33.

65. Gay, 1988, page 59; information from an interview with Helen Schur, June 3, 1986.

66. Roazen, *Meeting Freud's Family*, pages 147–148.

67. Melitta Schmideberg, "A Contribution to the History of the Psychoanalytic Movement in Britain," *British Journal of Psychiatry,* Volume 118, 1971, page 64; see Roazen, *Meeting Freud's Family,* page 153.

68. Roazen, *Meeting Freud's Family,* page 147.

69. Not everything was blissful with regard to Martha and the servants, as Jones seems to imply. To Minna, Freud laments the loss of a particularly capable one in a letter of April 27, 1893: "We have had a big palace revolution. Lene [a maid] was overthrown and, to my regret, has gone—she was the most capable, but there is no opposing Ammen, and Martha seems to have had something against her for some time"; see Hirschmüller, 2005, page 237. Esti Freud also tells us that Martha was careful to pick unattractive servants—"hags," as she calls them. Martha was concerned that good-looking servant girls might pose a temptation for her three boys; see Roazen, *Meeting Freud's Family,* page 160.

70. Jones, I, pages 151–152,

71. Gay, 1988, pages 59–60.

72. Appignanesi and Forrester, *Freud's Women,* pages 42–43.

73. Quoted in Gay, 1990, page 172.

74. Quoted in Young-Bruehl, *Anna Freud,* pages 308, 38.

75. Roazen, *Freud and His Followers,* page 59. He is quoting from page 44 of a paper by Dr. Max Schur, titled, "The Medical History of Sigmund Freud."

76. Billinsky, 1969, page 42.

77. Gay, 1988, page 60.

78. Sachs, *Freud,* page 80.

79. Ibid., pages 148–149.

80. Martin Freud, *Sigmund Freud,* page 205.

81. Young-Bruehl, *Anna Freud,* page 55.

82. Gay, 1988, page 162.

83. Ibid. See Richard Dyck, "Mein Onkel Sigmund," interview with Harry Freud in *Aufbau* (New York), May 11, 1956, pages 3–4. For a slightly different translation, see also *Freud as We Knew Him,* edited and introduced by Hendrik M. Ruitenbeek, Detroit: Wayne State University Press, 1973, page 312.

84. Martin Freud, *Sigmund Freud,* page 98.

85. Ibid., page 129.

86. Ibid., page 44.

87. Behling, *Martha Freud,* page 81.

88. Roazen, *Meeting Freud's Family,* page 179.

89. Martin Freud, *Sigmund Freud,* pages 180–181.

90. Sachs, *Freud,* pages 130–131.

91. Gay, 1988, page 61.

92. Masson, *The Freud/Fliess Letters,* page 154.

93. Gay, 1988, page 61.

94. Quoted in Ibid., page 39.

95. Sachs, *Freud,* pages 83–84.

96. Roazen, *Freud and His Followers,* page 59.

97. Behling, *Martha Freud,* page 137.

98. Masson, *The Freud/Fliess Letters,* page 177.

99. Behling, *Martha Freud,* pages 113–114.

100. Masson, *The Freud/Fliess Letters*, page 404; Gay, 1988, page 134.

101. Behling, *Martha Freud*, page 118.

102. Ibid., page 120.

103. Ernst Freud, *The Letters of Sigmund Freud,* page 89.

104. Behling, *Martha Freud*, page 80.

105. Letter of September 15, 1886, quoted in Jones, I, page 150; Behling, *Martha Freud*, page 61.

106. Jones, I, page 123.

107. Quoted in Jones, I, page 123.

108. Behling, *Martha Freud*, pages 78–79.

109. Jones, I, page 121.

110. Ibid., pages 123–126.

111. Ernst Freud, *The Letters of Sigmund Freud,* page 202.

112. René Laforgue, "Personal Memories of Freud (1956)," in *Freud as We Knew Him*, page 342.

113. Behling, *Martha Freud*, page 165.

114. Lucy Freeman and Herbert S. Strean, *Freud and Women,* New York: Frederick Ungar, 1981, page 47.

115. Quoted in Jones, III, page 209.

116. Appignanesi and Forrester, *Freud's Women*, page 42.

117. Roazen, *Freud and His Followers*, page 59.

118. Fichtner, *The Freud/Binswanger Correspondence,* page 221.

119. Jones, I, page 150.

120. Jones, I, page 122.

121. Puner, *Freud,* page 213.

122. Young-Bruehl, *Anna Freud*, page 54.

123. Behling, *Martha Freud*, page 133.

124. Ibid., page 76.

125. Gay, 1988, page 38.

126. Martha could not fall back on all her children: she never got along well with either Anna or Martin. We have already seen the tensions between her and Anna. With regard to Martin, Katja Behling writes: "Martha had her difficulties with Martin, and their relationship was a strained one. To her displeasure, her eldest son had … found his way into the gossip columns, the papers reporting duels, brawls, reckless sporting exploits, injuries and accidents, and for a while as a young man Martin was almost seen as the back sheep of the family" (Behling, *Martha Freud,* page 122).

CONCLUDING THOUGHTS

1. Hirschmüller, 2005, page 27.

2. Rosenzweig, *Freud, Jung, and Hall,* pages 4–10.

3. Gay, 1988, page 76: "The rumor, launched by Carl C. Jung, that Freud had an affair with Minna Bernays lacks convincing evidence."

4. See Chapter 3, page 38.

5. See Chapter 4, page 77.

6. See Jung, *Memories. Dreams, Reflections*, pages 159–160.

7. Behling, *Martha Freud*, page 77.

8. You'll remember how pleased Freud was ("relieved") on holiday in the Italian alps when Minna arrived on August 26, 1900, and he could rid himself of the group of people he was traveling with—many of them relatives—and be able to escape with her alone; see Freud's September 14, 1900, letter to Wilhelm Fliess, Masson, *The Freud/Fliess Letters,* pages 422–423.

9. Minna notes, in an August 6, 1898, letter that she and Freud send to Martha, that Freud loves "to sleep every night in a different bed"; see Hirschmüller, 2005, page 242.

10. August 10, 1898 letter from Freud and Minna to Martha. See Chapter 4, page 98.

11. Martin Freud, *Sigmund Freud,* pages 26–27: "My father began work at eight every morning and it was not uncommon for him to work through until perhaps three o'clock the following morning."

12. See Chapter 2, page 13. Also, see Maciejewski and Gaines, 2006, page 499; and Hirschmüller, 2005, pages 18–19.

13. This was before Anna became intimate with Dorothy Burlingham. For Anna Freud's letters to Eva Rosenfeld, see Heller, *Anna Freud's Letters to Eva Rosenfeld.* For the rumor of an affair between Freud and Minna with reference to Eva Rosenfeld, see Eissler, *Three Instances of Injustice,* pages 108–109.

14. Paul Roazen, *Meeting Freud's Family,* page 139; Silverstein, 2007, page 287.

15. McLynn, *Jung,* page 80.

16. Bair, *Jung,* pages 86 and 680 (Note 20).

17. Carotenuto, *A Secret Symmetry,* pages 92–93.

18. This is where he describes Minna as having "a great transference" to Freud and states that Freud "*was not insensible.*" This latter phrase was spoken in English by Jung—also, emphasis Jung's.

19. Kerr, *A Most Dangerous Method,* page 503.

20. McLynn, *Jung,* page 183.

21. Barbara Hannah, *Jung: His Life and Work, A Biographical Memoir,* New York: Putnam, 1976, page 117.

22. Behling, *Martha Freud,* page 164.

23. Appignanesi and Forrester, *Freud's Women,* page 42.

24. Sachs, *Freud,* page 77.

25. Jones, III, pages 208, 510.

26. New York: *New York Review of Books,* 1997; originally published in 1984 by Alfred Knopf.

27. Quoted in Malcolm, *In the Freud Archives,* pages 111–112.

28. Puner, *Sigmund Freud,* page xix.

29. Roazen, *Meeting Freud's Family*, pages 111–113.

30. Hirschmüller, 2005, page 18, Note 12.

31. Bair, *Jung*, page 688.

32. Hirschmüller, 2005, page 26.

33. I have my own horror story to tell in that regard. In trying to get a copy of Billinsky's handwritten notes upon which his published interview with Jung is based, I enlisted the help of a scholar who had obtained a copy. He was quite willing to provide me the notes but first wanted to check with the person who had provided him the material in the first instance, which seemed reasonable to me, as a courtesy if nothing else. To my dismay the person who had originally obtained the notes refused me permission and informed me in an angry, obscenity-laced email. Why did he do that, you may ask? The reason: I had written a novel about Freud, and apparently, in this person's way of thinking, that automatically disqualified me from obtaining a copy of the original notes. It is ironic that this person would refuse me, since he has been for years one of the most outspoken critics of Eissler and the Archives and their efforts to restrict the free circulation of source materials related to Freud and psychoanalysis.

34. I have found that the reluctance to reveal sources affects not only Freud scholarship but research on Jung as well. Bair notes that the Bleuler/Freud correspondence is not available because the Bleuler heirs have refused permission to publish it (see Bair, *Jung*, page 683). Perhaps this is a common problem for scholars working in the history of psychiatry. I have not come across similar problems in my work on Charles Darwin.

35. Roazen, *Freud and His Followers*, page 61.

Bibliography

Alliance for Audited Media, "The Top 25 U.S. Consumer Magazines for June 2013." Retrieved from http://www.auditedmedia.com/news/blog/2013/august/the -top-25-us-consumer-magazines-for-june-2013.aspx.

Anzieu, Didier (1986). *Freud's Self-analysis*. Translated from the French by Peter Graham, with a preface by M. Masud R. Khan. London: Hogarth Press.

Appignanesi, Lisa, and John Forrester (2000). *Freud's Women*. New York: Other Press.

Bair, Deirdre (2003). *Jung: A Biography*. Boston: Back Bay Books/Little Brown.

Behling, Katja (2005). *Martha Freud: A Biography*. Translated by R. D. V. Glasgow, Cambridge, England: Polity Press.

Bernays, Anna Freud (1940). "My Brother, Sigmund Freud," *American Mercury*, Volume LI, pages 335–342.

Billinsky, John M. (1969). "Jung and Freud: The End of a Romance," *Andover Newton Quarterly*, Volume 10, Number 2, pages 39–43.

Blum, H. P. (1998). "Freud and Jung: The Internationalization of Psychoanalysis," *Psychoanalysis and History*, Volume 1, Number 1, pages 44–55.

Blumenthal, Ralph (1981). "Historian Links Freud and Wife's Sister as Lovers," *The New York Times*, November 22.

Blumenthal, Ralph (2006). "A Century-Old Swiss Hotel Log Hints at an Illicit Desire that Dr. Freud Didn't Repress," *The New York Times*, December 24.

Bonaparte, Marie, Anna Freud, and Ernst Kris (1954). *The Origins of Psycho-Analysis, Letters to Wilhelm Fliess, Drafts and Notes: 1887–1902*. London: Imago.

Boyer, John W. (1978). "Freud, Marriage, and Later Victorian Liberalism: A Commentary from 1905," *Journal of Modern History*, Volume I, pages 72–102.

Brabant, Eva, Ernst Falzeder, and Patrizia Giampieri-Deutsch, eds. (1992). *The Correspondence of Sigmund Freud and Sàndor Ferenczi, Volume I, 1908–1914*.

Translated by Peter T. Hoffer, introduction by André Haynal. Cambridge, MA: Belknap Press of Harvard University Press.

Breger, Louis (2000). *Freud: Darkness in the Midst of Vision*. New York: John Wiley.

Brill, A. A. (1949). *Lectures on Psychoanalytic Psychiatry*, New York: Knopf.

Brome, Vincent (1978). *Jung: Man and Myth*. New York: Atheneum.

Burnham, John C. (1960). "Sigmund Freud and G. Stanley Hall: Exchange of Letters," *Psychoanalytic Quarterly*, Volume 29, pages 307–316.

Burston, Daniel (2008). "A Very Freudian Affair: Erich Fromm, Peter Swales, and the Future of Psychoanalytic Historiography," *Psychoanalysis and History*, Volume 10, Number 1, pages 115–130.

Carotenuto, Aldo (1982). *A Secret Symmetry: Sabina Spielrein between Jung and Freud*. Translated by Arno Pomerans, John Shepley, Krishna Winston. New York: Pantheon Books.

Clark, Ronald W. (1980). *Freud: The Man and the Cause*. New York: Random House.

Clark University. List of honorees for 1909 celebrations. Retrieved from https://www.clarku.edu/micro/freudcentennial/history/1909psych.cfm.

Donn, Linda (1988). *Freud and Jung: Years of Friendship, Years of Loss*. New York: Scribners.

Dyck, Richard (1956). "Mein Onkel Sigmund," in *Aufbau* (New York), May 11, 1956, pages 3–4.

Eissler, Kurt R. (1953). Interview with C. G. Jung. Unpublished manuscript, Library of Congress. In German. 61 pages. Tape Number 74, August 29, 1953.

Eissler, Kurt R. (1994). "C. G. Jung, a Witness or, the Unreliability of Memories," pages 107–84, in *Three Instances of Injustice*. Madison, CT: International Universities Press.

Elms, Alan C. (1982). "Freud and Minna," *Psychology Today*, Volume XVI, December 1982, pages 41–46.

Engelman, Edmund, Peter Gay, Rita Ransohoff (1976). *Berggasse 19: Sigmund Freud's Home and Offices, Vienna 1938*. Chicago: University of Chicago Press.

Ferenczi, Sándor (1988). *Ohne Sympathie keine Heilung: Das klinishche Tagebuch von 1932*. Edited by J. Dupont. Frankfurt am Main: Fischer.

Fichtner, Gerhard, ed. (2003). *The Sigmund Freud–Ludwig Binswanger Correspondence, 1908–1938*. Translated by Arnold J. Pomerans. New York and London: Other Press.

Fiebert, Martin S. (2010). "Sex, Lies, and Letters: A Sample of Significant Deceptions in the Freud–Jung Relationship." *Psychology*, Volume 1, pages 113–115.

Freeman, Lucy, and Herbert S. Strean (1981). *Freud and Women*. New York: Frederick Ungar.

Freud, Ernst L., ed. (1960). *Letters of Sigmund Freud, 1873–1939*. Translated by Tania and James Stern. New York: Basic Books.

Freud, Ernst L., Lucie Freud, and Ilse Grubrich-Simitis, eds. (1976). *Sigmund Freud: His Life in Pictures and Words*. With a biographical sketch by K. R. Eissler, translation by Christine Trollope. New York and London: Harcourt Brace Jovanovich.

Freud, Martin (1970). "Who Was Freud?" in *The Jews of Austria, Essays on their Life, History and Destruction*, edited by Josef Fraenkel, Second Edition. London: Vallentine/Mitchell.

Freud, Martin (1977; originally published 1958). *Sigmund Freud: Man and Father*. Lanham, MD: Jason Aronson.

Freud, Sigmund (1953–1974). *The Standard Edition of the Complete Psychological Works of Sigmund Freud, Translated from the German under the General Editorship of James Strachey, In Collaboration with Anna Freud, Assisted by Alix Strachey and Alan Tyson*. Twenty-Four Volumes. London: The Hogarth Press. *The Interpretation of Dreams* (1900), Volume IV, pages 1–338. *The Psychopathology of Everyday Life* (1901), Volume VI, pages 1–279. *Jokes and Their Relation to the Unconscious* (1905), Volume VIII, pages 9–238. "'Civilized' Sexual Morality and Modern Nervous Illness" (1908), Volume IX, pages 177–204. "On the Universal Tendency to Debasement in the Sphere of Love (Contributions to the Psychology of Love II)" (1912), Volume XI, pages 179–190. The *"Uncanny"* (1919), Volume XVII, pages 217–252. *An Autobiographical Study* (1925), Volume XX, pages 7–70.

Gay, Peter (1988). *Freud: A Life for Our Time*. New York: W. W. Norton.

Gay, Peter (1989). "Sigmund and Minna? The Biographer as Voyeur," *The New York Times*, January 29.

Gay, Peter (1990). *Reading Freud: Explorations and Entertainments*. New Haven, CT: Yale University Press.

Hale, Nathan G. Jr., ed. (1971). *James Jackson Putnam and Psychoanalysis: Letters between Putnam and Sigmund Freud, Ernest Jones, William James, Sàndor Ferenczi, and Morton Prince, 1877–1917*. Cambridge, MA: Harvard University Press.

Hannah, Barbara (1976). *Jung: His Life and Work, A Biographical Memoir*. New York: Putnam.

Heller, Peter (1992). *Anna Freud's Letters to Eva Rosenfeld*. Translated by Mary Weigand. Madison, CT: International Universities Press.

Hirschmüller, Albrecht, ed. (2005). *Sigmund Freud/Minna Bernays: Briefwechsel 1882–1938*. Tübingen, Germany: Edition Diskord.

Hirschmüller, Albrecht (2007). "Evidence for a Sexual Relationship between Sigmund Freud and Minna Bernays?" *American Imago*, Volume 64: Number 1, pages 125–129.

Jaffé, Aniela, ed. (1979). *C. G. Jung: Word and Image*. Princeton, NJ: Princeton University Press.

Jones, Ernest (1953–1957). *The Life and Work of Sigmund Freud*. Three volumes. New York: Basic Books.

Jung, C. G. (1957). Interview by Dr. Richard I. Evans, University of Houston, August 5–8. Retrieved from http://www.youtube.com/watch?v=-kdF-qV6PpE. Also available in printed form; see McGuire, William, and R. F. C. Hull (1977). *C. G. Jung Speaking, Interviews and Encounters*, below.

Jung, C. G. (1961). *Memories, Dreams, Reflections*. Edited by A. Jaffé, Revised Edition. New York: Vintage Books/Random House.

Jung, C. G. (1989). *Introduction to Jungian Psychology: Notes of the Seminar on Analytical Psychology Given in 1925 by C. G. Jung.* Edited by Sonu Shamdasani. Princeton, NJ: Princeton University Press.

Kerr, John (1993). *A Most Dangerous Method: The Story of Jung, Freud, and Sabina Spielrein.* New York: Knopf.

Laforgue, René (1973). "Personal Memories of Freud (1956)," in *Freud as We Knew Him.* Edited and introduced by Hendrik M. Ruitenbeek. Detroit: Wayne State University Press.

Lothane, Zvi (1999). "Tender Love and Transference: Unpublished letters of C. G. Jung and Sabina Spielrein," *International Journal of Psycho-Analysis*, Volume 80, pages 1189–1204.

Lothane, Zvi (2007a). "The Sigmund Freud/Minna Bernays Romance: Fact or Fiction?" *American Imago*, Volume 64, Number 1, pages 129–133.

Lothane, Zvi (2007b). "Sigmund Freud and Minna Bernays: Primal Curiosity, Primal Scenes, Primal Fantasies—And Prevarication," *Psychoanalytic Psychology*, Volume 24, Number 3, pages 487–495.

Maciejewski, Franz (2007). "Did Freud Sleep with His Wife's Sister? An Expert Interview with Franz Maciejewski, PhD," Interviewed by Alma Bond, *Medscape Psychiatry Mental Health.* Retrieved from http://www.medscape.com/viewarticle/555692.

Maciejewski, Franz, and Jeremy Gaines (2006). "Freud, His Wife, and His 'Wife,'" *American Imago*, Volume 63, Number 4, pages 497–506.

Maciejewski, Franz, and Jeremy Gaines (2008). "Minna Bernays as 'Mrs. Freud': What Sort of Relationship Did Sigmund Freud Have with His Sister-in-Law?" *American Imago*, Volume 65, number 1, pages 5–21.

Maddox, Brenda (2007). *Freud's Wizard: Ernest Jones and the Transformation of Psychoanalysis.* Cambridge, MA: Da Capo Press.

Makari, George (2008). *Revolution in Mind: The Creation of Psychoanalysis.* New York: Harper.

Malcom, Janet (1997, originally published in 1984). *In the Freud Archives.* New York: New York Review of Books.

Masson, Jeffery M., ed., trans. (1985). *The Complete Letters of Sigmund Freud to Wilhelm Fliess, 1887–1904.* Cambridge, MA: Belknap/Harvard University Press.

McGuire, William, ed. (1974). *The Freud/Jung Letters: The Correspondence between Sigmund Freud and C. G. Jung.* Translated by R. Manheim & R. F. C. Hull, Princeton, NJ: Princeton University Press.

McGuire, William, and R. F. C. Hull, eds. (1977). *C. G. Jung Speaking, Interviews and Encounters.* Princeton, NJ: Princeton University Press.

McLynn, Frank (1996). *Carl Gustav Jung.* New York: St Martin's Press.

Mendelsohn, Daniel (2011). "Heroine Addict: What Theodor Fontane's Women Want," *The New Yorker*, March 7, 2011. Retrieved from http://www.newyorker.com/magazine/2011/03/07/heroine-addict.

Nunberg, Herman, and Ernst Federn, eds. (1962). *Minutes of the Vienna Psychoanalytic Society, Volume I: 1906–1908.* New York: International Universities Press.

O'Brien, Michael T. (1991). "Freud's Affair with Minna Bernays: His Letter of June 4, 1896," *The American Journal of Psychoanalysis*, Volume 51, Number 2, pages 173–184.

Puner, Helen Walker (1992—originally published 1947). *Sigmund Freud: His Life and Mind*. Foreword by Erich Fromm, with a new introduction by Paul Roazen and an afterword by S. P. Puner. New Brunswick, NJ: Transaction Publishers.

Roazen, Paul (1976). *Freud and His Followers*. New York: Knopf.

Roazen, Paul (1993). *Meeting Freud's Family*. Amherst, MA: University of Massachusetts Press.

Roazen, Paul (2001). *The Historiography of Psychoanalysis*. New Brunswick, NJ: Transaction Publishers.

Rosenzweig, Saul (1992). *Freud, Jung, and Hall the King-Maker: The Historic Expedition to America (1909), Including the Complete Correspondence of Sigmund Freud and G. Stanley Hall*. Seattle: Hogrefe & Huber Publishers.

Rudnytsky, Peter L. (2006). "Rescuing Psychoanalysis from Freud: The Common Project of Stekel, Jung, and Ferenczi," *Psychoanalysis and History*, Volume 8, Number 1, pages 125–159.

Schmideberg, Melitta (1971). "A Contribution to the History of the Psychoanalytic Movement in Britain," *British Journal of Psychiatry*, Volume 118, pages 61–68.

Schoenwald, Richard (1975). "Review of The Freud/Jung Letters," *Journal of Modern History*, Volume 47, Number 2, pages 360–363.

Schorske, Carl E. (1981). *Fin-de-Siècle Vienna: Politics and Culture*. New York: Random House.

Silverstein, Barry (2007). "What Happens in Maloja Stays in Maloja: Inference and Evidence in the 'Minna Wars,'" *American Imago*, Volume 64, Number 2, pages 283–289.

Swales, P. J. (1982). "Freud, Minna Bernays, and the Conquest of Rome: New Light on the Origins of Psychoanalysis," *New American Review: A Journal of Civility and the Arts*, Volume 1, pages 1–23.

Time magazine (September 5, 1969). "People" section, page 32.

Tögel, Christfried (2002). *Unser Herz Zeigt Nach Dem Süden, Reisebriefe 1895–1923*. Berlin: Aufbau Tashchenbuch Verlag.

Young-Bruehl, Elisabeth (2008). *Anna Freud: A Biography*, Second Edition. New Haven, CT: Yale University Press.

INDEX

Abraham, Karl, 23, 109, 122, 149, 150
abstinence, 131–132, 137–138,
    139–140, 185
Adler, Alfred, 5, 17, 21, 149
Aeneid (Virgil), 32
Andover Newton Theological School, 15
Andreas-Salomé, Lou, 144, 147, 175
anti-Semitism, 134–137, 147–148, 156,
    192, 204n6
Anzieu, Didier, 146–147, 150–151
Appignanesi, Lisa: on Freud–Bernays
    affair, 52, 101, 199; on Freud's
    marriage, 161, 166, 175, 198
ars amandi ("art of love"), 145
Austro-Hungarian divorce law,
    131–132, 139

Bair, Deirdre, 49, 81, 108, 199–200,
    208n47, 218n68
Behling, Katja: on Freud's marriage, 162,
    163–164, 168, 172–173; on Martha,
    170–171, 174, 176–177, 231n126;
    on Minna and Anna, 107–108, 197
Berggasse apartment: anti-Semitism
    and, 136–137; laboratory issue,
    39–40, 45, 78–79, 88–89, 185–186;

life at, 124, 154, 158–177, 195,
    197–200; Minna's bedroom/
    liaison opportunities, 42–43, 50,
    86, 123–124, 187, 191; Minna's
    residency, 89, 124, 133, 150–151
Berggasse 19: Sigmund Freud's Home and
    Offices, Vienna 1938, 42, 86
Bernays, Anna. *See* Freud, Anna Bernays
Bernays, Anne, 49
Bernays, Eli, 25, 30, 112–113, 150
Bernays, Martha Freud: Anna and, 166,
    176; crisscross with Minna, 110,
    139, 146; differences from Minna,
    107, 148, 175; family of, 153; health
    of, 170–171, 195; Jung and, 18–19,
    62, 64, 88, 174, 192; marriage of
    (*see* Freud, Sigmund, marriage of);
    Martin and, 231n126; Minna's role
    in family and, 151–152, 176–177;
    personality of, 148, 153–154,
    162–166, 175–177, 185; physical
    appearance of, 154, 166, 184; on
    psychoanalysis, 174, 192
Bernays, Minna: Anna and, 107–108,
    151, 170, 227–228n227; Berggasse
    residency, 89, 124, 133, 150

Bernays (*continued*)
(*see also* Berggasse apartment);
commonalities with Freud, 111–112,
124–131; credibility of, 183, 188–
189; crisscross with Martha, 110,
139, 146; differences from Martha,
107, 148, 175 ; engagement of, 39,
109–110, 189; Esti and, 35, 69, 125,
151, 191; family relationships of, 13;
as Freud's confidante, 108–109, 112–
114, 152, 176–177, 194, 200–201,
212n16; Freud's death and, 105–106;
Freudian circle and, 109–110,
194–195; influence on Freud's
work, 200–201; intellectualism
of, 80–81, 106, 127–131, 147, 184,
201; motives of, 45, 72, 150–152,
188–189, 194–195; personality of,
106, 108, 124–131, 150–151, 180,
191; physical appearance of, 40, 49,
79–81, 106–107, 175, 184, 221n6;
psychoanalysis and, 125–126, 175,
184, 185, 200–201; relationship with
Jung, 71–73, 80–81, 90–91, 185,
193–194 (*see also* Freud–Bernays
affair, Minna's confession); role
in family, Martha and, 151–152,
176–177 ; rumored pregnancy/
abortion of, 26, 29, 31–33, 38, 51,
64–65, 75, 101; sexuality of, 52, 101,
184. *See also* Freud–Bernays affair
Bernays Heller, Judith, 13
Bernheim, Hippolyte, 41
Billinsky, John M. Jr., 19–20, 71, 211n117
Billinsky, John M., 15–16. *See also*
Billinsky interview
Billinsky interview: content of, 17–19, 179,
181, 192–194; Eissler on credibility
of, 43–48, 87–95, 183, 206n31,
208n38; Elms on credibility of, 38,
71; Gay on credibility of, 183; Kerr
on credibility of, 33–34, 183; Lothane
on credibility of, 48–50; Meier
and, 58, 182, 183; motives behind,

15–17, 71; Rudnytsky on credibility
of, 19–20, 71, 193; softening of, 19,
33–34, 71, 145, 183, 193, 211n117;
Time article and, 15, 16, 17, 71, 194,
206n31, 207n33, 207n35
Binswanger, Ludwig, 17, 21, 73, 77, 135,
175, 179, 208n51, 216n12
Bleuler, Eugen, 5, 7, 20, 23, 48, 72, 74,
91–92, 108, 195, 233n34
Blum, Harold, 42
Blumenthal, Ralph, 43, 87
Bonaparte, Marie, 147, 174–175, 212n16,
222n29, 226n193
Boston City Hospital, 15
Breger, Louis, 52, 101, 109
Breuer, Josef, 4–5, 23, 112, 133–135, 109,
149, 209n71
Brill, A. A., 22, 23, 25, 88
Brome, Vincent, 34, 68, 211n120
Burghölzli Mental Hospital, 5, 7, 20,
22–23, 72, 78, 92, 208n47
Burlingham, Dorothy, 13, 232n13
Burnham, John C., 207n35
Burston, Daniel, 12, 35–36, 69–70

C. G. Jung Institute, 15
Carl Gustav Jung (McLynn), 52
Carmen (Bizet), 127
Carotenuto, Aldo, 209n69
Carson, Johnny, 20
Charcot, Jean-Martin, 4, 127, 135
Charteris, Hugo, 34, 59, 68
cigar smoking, 169
"'Civilized' Sexual Morality and Modern
Nervous Illness" (Freud), 138
Clark University, 15, 24–26, 134, 144,
206n32, 208n37, 209–210n74
Clark, Ronald W., 37, 70–71
cocaine, 111, 141
Columbia University, 25, 61, 78
Committee, 109–110
*Complete Edition of the Letters of
Sigmund Freud to Wilhelm Fliess,
The* (Masson), 30

contraception, 137, 138
conversion neuroses, 171
counter-transference, 23, 197

Darwin, Charles, 233n34
DeLaurentis, Dino, 20
depression, 171
Deutsch, Helen, 147, 175
divorce law, 131–132, 139, 184
Donn, Linda, 52, 101
Doolittle, Hilda, 147
dream analysis: dream content, 138;
    Freud's dreams, 138, 144, 145 (see also
    triangle dream); Jung's dreams, 46,
    66, 92, 188; in psychoanalysis, 5, 7–8
"Dream of Irma's Injection, The" (Freud), 33
Du Bois-Reymond, Emil, 3

ecgonine, 111
Eckstein, Emma, 147, 175
education, anti-Semitism and, 135–137
Eissler, Kurt: Burton mistakenly attributes
    to, 12; criticism of Billinsky,
    43–48, 87–95, 183, 206n31,
    208n38; critique of Jung, 43–47;
    Freud Archives and, 198–199; on
    Freud's letters, 40, 73–74, 82; idyllic
    portrayal of Freud, 70, 195; on Jung,
    219n102; interview of Jung, 14–15,
    28, 56, 59–66, 143, 181, 182; on
    Meier, 58; on rumor origins, 13
Eitingon, Max, 109
elitism, 127–131, 132
Elms, Alan C., 38–39, 40, 45, 67, 80, 90,
    91, 186
Engelman, Edmund, 136
Erich Hoche, Alfred, 135
Evans, Richard I., 85–86, 186, 205n31
"Evidence for a Sexual Relationship
    between Sigmund Feud and Minna
    Bernays" (Hirschmüller), 50, 98–99
experimental psychopathology,
    209–210n74, 218n57
extraterritoriality, 127–131, 132, 157, 184

femininity, 147
Ferenczi, Sándor: Clark University
    event and, 24–26; on Freud's
    incontinence episode, 28, 66,
    121–122, 180–181; homosexuality
    and, 142–143; letters with Freud,
    27; psychoanalysis and, 23, 109
First International Congress for
    Psychiatry, Psychology, and the
    Assistance to the Insane, 22
Fliess, Ida, 141, 142, 148
Fliess, Wilhelm: break with Freud, 108,
    141–142, 148, 169, 194; as Freud's
    confidante, 39, 41, 108, 16, 194;
    homosexuality and, 101, 141–150;
    letters with Freud during holidays,
    27–33, 67, 76, 116–117, 128; letters
    with Freud on Martha, 170–171;
    letters with Freud on Minna, 108,
    123–124, 200; letters with Freud on
    Nietzsche, 133; letters with Freud
    on sexuality, 137, 138, 139, 145;
    Swales on, 36
Forrester, John: on Freud–Bernays affair,
    52, 101, 199; on Freud's marriage,
    161, 166, 175, 198
Fortress Freud, 166, 197–200, 210n75,
    233n33, 233n34
free association, 5
Freud: A Life for Our Time (Gay), 203n3
Freud, Alexander, 30, 39, 114
Freud, Amalie, 154–156, 175
Freud, Anna: birth of, 137, 169, 170;
    Fortress Freud and, 197–200,
    210n75; Freud's biography and, 12;
    Freud's letters and, 42, 47, 48, 82,
    226n189; friendships of, 13, 191,
    206n24, 232n13; Martha and, 166,
    176; Minna and, 107–108, 151, 170,
    227–228n227; relationship with
    Freud, 131, 147, 171–172
Freud, Anna Bernays, 25, 30, 49, 116,
    150, 156–159
Freud, Clement, 172

Freud, David, 172
Freud, Elfie, 111
Freud, Ernst, 47–48, 82, 205n8, 223n86
Freud, Esti: Freud's dominance and, 161,
    162; Minna and, 35, 69, 125, 151,
    191, 199, 230n69
Freud, Harry, 167
Freud, Jakob, 3, 154–157
Freud, Lucian, 172, 205n8
Freud, Lucie, 105–106, 180, 205n8
Freud, Martha. See Bernays, Martha
    Freud
Freud, Martin: on anti-Semitism,
    136–137; Esti and, 35, 124–125,
    161, 162; on family holidays, 76,
    96–97, 127, 128, 153, 160, 168,
    220n120; on Freud's personality,
    136, 160–163, 167–169, 213n34,
    219n79; on Freud's youth, 155, 157,
    158–159; on Jung, 21–22, 44, 73;
    Martha and, 231n126
Freud, Mathilde, 44, 73, 171
"Freud, Minna Bernays, and the
    Conquest of Rome" (Swales), 29–30
Freud, Oliver, 136
Freud, Sigmund: anti-Semitism and,
    134–137, 147–148, 156, 192,
    204n6; authority of, 16, 18–19,
    25–26, 28–29, 46–47, 48, 57–59, 66;
    autobiography of, 135, 217–218n48;
    break with Jung, 5, 16, 18, 19,
    25n26, 47–48, 93, 97–98, 121,
    207n35, 216n13, 217–218n48;
    childhood of, 155–159, 160;
    control/dominance of, 159–162,
    195; extraterritoriality and,
    127–131, 132, 184; family life of,
    133–134, 147, 159–170; financial
    pressures of, 133–134, 192,
    220n120; friendships of, 109–110,
    130, 138–147, 149–150 (see also
    specific individuals); health of, 143,
    171, 195, 210n75; homosexuality
    and, 48, 101, 138–147, 187–188,

226n179; ideology of, 19, 66;
    incontinence episode (see triangle
    dream/incontinence episode);
    Nietzsche and, 69, 132–133;
    personality of, 124–131, 147–150,
    158–159, 166–170, 200–201; poor
    judgment of, 148–150; private
    practice of, 4, 13, 124, 127, 134,
    224n116; professional ridicule
    of, 134–137, 147–148, 184, 192;
    self-analysis of, 5 (see also dream
    analysis); on sexuality, 41–42, 131–
    133, 134–137, 139–140, 216n20;
    sexuality of, 35–36, 52, 68–69, 101,
    137–147, 184–185; superior human
    belief of, 35, 69, 130–131, 132–133,
    184. See also Freud, Sigmund,
    marriage of; Freud–Bernays affair
Freud, Sigmund, marriage of: conflict
    and compromise, 185; dominance/
    submission and, 153–154, 159–162,
    162–166; engagement, 4, 112–113,
    161, 169; Freud's comments to
    Jung on, 18–19, 62, 64, 88, 174,
    192; Freud's view of, 172–175;
    lack of intimacy in, 35–36, 69,
    124, 137–138, 139, 146, 148, 192;
    Martha's view of, 175–177; Martha's
    wife/mother role, 27, 34, 153–154,
    162–166, 196, 230n69
Freud: Darkness in the Midst of Vision
    (Breger), 52, 101
Freud and His Followers (Roazen), 13, 52,
    80, 101, 105, 139
Freud and Jung: Years of Friendship, Years
    of Loss (Donn), 52, 101
Freud Archives, Library of Congress,
    13, 28, 42, 50, 59, 81–82, 198–199,
    210n75
Freud–Bernays affair: Anzieu on,
    146–147, 150–151; Appignanesi
    and Forrester on, 52, 101, 199;
    Berggasse liaison opportunities,
    42–43, 50, 86, 123–124, 187,

191; Billinsky interview and (*see* Billinsky interview); Breger on, 52, 101, 109; Burston on, 12, 35–36, 69–70; Clark on, 37, 70–71; corroborative studies on, 26–29; Donn on, 52, 101; Eissler on (*see* Eissler, Kurt); Elms on, 38–39, 40, 45, 71–76, 186; evidence against, 37–52, 68–102, 182–189; evidence for, 55–67, 179–182, 190–202; Freud and Minna's commonalities, 124–131; Freud's poor judgement and, 148–150; Gay on, 14, 34, 39–43, 58, 71, 110, 112, 122–123, 182, 224n95; gossip and, 13–15, 180, 182, 191; Hirschmüller on, 13, 50–51, 98–101; holidays/travels alone, 30–33, 114–124, 190, 191–192, 211n126, 223n63, 223n74, 224n95, 232n8 (*see also* Schweizerhaus discovery); interpretive accounts of, 29–33, 67–68; intimate vs. sexual nature of, 10, 98–99, 145–147, 189, 191; Jones on (*see* Jones, Ernst); Kerr on, 33–35, 59, 68–69, 209n69, 211n117, 220n112; laboratory issue and, 39–40, 45, 78–79, 88–89, 185–186; Lothane on, 48–50, 95–98, 112, 217n45; Maciejewski (*see* Maciejewski, Franz) ; McLynn on, 52, 101; Merano trip, 30–33; Minna's confession (*see* Freud–Bernays affair, Minna's confession); Minna's motives, 45, 72, 150–152, 188–189, 194–195; from Minna's perspective, 150–152; missing letters and, 40–43, 47–48, 50, 81–85, 180, 189; mutual attraction and, 10, 110–111, 144, 185; O'Brien on, 29–33, 67; pressures on Freud and, 133–137, 147–148, 192; Puner on, 10–12; Roazen on, 52, 101, 139, 145–146; Rudnytsky on, 28–29, 180–181;

rumor origins, 9–36; Schweizerhaus and (*see* Schweizerhaus discovery); Silverstein on, 35–36, 68–70, 130, 149; Swales on, 29–33; transference and, 56, 62, 64, 139, 146, 182, 186, 232n18; triangle dream and (*see* triangle dream)
Freud–Bernays affair, Minna's confession: Eissler and, 15; evidence against, 38, 40, 45, 71, 183–189; Freud's knowledge of, 90–91, 94, 183–184; Jung and, 26, 29, 40, 67, 77–78, 94, 179–189; evidence for, 55–57, 67, 98, 151–152, 179–182
Freud Museum, 42
Freud scholarship, secrecy, 197–200, 210n75, 233n33, 233n34
"Freud's Affair with Minna Bernays: His Letter of June 4, 1896" (O'Brien), 33
Freud's Women (Appignanesi and Forrester), 52, 101, 161
Freudian circle, 109–110, 194–195
Fromm, Erich, 36, 69–70, 98–99

Gay, Peter: on anti-Semitism, 204n6; criticism of, 76–87; criticism of Swales, 67; on Freud–Bernays affair, 14, 34, 39–43, 58, 71, 110, 112, 122–123, 182, 224n95; on Freud's family life, 161, 164, 169, 224n117; on Freud's letters, 40–41, 56, 212n16, 222n29, 224n95; on Freud's sexuality, 137–138, 141, 143, 144–145, 185; on Freud's youth, 155–156, 158; Jones's work and, 205n2; on Martha, 164, 165, 166; on Minna, 40, 49, 79–81, 221n6
Göttingen University, 6

Hall, G. Stanley, 15–16, 17, 21, 24, 134, 207n34, 207n35, 208n37
Halle University, 135

Hamburg, culture of, 128–129
Hammerschlag, Samuel, 134
Hartford Theological Seminary, 15
Harvard Psychological Clinic, 26, 49
Harvard University, 15
Hausfrau, 164–166
Heller, Peter, 206n24
Helmholtz, Hermann, 3
higher education, anti-Semitism and,
     135–137
Hirschmüller, Albrecht: on Freud–Bernays
     affair, 13, 50–51, 98–101; Freud's
     letters and, 47, 50, 78–79, 81–85, 180;
     199, 213n28, 223n74; on Minna, 129,
     212n14
Historiography of Psychoanalysis, The
     (Roazen), 52, 101
holidays: Freud family, 76, 96–97, 127,
     128, 153, 160, 168, 220n120; Freud
     and Minna at Schweizerhaus,
     26–28, 51 (*see also* Schweizerhaus
     discovery); Freud and Minna at
     Merano, 30–33; Freud and Minna's
     travels alone, 114–124, 190,
     191–192, 211n126, 223n63, 223n74,
     224n95, 232n8
homoeroticism, 142–147
homosexuality: 48, 101, 138–147, 187–188
Hotel Erzherzog Johann, 31
Humanistiches Gymnasium, 6
hypnosis: Breur's method, 4–5; Charcot
     and, 4; in treatment of hysteria, 4–5
hysteria, 4–5, 135, 137, 171

impotence, 137–138
In the Freud Archives (Malcolm),
     198–199
incontinence episode. *See* triangle
     dream/incontinence episode
infantile sexuality, 5, 217–218n48
intellectualism, 127–131, 147, 184, 201
International Psychoanalytic Society,
     217–218n48
Interpretation of Dreams, The (Freud), 5,
     7, 33, 86, 112, 186

Jaffé, Aniela, 218n57
*Jahrbuch für psychoanalytische und
     psychopathologische Forschungen*, 23
Jefferson, Howard B., 206n32
Jews, anti-Semitism and, 134–137,
     147–148, 156
*Jokes and Their Relation to the
     Unconscious* (Freud), 5
Jones, Ernest: on Berggasse layout, 8;
     criticism of Puner, 129; on Freud's
     death, 105, 221n2; in Freud's
     defense, 9–10, 14, 37, 70; on Freud's
     marriage, 110, 111, 161, 164–165,
     173, 175–176; on Freud's sexuality,
     139, 140, 143, 147, 185, 226n179; on
     Freud's trips with Minna, 32, 114–
     123, 223n74, 223n84; on Freud's
     youth, 155, 157; Gay's work and,
     205n2; idyllic portrayal of Freud,
     70, 76, 195; information sources of,
     12–13, 21, 29–30, 212n16, 222n29;
     on Minna, 107, 110; psychoanalysis
     and, 9n1, 23, 109
Jung, Emma: letter to Ferenczi, 28–29;
     letters with Freud, 138; professional
     career, 175, 201; Spielrein and, 74,
     197; visits with Freud, 17, 21, 64, 73,
     179, 216n12; Wolff and, 34, 74, 197
Jung, Franz, 21, 208n50
Jung, Paul Achilles, 6
Jung, Carl Gustav: admiration of Freud,
     46, 74, 187–188, 194, 216n13,
     219n102; autobiography of,
     20–21, 47, 58, 93–94, 181, 182,
     217–218n48; Billinsky interview
     (*see* Billinsky interview); break with
     Freud, 5, 16, 18, 19, 25n26, 47–48,
     93, 97–98, 121, 207n35, 216n13,
     217–218n48; childhood of, 6–7,
     93–94, 204n16; Clark University
     and, 24–26, 209–210n74; credibility
     of, 77–79, 85–86, 102, 180–184,
     196; credibility of memory, 50, 77,
     186–187, 216n12; credibility of use
     of the term "laboratory," 39–40,

45, 78–79, 88–90; and, 50, 77, 186–187, 216n12; Eissler interview, 14–15, 28, 56, 59–66, 143, 181, 182; Eissler on credibility of, 43–48, 50, 102; Elms on credibility of, 38, 186; Evans interview of, 85–86, 186, 205n31; Gay on credibility of, 39–40, 42, 182; Hirschmüller on credibility of, 50; homosexuality and, 48, 142–143; ideology of, 19, 66; marriage to Emma, 34, 74, 197; Martha and, 18–19, 62, 64, 88, 174, 192; Meier and, 14, 34, 56, 57–58, 59, 68, 74, 85, 87, 94, 181–182; personality of, 21–22, 72, 93–94, 185, 193–194, 196–197; psychoanalysis and, 3–5, 7–8, 22, 195, 201–202, 215n2; relationship with Minna, 71–73, 80–81, 90–91, 185, 193–194 (*see also* Freud–Bernays affair, Minna's confession); revelations of, 57–59; revenge motive, 183–184; Rosenzweig and, 24–26, 58, 181–182; on sexuality, 7–8, 22, 48, 217–218n48; sexuality of, 39, 196–197; Spielrein and, 23–24, 33, 38, 74–75, 196–197, 209n69, 217n44, 217n45; Wolff and, 34, 197, 217n47; Zürich lecture, 46–47, 58, 77, 93–94, 181, 182
Jung: Man and Myth (Brome), 68
Jung Oral History Archive, 34, 59
Jung scholarship, secrecy and, 233n34

Kann, Loe, 147
Kerr, John, 33–35, 59, 68–69, 181–183, 209n69, 211n117, 220n112
Klein, Melanie, 164, 206n24
Koller, Karl, 111

La Salpêtrière, 4
laboratory issue, 39–40, 45, 78–79, 88–89, 185–186
Laforgue, René, 174

Lampl-de Groot, Jeanne, 147
libertarianism, 132
libido, 7, 38, 135
Lothane, Zvi, 48–51, 95-99, 112, 190, 217n45

Maciejewski, Franz, 13, 26–29, 36, 45, 48–51, 66, 69, 86–87, 95–97, 99, 100. *See also* Schweizerhaus discovery
Mack Brunswick, Ruth, 147
Maddox, Brenda, 205n1
Malcolm, Janet, 198–199
marriage: divorce law and, 131–132, 139, 184; sexual freedom and, 131–133, 139–140
Martha Freud: A Biography (Behling), 107–108
masculinity, 10, 147, 185
Masson, J. M., 30–31, 211n14, 226n189
McGuire, William, 210n100, 212n7
McLynn, Frank, 52, 101
medical field, 136, 147–148, 160, 184
Meeting Freud's Family (Roazen), 52, 101
Meier, C. A.: Billinsky interview and, 33–34, 42, 49, 183–184; credibility of, 44, 183–184; Jung and, 14, 34, 56, 57–58, 59, 68, 74, 85, 87, 94, 181–182
Memories, Dreams, Reflections (Jung), 47, 58, 92, 93, 209–210n74, 215n2, 218n57
Meumann, Ernst, 210n74
Meyer, Max, 161
Meynert, Theodor, 4
"Minna wars," 35–36, 68–70
morality, 131–133, 184
morphine, 141
Most Dangerous Method: The Story of Jung, Freud, and Sabina Spielrein, A (Kerr), 33
motivation, sexuality and, 139
Murray, Henry, 26, 34, 48–49, 59, 68, 227n211

Nameche, Gene, 34, 59
Nazis, 136–137, 212n16

neuroses, etiologies of, 5, 137, 139–140, 142, 171
New York Times, The, 40, 42, 43, 47, 81–82, 85, 87
Nietzsche, Friedrich, 69, 132–133

O'Brien, Michael T., 29–33, 67–68
Occam's Razor, 68, 189
Oedipus complex, 5, 217–218n48
On Aphasia (Freud), 112
"On the Psychology and Pathology of So-Called Occult Phenomena" (Jung), 7
"On the Universal Tendency to Debasement in the Sphere of Love" (Freud), 140
Ovid, 145

paranoia, 142
Phillips, John, 34, 68
polygamy, 131–132, 184
positivist school, 3–4
post-partum depression, 171
Preiswerk, Emilie, 6
prostitution, 144
Psychiatric Clinic, Columbia University, 25
psychoanalysis: acceptance of method, 56, 72; beginnings of, 4–5, 20, 208n47, 215n2; dream analysis in, 5, 7–8; Ferenczi and, 23, 109; Freudian circle and, 109–110, 194–195; implications of affair and, 199–200, 201–202; Jones and, 9n1, 23, 109; Jung and, 3–5, 7–8, 22, 195, 201–202, 215n2; Martha on, 174, 192; Minna and, 125–126, 175, 184, 185, 200–201; ridicule of, 134–137, 147–148, 184, 192; schizophrenia and, 23; support for, 20, 23, 194–195, 200–201
Psychology Today, 38, 71
psychopathology, 209–210n74, 218n57
Psychopathology of Everyday Life, The (Freud), 5, 32, 38, 75, 143–144

psychosomatic illness, 18, 170–171, 195
Puner, Helen Walker: on Freud–Bernays affair, 10–12; on Freud's marriage/family, 10–12, 124, 137, 139, 155, 160, 163, 176; on Freud's practice, 135; Jones's criticism of, 15, 70; treatment of by Freud's family, 199, 205–206n17
Puner, Samuel P., 205n17
Putnam, James J., 41, 68–69, 131, 139

racism, 134–137
Rank, Otto, 109, 149, 194
Reading Freud: Explorations and Entertainments (Gay), 42, 85
Reik, Theodor, 174
repression, 5, 21, 139
"Rescuing Psychoanalysis from Freud: The Common Project of Stekel, Jung, and Ferenczi" (Rudnytsky), 28
Rie, Oskar, 34–35, 68
Riviere, Joan, 147, 175
Roazen, Paul: Anna and, 199, 206n24; Esti and, 69; on Freud–Bernays affair, 52, 101, 139, 145–146; on Freud's death, 105; on Freud's dominance, 159, 162; on Freud's personality, 131, 168; on Freud's practice, 224n116; on Minna, 80, 175, 201; Murray and, 48–49, 227n211; Puner and, 12, 139; on Rosenfeld interview, 13; Silverman and, 35
Rosenfeld, Eva, 13, 34, 191, 206n24, 232n13
Rosenzweig, Saul: Clark University and, 24–26, 206n32, 207n35, 207n36, 209–210n74; on Freud's fainting episode, 210n75; Jung interview, 58
Rudnytsky, Peter L., 19–20, 28–29, 66, 71, 180–181, 193

Sachs, Hanns: on anti-Semitism,
    135–136; on Freud's letters, 120; on
    Freud's personality, 125, 126–127,
    128–129, 130, 131, 167, 168–169;
    friendship with Freud, 109, 130,
    149, 166, 198; on Minna, 126, 166
schizophrenia, 23
Schmid, Karl, 18
Schmideberg, Melitta, 164
Schoenwald, Richard, 36, 212n136
Schönberg, Ignaz, 39, 79–80, 109–110,
    113, 150, 184, 189, 221n6
Schorske, Carl E., 218n68
Schreber, Daniel Paul, 48
Schur, Helen, 40, 79, 229n65
Schur, Max, 40, 79, 164, 165, 230n75
Schweizerhaus discovery: Burston on,
    36, 69; Gay on, 43, 86–87, 190;
    Hirschmüller on, 99–100, 190;
    Jung's credibility and, 66; Lothane
    on, 48–51, 95–97
secrecy, Freud/Jung scholarship,
    197–200, 210n75, 233n33, 233n34
Seven Rings, 109, 130
sexuality: abstinence and, 131–132,
    137–138, 139–140, 184; ars
    amandi, 145; etiology and, 5, 7–8,
    48; Freud on, 41–42, 131–133,
    134–137, 139–140, 216n20;
    infantile, 5, 217–218n48; Jung vs.
    Freud on, 7–8, 22, 48, 217–218n48;
    motivation and, 139; neuroses
    and, 137, 139–140, 142; ridicule
    of Freud and, 134–137; sexual
    freedom, 131–133, 139–140;
    sublimation and, 139–140,
    146–147, 185; Victorian morality,
    88, 131, 135
Siegfried Bernfeld method, 40, 67
"Sigmund and Minna? The Biographer
    as Voyeur" (Gay), 40, 81
Sigmund Freud, Unser Herz zeigt nach
    dem Süden, Reisebriefe 1895–1923
    (Tögel), 82

"Sigmund Freud/Minna Bernays
    Romance: Fact or Fiction?"
    (Lothane), 48
Sigmund Freud: Man and Father (Freud),
    168
Sigmund Freud—Minna Bernays:
    Briefwechsel, 1882–1938
    (Hirschmüller), 50
"Sigmund Freud and Minna Bernays:
    Primal Curiosity, Primal
    Scenes, Primal Fantasies—and
    Prevarication" (Lothane), 49
Silverstein, Barry, 35–36, 68–70, 101,
    130, 149
Simmel, Ernst, 154
social class, 127–131, 158–159
Sperl Gymnasium, 3
Spielrein, Sabina, 23–24, 33, 38, 74–75,
    196, 209n69, 217n44, 217n45
Stein, Philip, 216n12
Storr, Anthony, 49, 214n80
Studies in Word Association (Jung), 8
Studies on Hysteria (Freud and Breuer), 4
sublimation, 139–140, 146–147, 185
successive polygamy, 184
superior human concept, 35, 69,
    130–131, 132–133, 184
Swales, Peter J.: Elms's criticism of,
    38, 75–76; Freud Archives and,
    198–199; on Freud–Bernays affair
    29–33; Gay's criticism of, 40;
    interpretive accounts and, 67–68;
    on Minna's possible pregnancy,
    64–65, 117

Three Essays on the Theory of Sexuality
    (Freud), 5
Three Instances of Injustice (Eissler), 13,
    43, 48, 102
Tiffany, Louis Comfort, 13
Time magazine, 15, 16, 17, 55, 71, 194,
    206n31, 207n33, 207n35, 208n37
Tögel, Christfried, 82–84, 100, 118,
    210n84, 223n74, 223n86, 224n120

Tonight Show, The, 20
transference: in Freud–Bernays affair,
    56, 62, 64, 139, 146, 182, 186,
    232n18; homosexuality and, 143; of
    patients, 23–24, 74, 197
triangle dream/incontinence episode:
    Eissler on, 93; Ferenczi on,
    28–29; Jung's analysis of 16, 19,
    25–26, 46–47, 61, 78, 216n11; Jung's
    sharing with others, 18, 28–29, 48,
    57–59, 94, 180–182; Lothane on,
    97–98; Minna's motives and, 189

Übermensch, 132–133
unconscious, 20, 21, 65, 174
universities, anti-Semitism and, 135–137
University of Basel, 6–7
University of Heidelberg, 126
University of Houston, 85, 186, 205n31
University of Münster, 209n74
University of Vienna, 3, 126, 130, 135
University of Zürich, 7

"Very Freudian Affair: Erich Fromm,
    Peter Swales and the Future of
    Psychoanalytic Historiography, A"
    (Burston), 12, 35–36
Victorian morality, 88, 131, 135
Vienna, culture of, 128–129, 131, 218n68
Vienna General Hospital, 4
Vienna Medical Society, 135

Vienna Psychoanalytic Society, 74
Virgil, 32
von Brücke, Ernst, 3, 140
von Fleischl-Marxow, Ernst, 101, 134,
    140–141

Wahle, Fritz, 161
Wednesday Psychological Society: *ars
    armandi* and, 145; beginnings of
    psychoanalysis and, 5; history of,
    222n31; members of, 21, 44, 73,
    108, 109, 14, 227n2209; Minna and,
    194–195
"What Happens in Maloja Stays in
    Maloja: Inference and Evidence in
    the 'Minna Wars'"
    (Silverstein), 35
Wolff, Toni: Minna confession and, 49,
    56, 59, 68, 74, 94, 181, 182, 183,
    197; professional career of, 175,
    201; relationship with Jung and
    Emma, 34, 197, 217n47
women, masculinity and, 10, 147, 185
word associations, 21
World War I, 124–125, 136, 168
writing paralysis, 170–171

Young-Bruehl, Elizabeth, 108

Ziehen, Theodor, 135
Zweig, Arnold, 198

About the Author

BARRY G. GALE, PhD, taught at Cambridge (as a National Science Foundation Dissertation Fellow) and Johns Hopkins University (at the Paul H. Nitze School of Advanced International Studies). He is the author of *Evolution Without Evidence: Charles Darwin and the Origin of Species* and *Belle Vue: Sigmund Freud, Minna Bernays, and the Meaning of Dreams.*